Praise for

A PLACE TO BELONG

"Amber O'Neal Johnston has penned an engaging and comprehensive guide for families of all backgrounds who are curious or committed to engaging in a diverse and inclusive lifestyle. Johnston's book is a refreshing reminder that humanity is shared, imperfect, and beautiful. Highly recommended."
—Charnaie Gordon, creator of Here Wee Read

"In *A Place to Belong*, Amber O'Neal Johnston offers a pathway toward inclusivity that is marked not with trite words and meaningless gestures, but with practical steps and helpful encouragement. She puts forth a beautiful vision for celebrating the uniqueness of your family while cultivating respect and appreciation for the differences of others."
—Jasmine L. Holmes, author of *Carved in Ebony*

"*A Place to Belong* captivated me from the very start. Amber offers a wealth of tools to help every family grow in their appreciation and connection to people who are different from them, racially, socially, or culturally. And she does it all in a way that is laced with hope and joy! *A Place to Belong* is going to change hearts and lives for years to come."
—Greta Eskridge, author of *Adventuring Together*

"Amber O'Neal Johnston gets it! *A Place to Belong* acts as a compass in navigating tough history and cultural identity conversations within a family. It reminds us to embrace our culture and to honor our history."
—Sheva Quinn, EdD, coauthor of *African American Families: Why We Homeschool*

A
PLACE
TO
BELONG

A
PLACE
TO
BELONG

Celebrating Diversity and Kinship
in the Home and Beyond

AMBER O'NEAL JOHNSTON

A TarcherPerigee Book

tarcherperigee

an imprint of Penguin Random House LLC
penguinrandomhouse.com

Most TarcherPerigee books are available at special quantity discounts for bulk purchase
for sales promotions, premiums, fund-raising, and educational needs. Special books
or book excerpts also can be created to fit specific needs. For details, write:
SpecialMarkets@penguinrandomhouse.com.

Hardcover ISBN: 9780593421857
Ebook ISBN: 9780593538289

Printed in the United States of America
1st Printing

Interior art: Painted background © Artem Kovalenco / Shutterstock
Book design by Alison Cnockaert

We find these joys to be self-evident: That all children are created whole, endowed with innate intelligence, with dignity and wonder, worthy of respect. The embodiment of life, liberty and happiness, children are original blessings, here to learn their own song. Every girl and boy is entitled to love, to dream and belong to a loving village. And to pursue a life of purpose.

—THE RAFFI FOUNDATION FOR CHILD HONOURING

CONTENTS

FOREWORD

THE FIRST TIME I MET AMBER, WE WERE BOTH SCHEDULED speakers for a homeschool conference. I sat in the audience as she came to the podium to share. Everyone around me fell into a hush and waited for this stately, elegant woman to begin. No words followed. Instead a quiet, deep-voiced "hmmm-mmm" emanated from Amber's body over the microphone, increasing in volume—melodic and ambient, slow and smooth. We were under her spell as Amber hummed the melody line of a Negro spiritual she'd learned at her grandmother's knee.

She opened her voice and heritage to us. She drew us into her experience, to her heart, and to her story without saying a word. At an inflection point, she unfolded a journey that riveted us to our seats. Amber taught us what it was like to be a Black woman raising a family in these United States—wanting her children to have a rich education with all the beauty, literature, art, and music she could bring to her family.

Despite Amber's conscientiousness, however, her children longed to see themselves represented in the education they were receiving—but the voices of Black people were absent from the traditional curriculum. One of Amber's daughters, in particular, identified the contradictions that lived in their family with the artless innocence of a child looking for her place in the world. Her inability to thrive in a place where her Black identity and culture weren't acknowledged or celebrated brought about a crisis. As Amber tells it, "To heal my daughter, I had to wreck myself. Not my body, mind you, but my sense of self." Amber began a journey to reclaiming herself and healing her daughter by delving into her cultural and family heritage. I find Amber's choice of words here powerful and a challenge to each of us. How are we perpetuating a world that treats some of our fellow citizens as invisible? Do we have the willingness to wreck ourselves (our beliefs, habits of practice, and understanding of history) to heal our families and our communities?

This is the heart of Amber's message and she delivers it with grace, conviction, and love—not an ounce of antagonism. *A Place to Belong* is the right book at the right time to teach each of us how to be brave enough to wreck ourselves in order that others may be liberated from the societal cages we have both consciously and unconsciously created for them. Amber amplifies that vision with poetic sensitivity and insight, as well as actionable practices that will transform any family who undertakes them.

I am honored to write the foreword to this book. It must be said, however, that I am a white woman. Let me be clear—I'm the student here. I read Amber's book eager to learn. I was moved repeatedly and transformed by the end. I remembered as a homeschooler the difficulty of finding texts that included the voices of the oppressed, and capitulating too often to the status quo (whitewashed) accounts of American history. I read the questions Amber poses in her chapters and wished I had had them to anchor my research and values as I taught my children when they were growing up.

Amber believes in the power of honest self-examination. She contends that identifying our beliefs is a first step in claiming our heritage. She asserts that telling our stories and illuminating them (even the hard parts) will result in a more humane society. I believe her! Amber doesn't leave us to find our own way. She shows us how to create what she calls "colorful" homes rather than taking refuge in the harmful philosophy of being "colorblind." As Amber puts it, "Pretending that race doesn't exist is not the same thing as promoting equality. While the intention may be to convey that race shouldn't matter, the message children receive from a colorblind mentality is that race doesn't matter, and that simply isn't true. In today's world, it matters immensely."

Understanding our relationship to race is as urgent today as it's ever been. Amber trusts each reader to grapple with their current biases. She provides a wide array of questions to pose to ourselves to help us dig a little deeper into how we understand race and what impact those beliefs have on our families. She recommends curating a diverse library of books and media choices. She addresses the thorny topic of what to do with the classic "white-centric" Western canon, balancing the enduring value of the stories against the disappointing lack of diverse representation. She talks about the difference between a "living" book and a "life-giving" book as a way to acknowledge that not all revered literature enables all readers to feel seen and enriched. In fact, Amber also gives a rousing thumbs-up to the value of visual media (films, YouTube, television) to aid this process of becoming more attuned to those who are not like us, as well as those who are.

I was particularly moved by the gorgeous vision outlined in part 3 that shows anyone how to cultivate a family heritage steeped in personal meaning. Amber's creativity and depth really shine here. She instructs us to honor our roots while also showing us how to leave a legacy, even if your family heritage is too painful to recall and celebrate. She confronts the challenge of teaching "hard history" (as she calls it) when the historical record includes painful reminders of our inhumanity toward one another. Amber has no shortage of ideas to help us in this mission: from interviewing relatives to collecting family recipes to building a keepsake chest. I found her suggestion to commission a work of art as a family heirloom inspired!

This quest to create a rich family culture is not the end of the journey in finding our place to belong. Amber reminds us that there are other ways of life equally worthy of exploration. She and her husband have made it a priority to raise global citizens. To that end, Amber describes her family's "worldschooling adventures" (delightful!) and even thoughtfully provides ideas for how to afford the cost of that kind of family travel (practical).

Most of us would agree with Amber that an important goal in parenting is to broaden our children's imaginations to value everyone, including themselves. Mere exposure to others of different backgrounds is not enough, however. Exposure is not the same as finding connection. Amber reminds us that "finding connection is not always the same as standing in agreement." In today's world where agreement seems in short supply, it was a relief to discover that connection to our stories and one another is enough to build bridges to a more just world.

For historically marginalized communities, that may mean letting go of unhealthy practices that accommodate the larger culture while over-looking the beauty and power of one's own. For those who are in the dominant community, that means working toward justice and fairness for all races and abilities, sexual identities, and religious backgrounds. Amber is a realist. She knows that these goals aren't met in a day. She reminds us: "We value progress over perfection, and we stand on the heels of hope . . . It's our responsibility to help our kids stretch in purposeful and sometimes uncomfortable ways."

My children are now adults, and I wish I had had a resource as filled with actionable practices and thoughtful philosophy about family heritage and race as this one when they were growing up. I'm eager to use the ideas with my grandchildren, nature's great parenting do-over. You with your children still at home can begin now.

I hope you'll read this book cover to cover and put into practice both the attitudes and abundant activities that Amber provides. I'm convinced they can heal all of us. I look forward to living in a world informed by people honest and fearless enough to value each person's story, heritage, and future aspirations. I'm grateful that Amber has provided a well-traveled footpath to get us there.

—Julie Bogart, author of
The Brave Learner and *Raising Critical Thinkers*

INTRODUCTION

As far back as I can remember, there has always been a place to which I belonged with a certainty that nothing has been able to take from me. When I say place, that means less a geographical locality and more a group of people with whom I am connected and to whom I belong.

—Sindiwe Magona, *To My Children's Children*

WHEN I BECAME A MOTHER, I ASSUMED THAT MY CHILDREN would always feel secure, valued, and loved in my arms. I saw myself as a mix between Ma Ingalls and Clair Huxtable, affectionately shepherding a flock of kiddos with down-home values, lively humor, and a dose of modernity. I knew the world would send rainy days, but I pictured our home as a bright light where babies grew, little ones played, and adolescents bloomed.

And I wasn't entirely wrong. My husband, Scott, and I are raising four children in different developmental stages: a nearly teen girl and her solidly tween sister, along with two elementary-aged little brothers. And in many ways, our family has unfolded much as I expected. Our children frolic outdoors amid pink and white cherry blossoms and enormous loblolly pine trees, and they catch frogs and fish with homemade nets in the lake across the road. We enjoy nightly family dinners inspired by food-spattered cookbooks and laced with veggies and herbs we've grown out back. Our family relishes movie nights and fireside read-alouds, and laughter is the soundtrack of our lives. We spend our days living and learning together, and our kids certainly feel loved. Our lives are comfortable.

But not long ago, I realized that I had confused comfort with belonging. I discovered that growing alongside our beautiful children were weeds of confusion, choking our best child-rearing efforts. We were following a cookie-cutter approach to parenting and education that left our children feeling unacknowledged and invisible despite our engaged presence and persistent affection.

We are an African American family living in a predominantly white community. Despite being near a major metropolitan city, our local gathering spots and extracurricular activities were completely white environments. We did what everyone around us was doing, so we expected to see positive results, but what we saw instead were children who felt like visitors in their own home, surrounded by the stories, voices, and images of others. We were raising little people who struggled to see themselves and understand their relationship to the broader world.

Every child longs for a place to belong. A place where cultural awareness, self-acceptance, celebration, and kinship are the norm. And this natural yearning for affiliation and attachment is best satisfied within the context of home and family life. Home is where lifelong attitudes are rooted and affirmed, where children learn the values that will inform how they move through the world.

At times, those values are overtly taught, and at other times, they're subtly caught. Though we told our kids that all people are equal and important, our actions taught them that perhaps that wasn't entirely true. Our silence about our own ethnic identity and family history combined with our reliance on white-centered homeschooling curricula planted seeds of doubt, causing our kids to consider that maybe there were some people worth studying or honoring more than others.

Thankfully, our oldest was born with an audacious spirit, and she quickly showed me in heartbreaking yet inspiring ways that what we were doing was not enough. She let me know that ignoring her brown skin and curly hair was not an enlightened colorblind path but rather a breeding ground for shame and alienation. At first, I couldn't hear her through the noise of my own insecurities and entrenched expectations, but in the words of filmmaker Darnell Lamont Walker, she silently expressed that "a seat at the table is desired. But I'll scream from the street if I need to."

Her screams could not be ignored, and by learning to see the world through her eyes, I was able to shift our family culture to one that honors my children's background, individuality, and sense of self-worth. And with that shift came an unexpected connection to others who are racially and culturally different from us. By acknowledging and embracing herself, my daughter was better able to love on our neighbors. That realization marked a turning point, one that resonated beyond the walls of our home.

On the heels of protests and political divisiveness, our nation is bursting with social unrest as Americans wrestle with defining who we are and what we stand for as a disparate yet connected group of individuals. The drive for inclusivity and equity alongside a heightened urgency to raise self-confident children who hold genuine affection for others is burning brightly within my heart and the hearts of many other parents.

Gone are the days when socially conscious parents feel comfortable with their children merely tolerating or empathizing with others. Intentional parents, those committed to making informed and culturally aware parenting decisions, are looking for a path to authentically embrace the fullness of our diverse communities. But we need strategies that acknowledge the intricacies and daily challenges of home. Realistic actionable steps toward progress that complement and embrace family life.

In many cases, messages on diversity, equity, and inclusion get mired down in polarizing ideologies. They're lost in a sea of politics and religion and covered over with blame, shame, anger, defensiveness, and criticism. That's not what I'm about. *A Place to Belong* begins with the fundamental premise that we all love our children, value our communities, and want the best for both. This book is a joyful ode to childhood, a time of exponential emotional growth, and to the home, the treasured space where our children form their first attachments and perspectives on the world.

Within the following pages, I'll offer a path forward for parents of all backgrounds who crave a culturally rich, life-giving home that fosters values of organic diversity and togetherness. We'll talk parent-to-parent and discover the magic of an inclusive learning environment where culture and childhood are honored in a cohesive and celebratory way.

And by learning environment, I don't just mean the physical space occupied by homeschooling families. Yes, I am a home educator, but I'm also the daughter of two principals and a product of public education. These experiences have shown me that cultivating a home culture is something every parent can do, regardless of personal education choices. Whether home and "school" are distinct locations for your family or combined at your dining room table, teaching is the charge of every parent. Learning happens outside the confines of formal lessons as much as within, and we all have the inherent freedom and responsibility to educate the whole child.

The COVID-19 pandemic showed so many of us that we were exhausted and overscheduled with days fueled by obligation and habit rather than intention and purpose. Through unexpected and sometimes traumatic circumstances, we learned that prioritizing family life is meaningful. Uninterrupted moments of deep connection and consistent time spent engaged in meaningful conversations provide crucial opportunities to spark ideas in our children's hearts. When mothers and fathers became primary teachers, many saw how relational living builds confidence in our children and inspires hope in our homes and communities, causing a generous ripple effect in galvanizing and changing the world, one family at a time.

If you've seen the fracturing of our communities, read books and articles about the tenuous state of cross-racial relationships, listened to socially conscious podcasts and experts talk about the shift that needs to occur, or feel moved to ignite a revolution of camaraderie and belonging in your home, this is the book for you.

I know that change and growth can be challenging, especially when dealing with hot-button topics. I've been there, and though it may feel like daunting work, I want to reassure you that the effort you put into considering the questions posed in these chapters will have tangible and lasting effects. Please don't feel discouraged or overwhelmed as you take the necessary steps to build or shift your family culture. You're doing important work in this space, it becomes easier and more natural over time, and the payoff is substantial.

Written from my perspective as a mother who has successfully shifted our home culture from a siloed pursuit of academic excellence to an inclusive celebration of self and others, these chapters will give you the tools to raise children who embrace their unique identities while feeling beautifully tethered to people who are racially, ethnically, culturally, or socially different than themselves.

In part 1, we'll start at the family table where honest conversations and openness lay the foundation of a secure home. After examining what we, as parents, bring to the table and establishing a blueprint for the type of home environment we hope to create, we'll move into the home library in part 2. This may be a literal room of shelves for your family, or all the little nooks and crannies sprinkled about where books can be found. I focus our attention there because books are some of the loudest communicators in a home, but they're not everything. In part 3, we'll see that other aspects of the broader family space are equally important: how our children feel in our home, the images they see and internalize, and the experiences and lessons they have, both formal and informal. They all matter. In the end, we'll move beyond the four walls of our homes as we seek to guide our children toward a firm footing in an uncertain but hope-filled world.

I'm writing this introduction to you on our screened-in back porch after a fresh rain. I have a huge cup of strong spicy tea—no milk, no sugar—and a small lap blanket keeping me warm. I invite you to join me. Grab a few creature comforts, cozy up, and get settled as we explore the inner workings of an inclusive and colorful home.

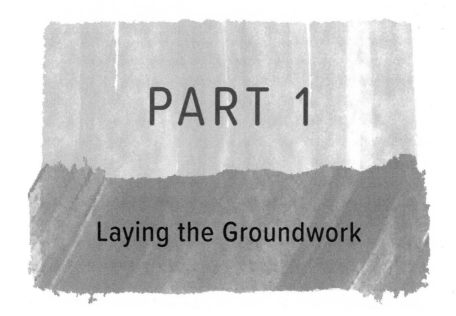

PART 1

Laying the Groundwork

I GREW UP HEARING MY GRANDMOTHER HUM OLD SONGS WHILE making cornbread muffins in the kitchen each afternoon during our visits to my grandparents' small town in southern Illinois. In my twenties, I learned that her familiar music was the melody of Negro spirituals. About a decade later, my ears perked up as I recognized one of the songs, "Wade in the Water," while watching Alvin Ailey's breathtaking 1960s signature ballet, *Revelations*, in the front row of Atlanta's Fox Theatre.

But it wasn't until I began homeschooling my children that I understood the full backstory of the song. What seems like a straightforward biblical reference to the Israelites' escape from Egypt was actually a coded song containing explicit instructions to fugitive slaves on avoiding capture and successfully making their way to freedom. That information was so eye-opening that I began to learn more about the Fisk Jubilee Singers, the first to popularize the song. And my hunger to know the backstory of other familiar songs from my childhood led me to *Like a Bird: The Art of the American Slave Song* by Cynthia Grady, a book I immediately studied with my children.

The book became a way for my kids to understand more about their heritage and to link the songs I share with them to the great-grandmother they never had the delight of knowing and to older generations of our family. Today, some years into our journey, I can rattle off dozens of stories and give many examples of relics that help connect my children to our family's past, but it hasn't always been this way.

In her poem titled "Caged Bird," Maya Angelou wrote that a bird confined to a limiting cage struggles to see beyond the rage induced by his confinement. He's bound and stripped of his ability to spread his wings and fly, "so he opens his throat to sing" of freedom.[1] I relate some of my parenting story to that idea because my daughter was in a narrow cage about five years ago, so she opened her throat to sing. She first responded to her confinement with silent protest when she rejected and hid her Black baby dolls. When asked about her peculiar behavior, she shared that the "dolls with brown skin are ugly," and she only wanted to play with the "pretty white dolls."

Following that encounter, she began incessantly questioning whether she would be the only Black girl at ballet, the park, or a birthday party. She would count "brown" people wherever we went: up and down the aisles of Costco, around the stalls of the farmer's market in our town square, at the gas station, and on hiking trails. And she would always tell me that she didn't want to go if there weren't any other Brown people there.

I knew her fixation on skin color was unhealthy, but I didn't know how to stop it. I wanted to rip out the intrusive thoughts crowding her mind, but I couldn't find the source. My husband and I had gone out of our way not to talk about race with her. We taught her that all people were valuable, and we were called to love everyone. We never made differences between people of one ethnicity or another. We were always careful to shade her from the evils of racism in any form it may present itself, and we did our best to create a colorblind home. But she persisted.

One night, I was awakened by the presence of something in my room and was startled to find my little girl standing at my bedside, staring at me with tears streaming down her face. I assumed that she'd had a bad dream, but when I asked her what was wrong, my caged bird opened her throat and said, "I can't sleep because I can't stop thinking about how ugly I am. I hate my skin, and my hair is disgusting. I don't want to look like this anymore."

The lies she believed about herself were absurd. This girl with the sweetest brown skin and delightfully curly hair felt that her Blackness was weighing her down. As I thought of how I could help my daughter become free, I couldn't shake the thought of one thing she said in my arms that night. I told her how beautifully and wonderfully made she was, how every fiber of her being was known and knitted to perfection. While I earnestly tried to get her to accept her skin and hair the way they were intended to be, she asked me in the middle of sniffles, "Well, why don't you wear your hair the way *you* were made?"

The wounds inflicted by an honest child are among the most painful.

The mother she knew had bone-straight hair. Though my hair comes out of my head curly and big, I had never seen that hair as an adult and had no clue how it looked. My mom (bless her heart, as we say in Georgia) began putting a chemical relaxer on my hair—as did most Black moms in the eighties—when I was only eight years old. Every six weeks or so for the next thirty years, until that night with my daughter, I would return to a salon wherever I happened to be in the country, or the world, to have my roots straightened or "touched up" with toxins that would often burn small sores onto my scalp.

I never questioned this process because, essentially, it was all I knew. And over the years, I gained a reputation with my hair. My long straight tresses hung down my back, and they became a point of compliment from everyone. My hair was part of my signature look, and I wore it as a crown of glory.

I encouraged my daughter to embrace her natural hair and love how she was made, but I was not setting an example. Having my daughter innocently question the motives and actions behind my hypocrisy was bone-chilling. I had to ask myself what kind of skin I was willing to put in the game on behalf of my little girl.

While I was wrestling with this, I remembered a movie I'd watched, ironically, when I was pregnant with her in 2009. In *My Sister's Keeper*, actress Cameron Diaz plays the mother, and her oldest daughter has leukemia. Her hair has fallen out, and she doesn't want to get out of bed to go on a family outing. When her mom keeps pushing and challenging her, the girl sits up in bed and exclaims, "I'm tired. Don't you get that? I'm sick, and I'm tired, and I'm ugly. Don't you dare tell me that I'm beautiful because I'm not! Don't you dare tell me that nobody's gonna stare at me because they will! I'm a freak!"[2]

With that, her mom walks out of the room, and the next thing the family hears is the clippers. She went into the bathroom and shaved off all her hair so her daughter wouldn't have to be bald alone. At that moment, that mom realized there were no words because sometimes words aren't enough. There are times when we, as parents, are called to show, with actions, a type of love that words can't express.

Please know that I'm not sitting here today comparing my daughter's identity issues and feelings to having leukemia, because they don't compare. But self-hatred born of invisibility is an affliction that spreads just like cancer. And while the body may sustain, it kills the soul.

The chemicals that some Black women use to permanently straighten their hair—to make their hair more "manageable" and "beautiful" according to mainstream society—cannot be reversed. You can't change your mind. The processed hair has to be cut off. That night, as I held my girl, my mouth and heart made a vow that my mind was not on board with. And the following day, I felt physically ill because I vividly recalled promising her that I would stop straightening my hair, and I didn't want to do it.

To heal my daughter, I had to wreck myself. Not my body, mind you, but my sense of self. I had to come face-to-face with who I was and what I felt about myself and my heritage, and it was so much more than just the hair. How could I ask my child to show up authentically in this world when I couldn't even do it? How could I ask her to be confident in who she was when I was still wearing the plastered smile I'd learned to put on when I was her age?

There was no chance of me going back on my word, so I grabbed the metaphorical clippers and went to work. No, I didn't shave my hair off all at once. But I vowed not to alter a single curl that grew from my scalp, and I slowly cut off the straight crown and let a giant curly wreath grow in. The transition was painful, but it was worth it. Now I'm on the other side, and this "big hair, don't care" mama can look at her little girls with a wink and a smile and say, "We got this, girl."

You may be wondering what in the world all of this has to do with family culture, and my answer is "Everything." Hair was one of the first ways we began to grapple with our heritage, but as the "awakening" process was happening, a radical shift occurred within our home because I had to contend with much more than just hair. I was also forced to evaluate the entire narrative woven into our home life, and I needed to discover how to let my children know that they mattered.

You may recognize bits of your own story within mine, but most likely, the path that led you to this book is an entirely different one. What matters most is not the particularity of your story but the acceptance that you have one and your willingness to stare into it to determine how it's manifesting in your children. As we look toward establishing a blueprint for an inclusive and colorful family culture, we'll start with what we, as parents, bring to the table. We'll discuss how open dialogue and conscious family practices can breathe life into our homes, setting a compass toward the hopes and dreams we hold for our treasured families.

1

EVALUATING YOUR FAMILY CULTURE

What Are You Bringing to the Table?

> To put the world in order, we must first put the nation in order; to put
> the nation in order, we must first put the family in order; to put the
> family in order, we must first cultivate our personal life; we must first
> set our hearts right.
>
> —Confucius, Chinese philosopher

MY CHILDREN LOVE PLAYING WITH THE CHANDELIER HANGING
in our dining room when sunlight pours in from the high foyer window.
We inherited this formal lighting fixture from the previous homeowners,
and it doesn't match the relaxed decor of our home, so it was one of many
things I'd planned to change as soon as we moved in. But seeing my kids'
joy in chasing rainbows formed by the hanging prisms led me to leave it
untouched. And even though it initially struck me as fussy and unappeal-
ing, the ornate light has become a fun focal point in the center of our
home.

One day, I found my youngest kiddo standing atop the table, jangling
the prisms, and before I could chastise him for having his chubby toes
where they didn't belong, he squealed with delight and exclaimed, "Look,
Mama! We have colors everywhere!" Forgetting my plans for admonish-
ment, I smiled at how delighted he was at that moment, and it was then
that the idea of having a colorful home began to cement in my mind.

Though my son's experience was quite literal, I envisioned a home atmosphere where we metaphorically celebrate colorful people like danc-ing rainbows. Each stripe dons its own unique shade while blending with its neighbor to create something more spectacular than any single color can achieve on its own. The afternoon rainbows on our walls remind me of the beauty of both individuality and togetherness lying alongside one an-other, and that's an idea I want to permeate my home.

I do hope that my children always feel magnificent in their skin. Not because they're convinced that they are somehow more special than others but because they embrace their differences while recognizing that we're better together. In short, I want them to form an identity around being a meaningful member of a colorful local and global community.

In her memoir, actress Tembi Locke considered the question "Do I belong here?" And after decades of trying to answer the question for strangers, the world, and herself, she concluded, "I had learned that iden-tity is prismatic, that belonging requires claiming."[1] I loved her words from the moment I read them. I understood, instinctively, that the concept of identity as a prism was compelling. Still, I had to sit with the thought for a while before assimilating it with my hopes for a colorful family culture.

Aside from the obvious connotation of being related to a prism, "pris-matic" means varied and brilliant. Colorful. Another definition is "formed, separated, or distributed" by something acting as a prism.[2] Identity is not a simple one-dimensional concept. It is a complex and colorful notion that actively develops through the prisms of experience and affiliation. Identity is not something that someone can put upon another person, but the home environment plays a crucial role in our children's identity development. Identity can be strengthened and supported under the careful watch of loving parents or marred by indifference and trauma. But for it to be au-thentic, it must be claimed.

For some families, including my own, a significant aspect of formed identity relates to religious convictions, and for the longest time, I felt like no further thinking on the matter was required. But I've since come to realize that parents have a responsibility to teach and guide within the context of our faith or without the overlay of any spiritual beliefs at all, depending on our personal convictions. So how do we go about helping our children claim an identity or self-concept that honors who they are while assuring that they can and do embrace others?

We are all individuals, but we are also part of something greater. To ignore either aspect can foster a poor sense of self, one of self-deprecation or self-adulation, situated at polarizing ends of the spectrum of belonging. Take the time to consider the messages your children may absorb from how you communicate your cultural identity and how you think and speak about others. Just as children have front-row seats to our passions and preferences, they also absorb our indifferences and insecurities. And sometimes those are communicated more loudly than we imagine.

What are you bringing to the table? The following sections include some questions to consider as you prepare to address past beliefs and behaviors, challenge the status quo, and welcome change within your home.

CULTURAL HERITAGE AND FAMILY BACKGROUND

Explore who you are, where you come from, and how your past informs what you currently think, do, and say because your children will draw from the strengths and inconsistencies of your identity as they claim their own.

- Who are you? What makes up your identity, and how does that shape your daily life?

- How does your cultural heritage manifest physically, and how do you feel about it? And by physically, I don't just mean how you look. I also mean your physical space. Are there things in your environment that speak to who you are and where you come from?

- How do the physical manifestations of your cultural heritage align with or differ from that of your children? If they differ, how is your child's cultural heritage manifested in your home?

- How do you feel about who you are? What about the people from whom you have descended? Do you know anything about your ancestors? Are there parts of your lifestyle, celebrations, thoughts, or speech that reflect them or their lived experiences?

- Do you help your children connect the dots between their immediate family, the generations before, and those who will come after them?

- Did your parents or other members of your family hold biased or racist views as you were growing up? Do you still believe some of what you heard? If not, how were you able to grapple with what was said? How does the memory of it impact you today?

- Why are you interested in creating an inclusive home environment? What do you want to do differently in your home versus the home in which you were raised?

- Which aspects of your childhood home would you like to replicate?

SOCIALIZATION AND COMMUNITY

Take inventory of who your family does life with and ascertain how your micro-community came to be. Acknowledge what's working in your social circles, and parse through any disconnect between the environment you want your children raised in and the environment your family swims in today.

- If you're white, do you have or have you ever had many close friends of color?

- Do you believe that having close friends of color helps with cultural understanding? If so, how? If not, why not?

- If you're a person of color, how much of your time is spent in all or mostly white environments? Are you comfortable with your current social circle?

- What about your children? How do you (and they) feel about the community in which they're being raised?

- If applicable, what do your children think about often being "the only one" in their environment?

- How diverse are your social circles? Is the degree of inclusivity, or lack thereof, intentional? If your environment is homogenous (e.g., all white or all Black), what prevents you from engaging in a more diverse community?

- Do you think your social circles are exclusive? Why or why not?

- Do you find yourself consciously leaning into or avoiding friendships with people of color? What about friendships with white people? If so, why? How have your past experiences shaped that inclination?

- What do you think about people of underrepresented cultures intentionally supporting one another and connecting alone as a group?

- Can you easily connect with people who look different than you? Are you able to communicate easily? Do you see them as peers?

- What topics do you find challenging to discuss with white people? People of color? Why do they make you uncomfortable?

RACE, STEREOTYPES, AND BIAS

Evaluate how you feel about race and its impact on the world around you. Many of us have been raised not to talk about these things, but that shroud of silence is part of what got us here in the first place. Allow yourself to delve into these taboo topics and begin to evaluate the truths and fallacies you carry because it can be challenging to explore ideas with your children that you haven't fully contemplated yourself.

- People routinely and often unconsciously view white people and their behavior positively, representing what is good, moral, and standard. Are there areas of your life where you can see that this is the case?

- Do you consider the ways you see other ethnicities showing up in social or work situations distasteful? Where did you get those ideas? Are you open to challenging them?

- Do you take a person's appearance or cultural background into account when making judgments about competence or ability? How so?

- Do you recognize language that reinforces stereotypes? How confident are you in identifying this type of language? Do you intentionally avoid speaking this way? Do you consciously try to avoid thinking this way?

- Do you talk to your kids about racism, race, ethnicity, and culture? If so, how deep do you go? If not, what's holding you back, and when do you plan to start?

- What types of race-based scenarios or conversations elicit an emotional response from you, positive or negative?

- How do you feel when you overhear people speaking French in the United States? What about when you hear people speaking Spanish? Do you notice a difference in your thoughts about the people based on the language spoken?

- How does racism show up today? Is it a series of infrequent, isolated, or personal incidents, or is it systemic? Why do you think so?

- Do you believe good people can unintentionally say or do bad things?

- How do you feel about color blindness? Do you think it's a worthy goal, that it devalues a person's experiences, or something else? Why do you believe that?

- Do you think people of color are paranoid about their experiences with racism? If so, what causes you to feel that way? If not, what makes you believe them?

- Do you think that people of color play the race card too often? If so, why do you think so, and how can you tell when it's happening?

- Have you evaluated your worldview in terms of how it may affect your interactions with diverse groups? When you think about this, what do you come up with?

- What positive attitudes are you passing along to your children, and how?

ACTIVISM AND LEADERSHIP

Ultimately, we're not looking for our kids to just know the truth, but rather, we're hoping that they will act upon it. It may be comforting to teach our children to "do as I say, not as I do," but the reality is that children follow our example, not our advice. Consider how your thoughts impact your actions and what you're doing to be the change you hope to see in the world.

- Do you challenge others when they make offensive jokes or comments about race, ethnicity, or gender? Do you participate?

- Do you speak up when you witness another person being humiliated or discriminated against? Why or why not?

- Do you encourage culturally diverse people to speak up about their concerns? Do you validate their issues? What kinds of emotions do those conversations bring up for you?

- Do you listen to white people when they share their personal experiences and how they feel about race-based interactions?

- Are you comfortable speaking about social injustice, bias, or oppression? Do you participate in conversations on these topics? Are you usually tuned in or out? If applicable, do you think your silence could be interpreted as agreement with the status quo? How does that make you feel?

- What role do you see yourself playing in racial reconciliation or the restoration of cross-cultural relationships? What role do you see your racial group as a whole playing?

- Do you find yourself annoyed by the constant chatter about diversity, equity, and inclusion? Why or why not? What emotions do you feel when people bring these topics up in your presence?

- Is learning emotionally sensitive or hard history important to you? Will understanding how we got to this place help us as a society or harm us as we navigate the legacy of racial angst that we've inherited?

- Do you seek out opportunities to improve your understanding of the marginalization of diverse groups? What about the joys, ingenuity, and resilience of these same groups?

- Do you find yourself trying to justify acts of discrimination? Do you validate or explain away the stories that people of color share about their experiences?

- What are your thoughts on the Black Lives Matters movement? Are there parts you agree with? Disagree with?

- How did the uptick in violence against Asian people in the aftermath of the pandemic make you feel? What did you do about it?

- Did you know that Asian Americans have faced racial discrimination long before the pandemic? Have you ever heard Asian people referred to as the "model minority"? What do you think of that concept?

- How do you feel about immigration and its impact on the "browning" of America?

- What do you think it means to be racist? Where did you get that idea?

- Can people of color be racist? Do people of color have a responsibility to rid themselves of racist ideas, or is that work only or primarily for white people?

- What are you doing to help foster positive cross-racial or cross-cultural relationships? How has that action impacted your life?

- Do you consider yourself socially aware? Justice-minded? What can you do to progress along these lines?

- Do your children see you challenging racism, demonstrating kindness, and standing up for every person's right to be treated with dignity and respect?

This is not an exhaustive list of questions, but these are the types of things we need to grapple with as we engage in transformative work within our minds, our homes, and our communities. It's crucial to be radically honest with yourself as you sit with your thoughts and the tension they may cause before engaging with others on these topics. If you have a safe person or group to explore these ideas with, it can sometimes be helpful to share your thoughts with others as you hear their perspectives.

Based on our past experiences and current circumstances, we'll each have different areas that need our attention most, but here is some of the work we can begin to do as we learn more about ourselves and others:

Train your brain to think differently. Consciously observe how you feel and behave and how your beliefs lead you to make positive or negative assumptions about people you encounter. Recognize opportunities to examine or reject your learned responses and replace them with healthy thinking when necessary. Deliberately expose yourself to counter-stereotypes in media, books, and relationships.

Question your objectivity. Ask yourself whether you would have spoken or behaved otherwise in a particular situation if the person you were dealing with was in a different social, racial, or cultural group. When making decisions that impact people in other groups, examine whether you can truly justify the choice or if bias may be playing a role.

Change your circumstances. Put yourself in someone else's shoes and try to see a situation from their perspective. Commit to placing yourself in environments where you're the minority and note aspects of the experience that feel challenging.

Reframe the standard. In so many circumstances, white people are seen as the standard in various ways (style, behavior, preferences, norms, etc.). This is obviously an issue for white people trying to see the world differently, but it's also an issue within communities of color. When you notice that someone is not doing something the "right" way, ask yourself whether it's truly a universal moral failure or rather a cultural preference.

Commit to extending yourself. This book is not an academic exploration of cultural differences or a review of models developed to overcome racism. It's very simply a guide for families choosing to live differently. It's so easy to remain in our bubbles, doing what we've always done, but if we're going to raise our children to see and value others in an authentic and committed way, we have to extend ourselves. We must expand our thinking, social circles, learning, adventures, and relationships.

AS YOU SPEND TIME CONSIDERING THE BAGGAGE AND GIFTS you bring to the family table (we all carry both), and how they may support or harm your family's culture, keep in mind the following foundational ideas.

Inclusivity is a way of life. When some people talk about diverse and inclusive environments for children, they think of pulling together a lesson on piñatas and Frida Kahlo for Hispanic Heritage Month or making lanterns and homemade sushi during Asian American and Pacific Islander Heritage Month. Then, of course, there's adding a little Frederick Douglass and Rosa Parks to the mix in February, too. Don't get me wrong, it's nice to join in celebrating various cultures throughout the year, but it's a mistake to think that these things alone will bring about satisfactory outcomes.

It's how our children listen and interact with the multifaceted nature of different people's experiences that matters. It's their engagement with the stories shared by and about others and how our children are able to weave in their own personal narratives with humility and confidence that shapes our kids' hearts and minds as they form opinions about whose stories matter and why. Promoting curiosity and infusing our home environment with colorful perspectives all year long, every year, is how we naturally guide our children toward an inclusive mindset that becomes second nature. Consistent and diverse stories and experiences create a compelling interest in seeing and being seen. This type of living inspires our children to act in the best interests of their neighbors as they seek to love them well.

Diversity is multidimensional and intersectional. There's considerable diversity among groups of people in terms of ethnicity, culture, and other characteristics. Typically, when we think about diverse stories, resources, or experiences for our children, we immediately picture colorful encounters that explore the world beyond white people, and understandably so. But at times, the needed diversity is that of people of color listening to the voices of other people of color. BIPOC may share commonalities born of historical circumstances, societal norms, underrepresentation, and prejudice or racism. Still, their context for those experiences will differ, and frequently, there is healing that needs to occur between non-white racial groups.

But what about other kinds of diversity? Admittedly, I sometimes find myself drawn so far into my experiences with ethnicity and culture that I've stopped listening for different entry points into this conversation. For instance, some time ago, I realized that I'd muted the voices of disabled people. Out of sight, out of mind. Ignoring them was relatively easy because listening requires active engagement, and I wasn't looking for relationships and understanding. I hadn't intentionally rejected a connection with communities of disabled people, mind you; I just hadn't bothered to think about them, which is often the case. It took my kids to open my eyes.

My doll-collecting daughter likes to sew clothes for her favorites before posing them for photos. One day, she placed a doll in a chair, and the outfit she'd made got all bunched up. Nina said, "I'm okay with this because my doll will get to stand up and show off her outfit in the next photo, but if she were usually sitting, like if she used a wheelchair, I'd need to change the way I make her clothes." That led to a discussion on where people who are seated most of their waking hours shop for clothes that look good on them because we'd never seen any clothes modeled by people in wheelchairs.

We followed that rabbit trail and landed at an article featuring disability fashion styling expert Stephanie Thomas. What she said in the interview stuck with me: "You can't market to or design for someone you don't value . . . you have more clothing for pets than you do for Disabled people in stores. . . . We see more value in a poodle, in a Labrador, in whatever . . . than we do in a fashion customer with a disability."[3] That's deep. And it's something we would never have thought of until we heard it from her. And as I was reading Stephanie's words, the intersectionality of her identity wasn't lost on me. She's disabled. She's a woman. She's Black. And in a single interview, she reflected all those parts of herself and more.

We choose who we hear from, and we can't just move through life expecting a diversity of messages to penetrate through osmosis. Our families need to actively seek expansion of thought and communion by looking beyond common conceptions of diversity. And while some fail to recognize or acknowledge the incredible diversity *within* groups of people, insiders are quick to let you know that they're not all the same.

Whether the differences stem from geography, language, socioeconomics, physical traits, or are born purely of personality and preferences, there is as much diversity of thought and ways within underrepresented (or "un-tapped," as entrepreneur Chike Ukaegbu likes to say) groups as there is among white people. This was never made more apparent to me than when I landed on campus my freshman year of college.

Because my high school had so few Black people, we were often seen as a single group. This may have been proliferated by the fact that we usually took up residence at one table in the cafeteria (read *Why Are All the Black Kids Sitting Together in the Cafeteria?* by Beverly Daniel Tatum for more on that), but there were many, many tables full of white kids, and no one ever considered them to be all the same. I'm not sure what I expected when I got to college because I had no frame of reference for being in a sea of Black folks, but what I experienced gave me a new perspective that propelled my thought processes on race and culture.

In the cafeteria at Florida A&M University, my alma mater, there were rows upon rows of tables filled with Black people. The entire room was Black, from the students to the person mopping the floor, all the cooks, and the professors sweating it out in a suit and tie in the Tallahassee humidity. At first glance, it seemed like it was just the high school table of Black kids amplified and on repeat, but a few weeks of casual observation taught me otherwise.

Within the sea of Blackness, I found separate tables of future engineers, business leaders, writers, and nurses. There were tables of students from Miami, Charlotte, Chicago, and Washington, D.C. Athletes, cheerleaders, sororities, and fraternities dominated some spaces, and others spilled over with international students from the Caribbean and various countries in Africa. There were even tables occupied by skaters and bikers and out-doorsy types, things that had always felt reserved for white kids. And then some seats were all jumbled up with no discernible form of categorization.

In high school, I was Black. The smart Black girl on some days. But in college, I was known as a marketing student who loved to babysit and spend time doing community service and having fun with her Alpha Kappa Alpha sorors while eating lasagna and working at the Gap or wait-ing tables at the local seafood joint. When I didn't have to take up space just being Black, people perceived me as so many other things along with being a young Black woman.

What I learned is that, given the opportunity to be themselves in a safe space, people will gladly show you all of who they are. What they'll reveal is that parts of themselves are shaped by the culture(s) with which they most identify, while other vital parts can't be pegged to any of our limited categories. That understanding of nuanced, ambiguous, complex, and fluid diversity is what our children need not only to see but believe, because it will inform how they interact with the people they meet and choose to do life with.

Understanding does not lead to imitation. I've witnessed parents who resist teaching their children about anyone with a different worldview because they're afraid that the "undesirable" aspects of a culture or people group will rub off on their kids. The thing is, I've never heard of that happening, and it feels far-fetched, at best, especially if your children are regularly grounded in your family's values. Many parents are okay with introducing their kids to recipes and songs from other countries, but their fear of digging into what others believe and how they see the world is so palpable that it can almost be mistaken for scorn.

I get that it can be scary to consider that our children may form their own thoughts about something once they know that there are options. Some parents may not like that idea, but ultimately, our kids are not us. They are less experienced people, and we are to guide them through wise counsel and by example. Not by using ignorance as a shackle.

Age-appropriate dialogue based on maturity and readiness coupled with a healthy unfurling of information as you go along is a good thing. Teaching children moral imperatives on things that matter is crucial. You can disagree with something that a particular group of people commonly believe or practice and still commit to understanding their perspective. Recognizing a person's or group's value and their right to be treated with dignity, celebrating the beauty found in their culture, and empathetically listening to their experiences while seeking to know them better does not mean that you support all they do. Finding connection is not always the same as standing in agreement.

It's okay to tell your children that a particular custom often practiced by a specific group of people is not something your family supports, but check yourself for bias before doing so. Ensure that what you're resisting is something rooted in your family's core values and not merely an opinion based on your frame of reference. For example, when we encountered the practice of female genital mutilation in a book, I discussed it with my oldest daughter and expressed that it was not something that our family supports. I explained the consequences of the practice and precisely why we stand against it. I also pointed out that the procedure does not represent the totality of the people we were learning about. We cannot dismiss them as inconsequential or undeserving because we disagree with something they hold dear, but we can also stand firm in our convictions.

It's possible to care and connect without demolishing your moral compass. But completely ignoring the existence of entire groups of people or sheltering your child from different perspectives for fear of your child wanting to leave your family ways behind to embrace a different way of thinking or living may satisfy you in the short run, but it rarely turns out well in the end. Lead your children, but allow them to learn, grow, and form their own thoughts.

If we do our jobs well, our children will leave our homes and launch into independence prepared to find their footing. You can't embrace authentic learning and growth with your children when you're leading from fear. You don't have to agree with all the values and beliefs of particular cultural, religious, or social groups to teach your children to recognize the value of their humanity. Give your kids a chance to understand how the world and its people operate within the sanctuary of the home before they must face it on their own.

Not all diversity is good diversity. To be frank, many of the diverse learning resources I've seen are mediocre, at best. They're often heavily politicized one way or the other, removing all opportunities for nuanced thought or consideration. Or they're flooded with dry facts: country flags, highest peaks, gross domestic products, etc. Sometimes, diverse resources are good but limited by only focusing on cultural celebrations.

Filling out worksheets and learning what some people do one day a year isn't what we're here for. If you want to talk GDP, discuss how it impacts the people and their way of life. Rather than just coloring the flag, find out what it means and discuss how it relates to a country's past, including any ties to colonialism. When you're looking at the highest peaks, learn whether the inhabited parts of the country are mountainous and how the terrain influences the food they grow, housing options, professions, and transportation. And when you discuss cultural celebrations, be sure to spend even more time learning about the everyday and the mundane. And then keep going.

Sometimes we can improve mediocre resources, but it's best to avoid some things entirely. When you encounter materials, books, lesson plans, videos, or activities that seem flat and one-dimensional or when they reinforce stereotypes, start asking questions. If something you see or read feels "off" or questionable, stop and evaluate the source. Is an entire group of people ignored, demonized, or always portrayed as heroes or victims? Where did the resource come from? Who else is using it? Who wrote it, and what did they receive in exchange? On what authority are they making claims? Do they have firsthand experience? Where and how did they conduct research? Has the resource been created or vetted by multiple people within the group it claims to represent? What ideologies does the resource present?

Guard the minds of young children fiercely when it comes to propaganda and false teaching. As they get older, starting in middle school and definitely by high school, begin to share some of the biased and poorly done resources with them so they'll understand what to look out for as they start to receive inputs from more outside sources.

And keep in mind that multiculturalism is not the end game. Yes, we want our homes and communities filled with diverse representations of racial, cultural, and social groups, but not just because it's trendy. Many people in our society have gotten caught up in the game of glorifying multiculturalism just for the sake of showing that all people are equal, and that's not wrong, but it's incomplete.

The idea behind this book is to bring people together. We're all working on teaching our children to feel secure in who they are and to understand and value others so that they can naturally grow closer. We want to close gaps, build bridges, form relationships. Diversity just because is a weak aim. It seems like a feel-good vibe or virtue signaling more than anything else. Without the ultimate goal of unity, much of what we're discussing here can lead to divisive and polarizing positions. If you're teaching your children the value of colorful and inclusive living for any reason other than togetherness, you may need to reconsider your motives.

Similarities bind us together. Before we know it, our kids can drown in the Sea of Differences. Constantly pointing out everyone else's divergence from our own experiences without allowing space for children to assimilate our many similarities can lead to an "us versus them" way of thinking. The consistent and natural integration of inclusive learning throughout childhood diminishes the risk of children approaching others from a place of foreignness.

The distinction may be lost on some people, but I hope you understand that we aren't looking to point out how people are different and demand that our kids love them anyway. We're looking to celebrate differences amid kinship. We are simply helping our children to see clearly.

In his book *The Courage to Teach: Exploring the Inner Landscape of a Teacher's Life,* Parker J. Palmer expresses that "we cannot see what is 'out there' merely by looking around. Everything depends on the lenses through which we view the world. By putting on new lenses, we can see things that would otherwise remain invisible."[4]

We need clear lenses, and our children deserve them, too. Through clear lenses, our families will see whole people. People who are just like us in a few ways, similar in many ways, and entirely different in big and small ways. People aren't linear. They're beautifully abstract, and our children's hearts and minds need to stretch to handle the fullness of what our sisters and brothers around the world, and next door, bring to the table.

Colorblindness is not the goal. Not too long ago, a white neighbor sent me a video of two people talking about how things in our country will be better when everyone stops talking about race and becomes colorblind. The interviewees acknowledge that no one can actually be colorblind, but they feel that the key to success is to fake it until we make it. Their premise is that if we all *act* colorblind, we'll see that everything is fine.

The video was bizarre, and the fact that one of the people speaking was Black doesn't deter me from that position. I think he and the woman he was speaking with were well-meaning but misguided. Besides being naive, their plan didn't offer any ideas for dealing with the real and present pain of racism. And neither of them had children.

It's so much easier to develop plans for navigating the muck of racism when you don't have kids. Before I had little faces looking up to me for direction and coming to me in confusion, I had all the answers. In many ways, I shielded myself from the blows of racism because I had constructed a protective little bubble of "sticks and stones may break my bones, but words will never hurt me."

But messing with my kids does hurt me. Watching my children grasp for shreds of positive identity as our nation, our world, fumbles around with race relations awakens my mama bear instincts. And presenting kids with a plan to erase their color in favor of everyone blending in isn't an option.

Race is a social construct, but that doesn't mean racism doesn't exist. Yes, we're all part of one race, the human race. And we need to teach that to our children. But at the same time, humans began categorizing themselves by skin color and other physical traits, and many of those categorizations have significant social consequences for all involved. Acknowledging that people artificially devised race is critically important, but it doesn't negate that racism is real.

Pretending that race doesn't exist is not the same thing as promoting equality. While the intention may be to convey that race *shouldn't* matter, the message children receive from a colorblind mentality is that race *doesn't* matter, and that simply isn't true. In today's world, it matters immensely.

By normalizing colorful living, we're not aiming to be colorblind—far from it. I don't want my kids to pretend to see, not see, do, or be anything. Acting isn't a path to belonging. What we want is to build naturally colorful communities based on authentic fellowship and mutual respect. We want to see each other as we are and believe that it's all good. Inclusive living is cathartic. Color and culture are beautiful. Our differences don't divide us; negative judgments and lackadaisical ignorance rupture society. People assign ugly designations to our differences and then claim that the ugliness will disappear if we don't acknowledge what's right before our eyes.

This way of thinking reminds me of when my kids were little and they would hide from me by covering their eyes. Their flawed thinking led them to believe that if they couldn't see me, I couldn't see them either. But as they matured, they came to realize that I could, in fact, still see them even if they were pretending not to be there. Success is not that our children don't notice diverse images, people, and experiences. Success is that they see people for who they are, notice their beauty, value their presence, and quickly move on because they expected them to be there all along.

Once we've explored our social and cultural identity and personal perceptions, and perhaps wrestled with our misperceptions, it's time to start laying the foundation of our home environment. We'll begin with what families choose to discuss at the dinner table and the atmosphere in which those discussions take place.

2

·······

EMBRACING TOUGH TABLE TOPICS

Normalizing Weighty Conversations

However much we are affected by the things of the world, however
deeply they may stir and stimulate us, they become human for us
only when we can discuss them with our fellows. . . . We humanize
what is going on in the world and in ourselves only by speaking of it,
and in the course of speaking of it we learn to be human.

—Hannah Arendt, *Men in Dark Times*

TO INTERNALIZE THAT HOME IS TRULY A PLACE TO BELONG,
children must believe that it's safe to process feelings and information with
their parents. At home, children should voice their curiosity about others,
share honest thoughts on the world, and question the messages they encounter outside of the family structure without reproach or consequence. Foster-
ing this level of open dialogue around topics often considered impolite or
off-limits requires parents to radically accept and welcome all questions (the
pull), while initiating and normalizing age-appropriate weighty conversations (the push).

Many parents have a misperception that talking about race and racism
will put ideas into their children's heads. Often, parents feel that their
children's innocence will be marred if they're forced to think about ugly
or difficult things too early. I know these feelings well because my husband
and I held similar thoughts when we started our family.

We wanted our kids to continue playing and living the carefree life they appeared to be enjoying, and we figured that we'd get to the tough stuff later since they weren't even thinking about it. But we couldn't have been more wrong. Our children, like all children, were thinking about skin color and other physical differences long before we ever brought it up or made space for them to talk about it.

Discussions about discrimination, race, gender, and class will not be the same for every family. While there's no single right way to handle the conversations, experts agree that the earlier parents start talking to their kids, the better. Research has shown that infants notice and respond to skin color at three to six months. Toddlers start using race to choose playmates at around two to three years old, and even five- to six-year-olds associate race with status. By seven to nine years old, elementary school students have an increased understanding of societal norms relating to race. And by the time tweens are ten to eleven years old, white children avoid mentioning race while children of color exhibit greater racial understanding.[1]

Though they can rarely name it, children observe bias throughout their environments. Many witness or experience prejudice and racism but don't have the vocabulary or context to communicate what they've seen or heard. So while we may feel more comfortable avoiding or delaying conversations on tough subjects, our children are absorbing messages all around. We can leave them to assimilate these inputs and arrive at their own conclusions, or we can move past our fears and apprehensions to step up and guide them through a childhood of learning and growth. Culture-inclusive homes are committing to the latter, and one of the easiest ways to get started is to weave important topics into dinner table discussions consistently.

There's nothing particularly magical about the dinner table, so maybe your family will cultivate a different safe space for these conversations. But food is a social lubricant, and I find that my kids are more relaxed and ready to gab when our family is gathered around the table, filling our bellies with yummy food. Once you've established that yours will be a home where children can safely explore the tough stuff, begin an ongoing process of push and pull.

THE PULL

Anyone who has spent more than a few moments with young children knows that they are naturally curious. Children pull for information and figure out the world around them by watching closely, listening intently, and filling in gaps by asking lots of questions. Kids learn to keep quiet when we respond to their questions with irritation, hostility, silence, or shaming. But when we welcome their questions with expectant open arms and judgment-free, engaging dialogue, kids recognize that they have a safe space for working through their private thoughts aloud, a space where people who love them no matter what they say will guide them well. That sacred space is home.

Writer and activist Audre Lorde once said, "I have come to believe over and over again that what is most important to me must be spoken, made verbal and shared, even at the risk of having it bruised or misunderstood."[2] That compelling need to speak is something that burns brightly within children, and many are willing to risk it all just to be heard. Our job as culturally conscious parents is to listen well to help our children understand the complexities of identity, discrimination, privilege, racism, and exclusivity. Thankfully, we aren't required to have all the answers, but the questions must be asked and thoughtfully discussed.

Be an askable parent. The term "askable parent" was first coined by Sol Gordon, PhD, a clinical psychologist and sex educator who believed that parents should answer a child's questions about sex whenever they asked. I wholeheartedly agree with this idea, and I also think the same is true for questions regarding other tough subjects. Our goal, as parents, should be to become our children's number one go-to person when they aren't sure how to process things or when they want to know more about something they've heard or noticed. To be an askable parent, commit to the following:

1. **BE AVAILABLE.** It's difficult enough to get up the nerve to ask a tricky question, but it becomes nearly impossible if bold questions are met with indifference or swept aside with a promise to "talk about it later." Do your best to sit down and give your children your full attention when they want to talk to you about important issues. When

immediate attention is not possible, give them a specific time when you'll be available. Be sure not to forget—setting a timer on my phone has worked well for me in the past because my memory is not dependable.

2. **GIVE YOUNG CHILDREN PERMISSION TO WAIT.** Or put more directly, make sure your kids know that they can ask anything, but sometimes they have to wait until they get into the car. In our home, questions about people we encounter in public and how they look or act are "car questions" because I've trained my kids to hold them in until we get back to the car.

    I'd be lying if I didn't admit that I started using the term "car questions" to avoid personal mortification. But more important than parental embarrassment is avoiding making anyone feel like a spectacle simply because my child is curious or ignorant. I want to ensure that my children's need to know and ask doesn't override their responsibility to treat others well, and I'm always sure to commend little ones who have exercised patience with their burning questions.

3. **DON'T FREAK OUT.** During some of our deep dinner conversations, my children have said some wild things. Prejudiced things. Inaccurate things. Biased things. Insensitive things. Sexist things. Racist things. Ignorant things. When I hear their shaky premises and childlike conclusions, it takes everything inside of me not to react with swift and sharp admonition. But that will only train them to feel ashamed and keep quiet.

    I want to hear all the things: good, bad, or ugly. I'm not a mind reader, so I need my children to feel comfortable asking me anything and everything, and that requires me to stay calm and collected, even when they're dropping bombs. That doesn't mean that I never show emotion. Our children must see when something makes us sad or angry. Being upset about injustice is a good thing! It just means that I don't express anger or shock toward my children for something they may say.

    When your children say misguided things, be sure to let them know that you disagree with what they're saying and why. And if what they've said is hateful, make it clear that you don't condone their statements or the ideas feeding them. As you do this, try to keep them talking by asking questions about why they believe what they believe and listen carefully to their answers.

You may find that your child is eager to debate you on complex social topics; this can be particularly true with teenagers. When they're communicating in a respectful tone, don't shy away from the back-and-forth. They need to know that their opinions matter, and having a safe space to speak passionately helps develop their critical thinking skills (and yours, too!).

4. **KEEP IT WITHIN THE FAMILY.** Don't share your children's controversial questions or comments outside of the family without their permission. If you want them to share what's in their hearts without boundaries, you must treat their emotional meanderings as treasures. Having your child's trust is a great responsibility and privilege that requires sensitivity and care. I would never want someone to publicly share my private conversations with my husband, mom, or sister because I haven't carefully considered, criticized, and prepared those raw words for the world. They are a work-in-progress to be refined over time, and our children's naive, curious, and sometimes downright hurtful thoughts are the same.

5. **BE WILLING TO REVISIT THE SAME TOPIC REPEATEDLY.** Askable parents are not part of the "one and done" crew. We don't put on armor to head into battle for big hairy conversations. Instead, we spend our entire parenting journey dropping seeds here, there, and everywhere. Some tough conversations amount to little more than a statement, while others will be epic. There have been nights when I've practically had to hold my eyelids open to work through complex things with my nearly teen daughter, only to talk through the same thing again days, weeks, or months later. Growth is an iterative process, and askable parents are willing to show up every time.

6. **ELIMINATE THE CONCEPT OF "OFF-LIMIT" TOPICS.** There's nothing that my children can't ask me. Sometimes they catch me off guard, or they

ask things that I wish they wouldn't, but those are only opportunities for me to meet them where they are. I don't always share all I know or think on a particular topic because our conversations remain developmentally appropriate. Still, I try to fill the need they have to know something more.

7. **BE HONEST.** There's no quicker way to lose a person's trust than to lie. Children are complete and deserving persons, and losing their trust is avoidable. Do your best to be truthful and not sugarcoat hard truths or mislead your kids. It's far better to tell the truth about a little than to lie about a lot. And if you don't know the answer to a question, be willing to say that, too. "I don't know" is a brave answer, and realistically, it will be the truth in many a conversation when tough table topics are encouraged.

Being askable means that our kids may bring up things that we might not fully understand or have never felt comfortable discussing. Rest assured that few can claim expertise on the most challenging issues of our time and their sociological, political, religious, and cultural implications. We don't have the luxury of waiting for it all to be worked out before diving into the deep end with our kids. They're growing up today, where imperfect solutions for impossible problems abound, and yet we're charged with giving them a sense of hope for their future. We're the ones who will help our children understand that we don't expect them to fix all that's wrong in the world, but they're called to make a difference when and where they can.

THE PUSH

Every child is different. Some pepper you with important questions daily, some skirt around issues, and others fail to think deeply about the world and how they fit into it. Many kids don't know what they don't know, so they'll never ask questions that open the door for necessary conversations. Sometimes it's incumbent on us, the parents, to disseminate ideas or push opportunities for discussion by initiating and normalizing weighty talks. So while some topics may come up naturally, you may also find that you have to be quite intentional about how and when to broach ideas with your children.

Asking questions and leading an ongoing dialogue on race, culture, and inclusivity can sometimes feel awkward. But as author Dr. Ali Michael says, "Race questions are not meant to lead us into a quagmire of guilt, discomfort, or isolation. Sustained race inquiry is meant to lead to antiracist classrooms, positive racial identities, and a restoration of the wholeness of spirit and community that racism undermines."[3]

This willingness to engage is essential because it encourages us to lean into something that we may not know much about. Over the years, I've relied on intuition and personal experiences to initiate some table topics, but I've also committed myself to a habit of reading and listening as a lifelong learner. There are many books, articles, blogs, podcasts, films, and workshops from which I've gleaned ideas, even when I don't agree with them in their entirety.

For example, in the TV special *PBS KIDS Talk About: Race & Racism*, families had conversations about racial identity, racism, and how parents and kids can work together to help build a more equitable society.[4] Coming out of that work, they shared various questions that you can ask your children, including:

- Why do people look different from one another?

- Do you think it's okay to notice and talk about differences in people's skin color?

- Who are the heroes who have fought against racism across history and today? When we see something unfair, what are ways we can stand up for others?

The blog *Raising Race Conscious Children* also provides many inspiring examples for how to speak to children about race and other topics directly in an age-appropriate way. Some of their ideas include:

- "Usually people call people who look like us 'White,' even though our skin isn't actually White. Usually people call other people with dark skin 'Black,' even though their skin isn't actually Black."

- "The N-word is a terrible, horrible name used against Black people. It is a powerful insult meant to treat Black people as less than human."

- "You know sometimes we form hypotheses about people based on their race or their gender, and I think that Ruby's mom might have been making an assumption about you both because you are a boy and because you are brown—what do you think?"

- "We don't know what relationship people have with one another without asking . . . because you can't know which person belongs to another just by looking at them."

- "Slavery was when people with Black skin were enslaved. That means people with White skin owned them, and they didn't have any rights or freedoms. And because of this history, people with Black skin are still treated unfairly."

- "You know what? That boy wasn't just being mean. There's a word for what he was being. He was being 'sexist.'"

- "Mia is the only girl who looks like her . . . you are totally right! With straight, dark hair, and eyes shaped like hers and skin like hers. Mia is Chinese. She is the only Chinese girl in your class, and you noticed that."

- "I think that's a very rude and offensive thing to say, and I'm upset that you are speaking hatefully around my family."

- "I don't like when I hear other children ask questions about what language we are speaking in a negative way. It's an incredible thing to speak two languages. And we know a lot of people who speak two languages."

- "I don't like this video. It is making fun of people who are Asian."

- "Some mommies and children have a similar skin color, but other mommies and their children have different skin colors; did you know that?"[5]

This is only a sampling of the many different statements that can start compelling conversations in your home. They aren't intended to be instructions but rather examples of the type of natural age-appropriate language we can use with our children to help normalize race consciousness. It's important that our children understand that it's completely okay to talk about race and culture because they're such important parts of one's identity.

When my kids were younger, I had no idea which direction I wanted to go to educate them about race, but I knew that children of color needed to have a "building up" of their sense of self without being made to feel like victims. I wanted my kids to know that we did indeed "see" them despite our initial missteps in ignoring their color. Though we initially avoided discussing the social complexities wrapped up in race, ethnicity, and culture, I was ready to change the trajectory of conversations in our home and needed direction.

I was searching for themes to integrate into our family conversations when I came across the October 1919 issue of *The Crisis*. In it, historian and activist W. E. B. Du Bois outlined seven goals for *The Brownies' Book*, the first magazine published for African American children and youth. I updated his original language to match modern usage when I added the goals to my journal, and I've done the same here, but the essence remains the same.

He suggested that we should strive:

1. To make Black children realize that being "Black" is a normal, beautiful thing.

2. To make them familiar with the history and achievements of their race.

3. To make them know that other Black children have grown into beautiful, useful, and famous persons.

4. To teach them a delicate code of honor and action in their relations with white children.

5. To turn their little hurts and resentments into emulation, ambition, and love of their homes and companions.

6. To point out the best amusements and joys and worthwhile things of life.

7. To inspire them to prepare for definite occupations and duties with a broad spirit of sacrifice.

What blows my mind most about this list is how relevant the goals are over a hundred years later. Within this framework, I discovered foundational thoughts that could drive how I spoke to my children and what we talked about at the dinner table and beyond. These goals are incredibly relevant to my Black children and just as appropriate for other children of color regarding their own cultures.

In many ways, I believe that all children need to hear the same core messages while also learning and understanding ideas unique to their own racial, social, and cultural circumstances. Families will share overlapping discussions, and specific conversations will vary, but tough table topics, weighty conversations, and ongoing dialogue are essential for every home.

Balancing cultural appreciation and celebration with justice-minded thinking and living is the sweet spot for an inclusive home. One without the other leaves our children at risk of being activists who lack relational relevancy on one hand or empathetic but actionless members of society on the other. The total package propels families forward as we raise confident thinkers and doers who feel seen while seeing others.

It's okay to make mistakes. Fear is a driving factor for many things, including the avoidance of difficult conversations. Whether it's the fear of saying something wrong, the fear of not knowing, or the fear of robbing our children of their innocence, well-meaning parents can remain stuck in surface communication that never leads to meaningful discourse. And for some of us, it's the fear that we've waited too long to change course that holds us back from getting started, speaking up, and becoming askable.

If you find yourself crippled by fear, please know that it's okay to make mistakes. We're embarking on a road less traveled, and there is no perfect map. As we work to do our best on behalf of our children, there will be missteps.

Sometimes correcting course is as easy as doing it differently next time, but at other times we may need to apologize to our children or let them know that we messed up and need to start over on a different path. Now is always a good time to start. It's never too early or too late to aim for openness and dialogue. Just keep it straightforward with something like these examples:

- "Sweetheart, I apologize for things that I've said and allowed others to say in your presence. I want to set a better example of how we should think about, speak of, and treat others. I've learned and grown over time, and I'd like our family to commit to being better friends with people who are like us and different than us in various ways. I'm not perfect, so I'm sure that I'll make mistakes along the way, but I hope you'll join me in recognizing the value in other people and cultures as we get to know them through our learning and in real life."

- "Honey, I love you so much, and I always want to do what's best for you. In the past, I've shied away from tough conversations because they made me uncomfortable, and I wasn't always sure of what to say or how to say it. Sometimes I was even afraid to bring certain topics up at all. I'm sorry that I haven't always been easy to talk with, but going forward, I'd like to help our family speak openly about whatever is on your mind, without consequence. I'm committed to talking about anything you'd like to discuss or ask, and I'm looking forward to asking you about your thoughts on various topics, too. What do you think?"

Be as specific as possible and end with language that shows that you plan to partner with your child to make changes *with* them rather than do something *to* them. Though it can be difficult, exposing our fallible humanness to our kids is a gift because it makes it easier for them to see that there is no expectation or possibility of perfection.

Change requires work. Some of it will be easy work, but some of it may feel hard. Everyone will process the effort differently, but from my experience, the greater understanding and perspectives gained through this ongoing work have enhanced our quality of life in innumerable ways. The deeper we dig, the easier and more enriching it becomes, and the more committed I am to honoring our colorful and inclusive family atmosphere.

3

....

ESTABLISHING A BLUEPRINT

Inclusive Family Ways and Home Culture

There is no doubt that it is around the family and the home that all
the greatest virtues, the most dominating virtues of human society,
are created, strengthened and maintained.

—Winston Churchill, former UK prime minister

BEFORE BECOMING AN ENTREPRENEUR AND LATER STARTING A
family, I worked for several large corporations, and each had its own culture. Their business functions made them look similar from the outside,
but the atmospheres within felt vastly different. The same holds true for
families. Every family has its way of doing things that gives it structure and
personality. To help our children feel a sense of belonging, we need to
establish personal ways of doing life together: family ways.

Family ways are the learned behaviors within a home situated at the
intersection of culture, tradition, history, and daily life, and they are mal-
leable. Intentional parental influences can alter them, and as with folkways
and foodways, small shifts in family ways can be transformational over
time. Every family has the capacity for adaptive change, which requires
new learning and thinking. As we discover different approaches to better
support our children, we can confidently mold our family ways, on an
ongoing basis, in real time.

Some aspects of the culture within our homes depend on factors such as ethnicity, geography, religion, and socioeconomic conditions, but we still have a say in how we shape our family ways. They are typically the traditions, rituals, values, and practices situated within the rhythms of family life. They can be noticed and named, and they contribute greatly to our children's sense of belonging.

By identifying positive behaviors and coupling them with values that support an inclusive home atmosphere, family ways help provide direction and guide rails for children as they learn to embrace and uphold what their families cherish most. Though the specific practices vary from family to family, the commonality is that they're always rooted in home life.

Michael Allen Fox, the author of *Home: A Very Short Introduction*, writes, "Why is home so important to us, then? Because for better or worse, by presence or absence, it is a crucial point of reference—in memory, feeling, and imagination—for inventing the story of ourselves, our life-narrative, for understanding our place in time. But it is also a vital link through which we connect with others and with the world and the universe at large."[1] That connection with others and the world fuels the family practices within a socially conscious home, and those practices affect what you say, what you do, and how you do it.

When we first began shifting our home atmosphere toward inclusivity, I struggled with what that meant in terms of our daily living. I had ideas about where I wanted to land, but I had no blueprint for getting there. After flailing a bit while being tossed around by every new book or article I read, I finally nailed down a list of family ways that I want my children to associate with how they think about our family and what we stand for:

1. **WE CHALLENGE THINKING WHEN WE FIND OURSELVES OR OTHERS RANKING THE VALUE OF OTHER HUMANS.** It can be easy to default to positions that benefit us and others like us, but we try to hold steadfastly to the truth that everyone is important and deserving of an equitable life free of contempt, prejudice, and injustice.

2. **WE INTENTIONALLY SEEK CONNECTION WITH PEOPLE WHO ARE DIFFERENT FROM US, EVEN WHEN IT REQUIRES US TO STEP OUTSIDE OF OUR COMFORT ZONE.** Spending time in culturally or socially diverse spaces is not always easy. Building bridges can be exhausting at

times, but we don't permit ourselves to quit. Instead, we look for points
of connection and opportunities to show solidarity whenever possible.

3. **WE PROUDLY EMBRACE THE ORGANIC RELATIONSHIPS AND VILLAGES
    WE'VE CREATED WITH PEOPLE WHO SHARE OUR CULTURAL BACK-
    GROUND.** We acknowledge that having a safe space to commune with
    people who share our cultural expressions and experiences is good.
    These unique opportunities for belonging help us feel understood,
    valued, and connected to our micro-community. Safe villages help us
    connect authentically to our broader community with confidence.

4. **WE ACTIVELY REJECT RACIAL, ETHNIC, AND SOCIAL STEREOTYPES AND
    THE HARM THEY CAUSE.** Some stereotypes are so ingrained that we
    find ourselves thinking them before we can even catch ourselves.
    When that happens, we are committed to acknowledging the thought,
    looking for its source, and communicating differently going forward.
    We will reassess our positions before acting, and we are committed to
    not permitting harmful words to be spoken in our presence without
    speaking up.

5. **WE BELIEVE IN THE POWER OF STORYTELLING, AND WE SHARE OUR
    OWN STORIES HONESTLY AND WITH CONFIDENCE.** Storytelling helps us
    celebrate beauty and triumph while lamenting ugliness and tragedy.
    It is cathartic and worthwhile, so we make space for our own stories
    just as we do for others'.

6. **WE LISTEN TO THE STORIES OF OTHERS WITH HUMILITY, WHILE SEEK-
    ING TO UNDERSTAND AND AFFIRM THE IMPORTANCE OF THEIR EXPERI-
    ENCES.** We may not always relate, but we will actively listen and show
    respect when others share their stories. We will never stop trying to
    understand, and we will believe the stories of others, even when we
    haven't experienced what they've experienced.

7. WE USE OUR RESOURCES TO COME ALONGSIDE PEOPLE, INSTITUTIONS,
    AND ORGANIZATIONS THAT SUPPORT FAMILIES AND COMMUNITIES

WITH EQUITABLE, COMPASSIONATE PRACTICES. We commit our money, time, gifts, and hearts to others who choose to walk this journey with us. We help those doing good work, and we don't want or need public recognition or accolades in return.

8. WE BELIEVE THAT READING AND LEARNING ARE POTENT FORMS OF ACTIVE RESISTANCE, AND WE PROMOTE BOTH WITHIN AND WITHOUT OUR HOME. Our family uses books and education as tools to help ourselves and our community grow in wisdom, knowledge, and action. We seek to use all that we gain not to look good but to do good.

9. WE ARE HONEST WITH OURSELVES AND OTHERS, AND WE SEEK TRUTH AT THE CENTER OF HISTORY AND CURRENT EVENTS. Our allegiance does not lie with political parties or in social alliances. We are not looking to be right or to prove a point but to know and share truthfully.

10. WE RECOGNIZE OUR IMPERFECTIONS AND SHOW GRACE TO OUR-SELVES AND OTHERS WHEN MISTAKES ARE MADE. We have high expectations for truth, mercy, and justice, but we forgive and hope to be forgiven when we fall short of the mark. We look for sincere heart change and believe that everyone has the capacity to change, whether they choose to or not.

11. WE ALWAYS STRIVE TO DO BETTER WHILE RECOGNIZING THAT PERFECTION IS IMPOSSIBLE AND NOT EXPECTED. We are diligent and committed to colorful, inclusive, culturally rich living, but it's a never-ending growing process, and we will be kind to ourselves and others along the way.

12. WE USE WORDS TO INVITE PEOPLE INTO RELATIONSHIPS WITH US, LIFT OTHERS UP, AND DECRY INJUSTICE AND HATRED, BUT WE DON'T USE OUR WORDS AS WEAPONS OF SHAME OR DESTRUCTION. What we say, write, and share matters, and we'll speak to others with respect, even when we are not met with the same. We will never seek to embarrass or harass another person, regardless of their position, but we won't

remain silent in the face of opposition and ignorance. We will speak boldly, truthfully, and respectfully.

13. **WE ARE CURIOUS LIFELONG LEARNERS WHO VALUE INQUIRY AND CRITICAL THINKING.** We will always learn, ask questions, and grow. We listen to the wisdom of others and reject false teaching, excuses, and hate-laden crazy-making. We don't blindly accept the opinions or will of others, and we are prepared to sit through the tension sometimes caused by independent thinking.

14. **WE KNOW THAT PEOPLE ARE NOT ALL GOOD OR ALL EVIL, SO WE DON'T TREAT THEM AS SUCH.** We believe that all people are capable of doing both good and bad things, but we also don't choose to spend time with or give energy to abusive people or those unwilling to grow.

15. **WE NOTICE AND WILL REMAIN UNCOMFORTABLE WHEN FACED WITH OR WITNESSING MICROAGGRESSIONS, COVERT OR SOCIALLY ACCEPTABLE RACISM, OR HOSTILITIES.** We resist the urge to downplay or deny their existence, even if unintentional. We will not tolerate racism, prejudice, and oppression in any form, and we will confront it in our own lives and behaviors as we expose it to those around us, whether they be strangers, family, or friends. We will privately and publicly discuss their insidious nature along with the harm they cause.

16. **WE AIM TO RIGHT OUR WRONGS.** We are still learning, growing, and changing. We will inevitably make mistakes on our journey, and sometimes those mistakes may hurt people. We take full responsibility for our wrongs without making excuses. We offer sincere apologies and vow to listen, learn, and put in the work to get it right.

17. **WE ARE SAFE PEOPLE WHO ARE WILLING TO SUPPORT AND STAND OR SIT WITH THOSE WHO ARE HURTING.** We recognize that we can't fix every wrong, but we seek to show empathy, compassion, and solidarity with people hurt by individuals, organizations, systems, or governments.

18. **WE WILL ENTHUSIASTICALLY LEARN FROM PEOPLE WHO ARE SIMILAR AND DIFFERENT IN APPEARANCE, BACKGROUND, OR LIFE EXPERIENCE.** We want to seek out information, stories, and relationships that will help us understand ourselves, our neighbors, and other members of our local and global communities.

19. **OUR FINITE CAPACITY TO ELICIT CHANGE DOES NOT LIMIT OUR THOUGHTS, HOPES, AND DREAMS.** We know that we cannot rid the world of evil, hatred, bigotry, or discrimination. Nor will our efforts guarantee sustaining friendships among and across cultural and social groups. But we'll try anyway because we value progress over perfection, and we stand on the heels of hope.

20. **WHEN IN DOUBT, WE DEFAULT TO LOVE.** There's so much we don't know and can't see, but what we do know is that we will lead with love. Love for our own and love for others, in equal measure.

This list is not exhaustive, as I've only included the practices related to maintaining a culturally rich home atmosphere. There's no expectation that your family will adopt these as is. I only share mine here as an example of where you can go.

While your children are very young, you can simply embody these family ways in what you say and do, but as they grow in understanding, you'll want to explicitly teach your children what your family believes and how you've chosen to walk this journey. Show them your list in writing and refer to the practices frequently, especially when your family encounters something that supports or contradicts what you've said that you believe or how you'll behave in specific scenarios.

Take the time to think deeply about the family practices you wish to claim in your home because, from my experience, kids take them very seriously. My children recognize the importance of who we say we are, and they are the first to call out inconsistencies in our daily living. No one can spot hypocrisy like a child, and I find it refreshing, though not always easy, when my kids notice the discrepancies between what we say is important and how we act.

REMAIN CONSISTENT YET FLEXIBLE

Consistency is the difference between a nice platitude and a way of life. If you say one thing to your children at home but don't support or back it up in front of other people, you're teaching your kids that convenience and keeping the peace are more important than remaining true to your family's values.

You may find it easy to speak up against prejudice, racism, or injustice when dealing with strangers, but the situation can become stickier when it comes to family. Even if Grandma is the one making ignorant comments or dropping hateful bombs in passing, you still have a responsibility to say something to her and your children.

When I was little, I had a cursing granny. Swear words littered her speech regularly, and she most typically used them to describe people she didn't care for. In our home, comments like hers were never used or permitted, but I always received an earful when we visited my grandparents. One time, after a particularly lively string of coarse language, my dad asked his mom if she could refrain from cursing while I was in the room, and she responded, "No, I cannot. If you don't like it, don't bring her here." And there you have it.

So please know that I recognize how hard it may be to ask your parents, in-laws, or any other family members to avoid language that works against the atmosphere you're creating for your children. And I also realize that while we have the right to control what's said or done in our homes, we can't control what others say or do in their own homes. Pick your battles wisely, but don't forget that your first responsibility is to your children. And they need to know that what you've said is wrong is truly wrong.

Every case is different, but you may choose to limit time with certain people or avoid including them in your children's lives at all if their rhetoric is harmful and they have no interest in curbing their attitudes for your children's sake. Other options may be to firmly state, "What you just said is not true and goes against our family's values and beliefs. I wish you wouldn't speak like that in our presence." And if you cannot speak up due to the fear of retaliation or some other unfortunate situation, make sure that you circle back with your children as soon as possible with something like "What Grandma said today about *xyz* is not okay at all. I want you to know that she's wrong, and that is not something our family believes or values."

As your family grows, matures, and learns, you may find that the practices that served you well during one season are no longer the right fit. Author and activist Maya Angelou famously said, "Do the best you can until you know better. Then when you know better, do better." Revising or changing course is often a marker of growth, and that's a wonderful thing.

Once you've developed your list of family ways, with an understanding that you can update them at any time, begin to cultivate an atmosphere of trust and togetherness. Help your children experience the value of home. Show them the meaning of family and friendship by building a home culture where they can openly see themselves and celebrate others.

SOCIAL IDENTITY HINGES ON FAMILY CULTURE

My family has a rich heritage. Black people the world over, no matter their background, have a fantastic legacy to claim as their own. There are books to be read, recipes to be shared, music to be hummed, poems to be memorized, lyrics to be sung, words to be spoken, and gestures to be understood. There are stories to be told and sacred places and spaces to behold. Black people have a rich history to be brought into their homes and breathed over their children. There is much for me to pull from while making our culture and history accessible to my children.

Although the exact rendition of a Black person's cultural symphony is unique, we are in no way alone in this special treasure we possess. White people have an amazing heritage. Brown people have an amazing heritage. All people of color have an amazing heritage. We all have a cultural background to share with our children—to help them see where they fit in the story of our world.

But what does that mean? How can you genuinely reflect your culture and honor the heritage of others within your home? Parents' capacity to model the mindset and behaviors they're looking to promote within their families drives their ability to build or redefine an inclusive home culture successfully. The most critical parts of our children's environment are the voices and actions of the adults speaking into them. To create a culturally rich setting, we must begin with ourselves.

One of our goals, as parents, is to bind our children to a story they can claim as their own. To help them find clarity in their own culture. The question to answer first is "Who am I?" Chapter 1 established that we can help our children unpack that question by acknowledging that they're watching us, and our identity informs theirs. Leaning into family history and promoting a legacy mindset that recognizes our connection to future generations also pave the way for cultural identity to permeate our homes naturally.

I was the unwitting recipient of a childhood full of family lore shared by my grandparents, countless aunts and uncles, parents, and even siblings. Though I wish I'd cared enough to preserve the stories and properly engage in follow-up conversations, I accept what I was given as gift enough because I know that it has shaped me in incredible ways. As I considered how impactful family storytelling was for me, I realized that I'd overlooked its importance for my children.

While establishing our family ways, I intentionally began to take on the role of family storyteller for them, as others had done for me. In the beginning, I only shared epic stories, the tales that seemed worth memorializing. But eventually, I learned that my kids adore hearing every little tidbit I can scrape up for them. Even the most humdrum stories pique their interest, as evidenced by their repeated requests for the same anecdotes.

I remember an art teacher saying that great artists tell stories that are so real you can smell them through the canvas, and that's what I try to do with my storytelling. I want my kids to "smell" my grandparents' homes despite never having been inside. I talk about my Papa Henderson's farm and how he raised cattle and hogs for the family to eat plus a little extra to sell. They giggle and act disgusted when I recount how he tried to insist that his family eat every bit of the pig, including the snout, feet, and tail.

When we peruse antique shops, a favorite pastime of my younger daughter, I point out little trinkets and decor that remind me of something that took up residence in my grandparents' living room or sat on their nightstand. They know that Papa had a citizens band (CB) radio that alerted him of the comings and goings of townspeople and allowed him and his network of buddies to keep watch over their rental properties with keen interest. We laugh at Pawpaw's corny jokes and the way he used to talk about Grandmommy, saying, "She was the prettiest and smartest girl I'd ever met, so I proved my smarts and asked her to marry me. It's been seventy years, and I still can't believe she said yes!"

My husband and I talk about our parents, how they met, and how they poured into us in entirely different but equally beautiful ways. I've explained how the über-cool eat-ice-cream-for-breakfast-and-stay-up-all-night grandmother they know today is not the same mom who made the rules in my childhood home. And though they never got to meet my dad, my kids know so much about him that they speak of him as if they have firsthand knowledge.

I've shown our kids the exact spot where I met their dad, and I've taken them to the restaurant where we had our first date. I told them about the corny joke he shared that made me snort my tea that day and how strangely he acted the evening he proposed. They know that I played the cello growing up and that my first babysitter was a woman I affectionately called Mama Sara. And they know that she loved me well. My kids have heard all about my preschool teacher, Miss Gwen, and they know that we maintain a close relationship even to this day. My husband shares about his childhood outings to the lake, the time he broke both legs skiing, and why he hates olives so much. Each inane little story works to weave an ever-strengthening web of history and belonging for my kids, and they love it.

Many of the family stories that we share with our children reflect Black culture because that's how we identify, but I've also shared that our background is more complex than the buckets we use to label ourselves. I started that ongoing conversation by showing my kids an old family photo of my great-great-grandparents and their five children. Typically, there wouldn't be anything especially intriguing about this picture, but it feels strange for us because there are no Black people in it. Yet, my ancestors represented in the photo are not distant, unknown people. My grandmother knew them well, and their names and even their professions are known to me. But they have, in many ways, been completely dropped from my identity as a Black woman.

I can't help but wonder how Pascal (German Jew) and Mary Jean (Cherokee) Hickman would feel knowing that my racial identity does not include them, and the words I use to describe myself don't reflect their existence in any way. Yet, I have hope that my choice to pass along their photos and stories to my children to hold in their hearts and share with their little ones one day is something. Maybe not enough, but something that prevents them from being entirely erased.

I also hope that I've given my children a natural affection for our Cherokee and Jewish sisters and brothers. When my children hear of these cultures, or *any* culture, being ignored or maligned, I expect they'll think back to our photo and remember to stand in solidarity with an understanding that this is an "us" thing. Not a situation that only impacts "them." Culturally, I am unequivocally Black, and I raise my children as such, but not without acknowledging that we are all a mixture of many things, so to hate another is to hate ourselves.

In his 1970 book, *The Omni-Americans,* author Albert Murray famously shared, "The United States is in actuality not a nation of black people and white people. It is a nation of multicolored people. . . . Any fool can see that the white people are not really white, and that black people are not black. They are all interrelated one way or another."[2] At the foot of that heavy statement lies my desire to see my children engage in authentic cross-racial relationships. The kinds of relationships that preserve our heritage while blurring the lines of separation between people who aren't nearly as disconnected as today's news would have us believe.

My kids know much about our family because I've consciously chosen to talk about the minor parts, big ideas, and everything in between. In the words of researcher Marshall Duke, they have a strong sense of "intergenerational self," which is a critical step in helping our children develop healthy roots.

ENCOURAGE INTERGENERATIONAL KNOWLEDGE

Duke and his research partner, Robyn Fivush, tested the hypothesis that children who know more about their families will do better when facing challenges, and they reached an intriguing conclusion. In his book *The Secrets of Happy Families,* Bruce Feiler summarizes their results. He writes, "The more children knew about their family's history, the stronger their sense of control over their lives, the higher their self-esteem, and the more successfully they believed their families functioned. The 'Do You Know?' scale turned out to be the best single predictor of children's emotional health and happiness."[3] Some of the questions asked by the researchers included:

- Do you know where your mother grew up?

- Do you know where some of your grandparents met?

- Do you know the source of your name?

- Do you know which person in the family you act most like?

- Do you know the national background of your family (such as English, German, Russian, etc.)?

- Do you know some awards that your parents received when they were young?

- Do you know the names of the schools that your dad went to?[4]

Feiler also shares three types of family narratives he learned about from his time interviewing Duke. They are the ascending family narrative ("We were down and now we're up"), the descending family narrative ("We were up and now we're down"), and the oscillating narrative ("We've had our ups and downs"). Researchers found the oscillating narrative to be most compelling. Duke describes it as "Dear, let me tell you, we've had ups and downs in our family. We built a family business. Your grandfather was a pillar of the community. Your mother was on the board of the hospital. But we also had setbacks. You had an uncle who was once arrested. We had a house burn down. Your father lost a job. But no matter what happened, we always stuck together as a family."

Feiler highlights the researcher's conclusion that children who have a strong "intergenerational self" have the most balance and self-confidence because "they know they belong to something bigger than themselves." Family storytelling imparts this sense of rootedness. Yes, it's entertaining, but sharing the well-worn paths traveled by those who came before is also a way to strengthen your family culture.

CONFRONT DIFFICULT NARRATIVES

What if digging into your past is painful? The answer depends on your circumstances. If facing the discomfort or tension in your genealogy could bring healing and redemption to your family's complicated past, you can move forward knowing that you'll come out on the other side with a fresh perspective and stronger roots. Digging in may even help to reframe or reclaim your family's history triumphantly.

But for some people, the pain of the past is so pervasive that digging around in it will not bear healthy fruit. And for others, there simply is no known past to explore. If either of these situations describes your story, I want you to hang in here with me because I'm going to come back around to those very scenarios. But first, let's talk about hard truths.

People are complicated and messy. Families are made of people, so they're also complicated and messy. There's no way around that. And yet, there is still a reason to tie your children to their pasts, even if parts are painful. Learning of varied generational experiences helps our children contextualize their lives in a longer, more complicated story. And while we certainly should consider maturity levels and only share age-appropriate information, we do our children a disservice when we leave off parts of their story in an attempt to shelter them.

Oral storytelling has been woven into the fabric of our society from the beginning, and your children won't always be children. They will be torchbearers who carry your family's history on to your grandchildren and beyond. That history is not yours to withhold because your children have rightful ownership of their people's stories.

That's the mentality I held on to when I took my kids on a road trip to Kentucky, where we visited the former home of Revolutionary War veteran Major Richard Bibb, the head of the family from which Bibb lettuce arises. He was a white man known for eventually emancipating nearly a hundred enslaved people. While there, we attended the first-ever reunion of Bibb's descendants and the descendants of the men and women he enslaved. My children and I represented both sides.

We stand at the intersection of Major Richard Bibb's son and one of the women enslaved in his home. We exist because of a baby created under the worst of circumstances. At the reunion, I met white strangers whose lives and experiences were utterly foreign to me, yet we still felt connected. Whether society sees it as such or not, we are, in fact, family. That day, we chose to embrace each other. To cry, talk, hug, and wonder what our collective ancestors would think if they could see the beauty we've scraped from the ugly past we inherited.

When I returned home from that trip, a friend asked me how it went. I didn't have the words, so I borrowed some from Charles Dickens and wrote back, "It was the best of times, it was the worst of times, it was the age of wisdom, it was the age of foolishness, it was the epoch of belief, it was the epoch of incredulity, it was the season of light, it was the season of darkness, it was the spring of hope, it was the winter of despair." But mostly, it was amazing.

I share this with you as an example of the type of hard history you may come up with when you start digging around. Our children can read about these things in their schoolbooks, but if you're building a culturally rich home, you'll also want to take advantage of what you can find or explore within your own family.

What if digging up your family's past will do more harm than good? Or what if you can't even look back at the family tree? What if your child became yours through adoption, or you have the honor of raising a bonus child who doesn't share your biology? How can you represent your child's familial existence—both their family of origin and their forever family? I'm asked these questions all the time, and I'm always happy when I get a chance to talk about it.

APPROACH FAMILY HISTORY AS A TIMELINE

History is a timeline. For some families, knowledge of the timeline goes back many generations. For other families, the timeline started the day you and your child met. If you can't specifically pull from the past because of death, trauma, adoption, or whatever the reason, my heart goes out to you because I know that you've had to mourn what may be missing from your child's story. But don't feel at all discouraged, because you can still swim in the fullness of what you *do* know while building a legacy of timeline markers for the future.

Much of what we're exploring here is more about the process than the facts themselves. You can begin today with a family culture that includes telling stories from a decade ago, last year, or last night. Make it your job to build family traditions around what your family is doing right now. Treat the stories you're creating today with the same care and attention you would the stories of old because your children are watching you. They learn to value what you value, and more than anything, they simply want a place to belong.

If you know your child's birth country or state of origin, you can study it, celebrate it, and embrace parts of its culture within your own home. If you're a white American with German roots and your child is Ethiopian, your culturally rich home will reflect both Ethiopian and German culture with many American flavors. It's not going to look like anyone else's because you're creating something new. Your family has its own ways.

My niece and nephew came to our family through adoption, so I've walked this path with my brother's family. I've also seen it play out in other families, and I'm always amazed by the power of creative and intentional parents. I've followed Jamie C. Martin from SimpleHomeschool.net for about a decade, and I've so enjoyed reading about how her family approaches heritage and culture.

Jamie is American, and along with her husband, who is English, she is raising Jonathan (their biological son), Elijah (adopted from Liberia), and Trishna (adopted from India). With four nationalities represented in their family, she says they like to think of themselves as a mini United Nations. She shares stories about how her family celebrates each culture within their home, and I've periodically seen pictures of her children dressed in the traditional clothing of their homelands, sprinkled in with photos where they're wearing the typical jeans and T-shirt fare.

Jamie's family has a tradition of dedicated days when they formally celebrate specific cultural experiences. But in general, they have a casual, everyday, culturally rich, expanded home that looks different from everyone else's home. They created a new home culture where all their children feel rooted, even though they may or may not have extensive knowledge of their extended family history.

In addition to establishing a unique family culture built around traditions you create today, families with shorter timelines to work with can also focus on legacy building. The message to your children, which I also share with mine, is that the things they do and build now will be treasures for their descendants someday. Focus on the present and the years and generations to come instead of relying on an unknown past. There are always meaningful and worthwhile ways to build a family story, whether it looks back hundreds of years or highlights your current home with the understanding that today is tomorrow's history.

Now that we've built a foundation for celebrating heritage and inclusivity, let's embark on the beautiful journey of creating a colorful family culture on a daily basis. We'll approach the areas of home life not in order of importance because all of it matters, but in the order that my own family's journey unfolded. I'll spend the remaining chapters laying out actionable steps you can take to let this philosophy of education, life, and childhood fill your entire home with color and kinship. First, let's move into the part of the home that most immediately breathed life into my children's lives: the home library.

PART 2

Curating the Home Library

THERE WAS A TIME WHEN I THOUGHT BEAUTY WAS ALL THAT mattered in a book. I held fast to the belief that classic literature and quality nonfiction convey universal ideas that transcend any preoccupations with race. I accepted the promise that repeated exposure to passionate prose would transform my children into well-read lifelong learners, but in 2014, my oversimplified assumptions could no longer stand unchallenged. I took my children on a memorable field trip, but I was the one who got schooled that day.

It was our first time visiting a living museum—Historic Westville, in Columbus, Georgia—and we enjoyed a full day of exhibits, live interpreters, food, and crafts featuring southern life in the nineteenth century. By late afternoon, my kids were exhausted and ready to nap during the long ride home, so we took one last potty break before hitting the road. Seemingly, everyone had the same idea, so I settled into the ladies' room queue with my eldest while my friend watched the rest of our combined brood outside.

Nina and I patiently watched as each woman exited a stall and headed to the sink to wash her hands before quickly drying them under the strong gust of the environmentally friendly automatic hand dryers. After what seemed like an incredibly long time, it was finally our turn. When we finished, my daughter dutifully washed her hands and walked over to the dryer while dripping still-soapy water onto the rustic floor. I watched as she struggled to activate the automatic sensor on the dryer. She moved her little hands up and down, left and right, and around in circles before frustratedly throwing up her arms and loudly exclaiming in this quiet country bathroom, "Welp, I guess this dryer only works for white people!"

Heat rising in my face, I immediately ushered my daughter to the door and down the rickety steps, leaving my wet handprint on the back of her shirt as I reached for a water bottle to cool all the hot places that humiliation shows up in our bodies. After thanking my friend for watching my little ones, I dashed to our minivan. Once we were free from the staring eyes and pricked ears of bemused white people, everything inside of me wanted to turn around and scream, "What is wrong with you?!" Thankfully, wisdom took hold, and rather than transfer my insecurities and confusion onto my child's shoulders, I managed to ask in a quiet voice laced with forced nonchalance: "Honey, I noticed that you had a hard time getting the dryer to come on in the bathroom, and it looked like you got pretty frustrated. What was going on?"

She responded with matter-of-fact confidence, and what she said changed me forever: "I watched all of the white ladies put their hands under the dryer while we were waiting, but when I tried to do the same thing, the air wouldn't work for me, so I figured out that the dryer only works for white people because they made everything, and they know how everything works."

Sensing that we were on the brink of a watershed moment, I quickly followed up with "Why do you say that?" Without missing a beat, she responded, "Because you said we learn important stuff in our schoolbooks, and they only have white people in them."

At that moment, my mind flooded with mental snapshots of book lists, curriculum guides, and our very schoolroom. My heart sank as I grasped the truth. In my attempt to not make a big deal about skin color, I instead made my child feel as though she were invisible and that people like her did not matter. In the twenty-first century, I had crafted a learning environment within our home that made a little Black girl think that people like her couldn't even figure out how to dry their own hands.

And if my child felt that way, how many other children were forming similar conclusions about Black people? What about the other people of color so rarely mentioned in children's books and school lessons, if at all? I worried that the well-meaning attempts to present a colorblind education (at best), coupled with the intentional omission of BIPOC voices (at worst), were leaving our homes deafeningly silent when it came to celebrating the contributions of non-white people in our country and around the world. I found out the hard way that children often interpret silence as consent, leaving them feeling insignificant and unworthy of being seen.

Aside from a short paperback on George Washington Carver, I couldn't remember when we'd discussed a Black scientist. Why hadn't I taught her about the many Black inventors, mathematicians, environmentalists, and engineers who knew how things worked long ago and who still know today? I was aware of their existence, but their names never came up in our lessons or conversations because they didn't appear in the books we read.

Not only were our history and science lessons silent on the contributions and accomplishments of Black people, so was everything else. We had Harriet Tubman, Dr. Martin Luther King Jr., and Rosa Parks down cold, but they alone weren't enough to cement the idea that Black people could work a hand dryer. Aside from a small pile of picture books, nearly every title in our home library sent the same message: white is the standard, and black and brown are just colors.

As far-fetched as it may seem, this egregiously unbalanced inventory was born of high hopes and the most innocent of intentions. When my family was beginning, I stumbled upon several books and blogs that illuminated the lifelong benefits of raising children in a literature-rich home. I was an avid reader growing up, so the thought of encouraging my children to read was a no-brainer. Of course, my home culture would be a literary one.

To my mind, adopting this philosophy relied on two simple commitments: providing lots of good books and reading them. I was quickly inspired to collect award-winning books, classics, and not-to-be-missed modern titles. I embraced my role as curator of a lovely home library.

My daughter had become a reader thanks to my meticulous book curation paired with hours of family read-alouds. I had done all the "right" things. I couldn't understand how the perfect execution of a virtuous goal had culminated in her embracing such a flawed narrative. What had gone wrong?

Curiously, when I began to consider the source of the problem in my home, I found that a large part of the cause was also a significant aspect of the cure. My daughter had picked up countless cues from the books in our home, and yes, she'd formed misguided assumptions from the messages inside some of these books. However, the issue was less with what she had absorbed than what had been left out altogether. The books were not the issue. It was the mama librarian who had dropped the ball.

My vision for our home and the books within was not incorrect; it was simply incomplete. My definition of a "good book" was far too narrow, leading me to collect beautiful books without prioritizing the unique needs of my children.

While the books within each home will and should be curated differently, some ideas are universal. Every child should:

- Own books in which they can recognize themselves and the lived experiences of their families and communities.

- Have ready access to books that authentically express the humanity of people who look and live differently.

- Know that their personal story matters and that people like them are seen and valued.

- Read books that let them know that people who look or think like them are but a single part of our society.

- Be given opportunities to internalize the similarities and differences between people across a multitude of circumstances and conditions.

- Be supported by loving adults who will guide them through these books with genuine shared enthusiasm and rich discussions.

All children need books that are like mirrors in which they see themselves, as well as books that are windows into the wider world. And it's up to their parents and caregivers to provide them.

The realization that my home library was not "wrong" but merely incomplete gave me hope. I rolled up my sleeves and began the tedious but enriching work of shifting our bookshelves from liabilities to assets, and in the next three chapters, I'll share the lessons I picked up along the way.

These lessons are valuable for children of color who rarely see themselves reflected in books and also need to grapple with expressions of life beyond the borders of their own cultures. These lessons are essential for white children who need to form relationships with non-white characters in their literature. They need to encounter voices and perspectives different from their own, which will help them naturally form bonds within diverse communities. The goal is that our children will collectively know themselves and each other and hold both differences and similarities comfortably and lovingly in their hands.

To pave the way, I propose that parents focus on curating a home library filled with life-giving books that expand the traditional definition of a "good" book. A library that intentionally melds beautiful literature, contemporary stories, and books as mirrors and windows so children can see themselves, value and embrace others, and become part of a story that enlarges the borders of what is worthy, significant, and possible.

4

. . . .

MIRROR, MIRROR ON THE WALL

When Children See Themselves in Their Books

When children cannot find themselves reflected in the books they
read, or when the images they see are distorted, negative or laugh-
able, they learn a powerful lesson about how they are devalued in
the society of which they are a part.

—Dr. Rudine Sims Bishop, *Mirrors, Windows,*
and Sliding Glass Doors

THE FIRST TIME I READ THIS QUOTE BY DR. RUDINE SIMS BISHOP,
professor emerita of education at Ohio State University, I cried. I sat cross-
legged on the floor in front of our always-out-of-ink printer and quickly
wiped my tears before they dripped onto my screen. I had finally found
someone who could succinctly articulate the issue that had set off a bomb
in the middle of my home. My daughter was receiving messages that made
her feel devalued—not in school or on the playground, but in her own
home, at the hands of the person she trusted most in this world.

Dr. Bishop has been called the "mother of multicultural literature," but
that night, she felt more like an optometrist fitting me with powerful lenses
through which I could clearly see my home library for the first time. Don't
get me wrong. We had picture books featuring brown-skinned kids over
on *that* shelf, the one housing fun titles for quick reads, but those were not
the books we were savoring. Those were not the books I was checking off
my carefully cultivated list of "must-reads." The pages we were regularly

getting lost in on the sofa during family read-alouds did not include our kind of folks. The Black books in our home were merely peripheral.

How was it possible that I had received mothering messages on healthy foods, media consumption, time in nature, proper sleep, dental hygiene, gentle discipline, strong attachments, sharing meals, and savoring traditions, but not even a hint or suggestion that my brown-skinned girl needed to see herself and people like her in the books that our family valued most? Better yet, why did I, a Black woman, need someone to tell me what a Black girl needed? I know now that the shadows of my childhood experiences were there, but background noise often goes unnoticed until someone turns it off or calls our attention to it.

HOW COULD I NOT KNOW?

I grew up in a white neighborhood, attending predominantly white schools where there were not enough Black kids to spread across every classroom, and I never once had a Black teacher from kindergarten through twelfth grade. My parents were both principals in my school district, my father having integrated the ranks as the first Black administrator, but when I stepped outside my house, I entered a world where I was welcomed but rarely served.

I quickly learned a formula for pleasing the adults in that world: follow instructions, memorize, regurgitate, and don't complain. Having been born with the disease to please, I executed this simple plan with ease year after year with the precision of a well-oiled Stepford wife. And I did it all with a smile, never letting on that I felt like a tourist when I was at school, learning all manner of things about someone else's history, literature, art, and music. By the time I got to high school, I was beginning to grow weary from the self-induced pressure to silently perform, but I carried on because I didn't have another identity to fall back on. When senior year rolled around, three things happened that began to crack the veneer.

First, while most people assumed that I would go to an Ivy League or top-tier traditional school, I surprised everyone, including myself, by deciding to attend one of our nation's illustrious historically Black colleges and universities (HBCUs). That choice sent a ripple of whispers throughout my school as counselors, teachers, and classmates were unable to contain their shock. Prominent community members, including a local judge, expressed their dismay and disappointment that I was squandering opportunities to attend better (read: white) schools on scholarship.

The message I received was clear: white is right. But I still chose to take the only opportunity I'd ever had to sit in a classroom with multiple Black students. I chose the rare-for-me chance to be taught by teachers who looked like me, something most people take for granted. As a result, almost every part of my mostly white world communicated to me, in numerous ways, that I was intentionally and knowingly reducing my potential. The fact that I withstood the pressure and continued to the school of my choice should convey just how much I needed to know what it would be like not to be the only one.

The second thing happened when senior superlatives were announced at a school assembly in the gymnasium. These awards to honor the serious and funny aspects of the graduating class were something my friends and I had looked forward to all year. As the principal read the list amid cheers and laughter, she called my name three times:

Most Liberal

Most Likely to Be the Next Newt Gingrich

Most Likely to Succeed

If you're even slightly confused about how I could be voted incredibly liberal, exceptionally conservative, and extraordinarily successful at the same time, you can certainly join the club. I spent quite a bit of time contemplating the message behind these awards, and what I came up with is that I had the ability to make everyone feel that I was just like them. Perhaps this would please some people, but I mainly felt sorrowful. In my mind, the most accurate award would have been Most Likely to Hide What She Really Feels Inside.

In the home stretch of my final year of high school, I wandered the halls feeling like something was missing. I had everything going for me, but I was plagued with feelings of discontent and confusion. Maybe I was wearing this strange mix of emotions on my sleeve, or perhaps she was just intuitive and wise, but my English teacher asked me to stay after class one day.

She wondered whether I would be interested in writing about the work of a Nobel Prize–winning author for my final paper. This piqued my interest, and she went on to explain that a woman named Toni Morrison had recently won the coveted award, and my teacher thought I might enjoy reading her books. She suggested that I might even want to compare her work with that of other authors like Alice Walker or Zora Neale Hurston.

I thanked her for the idea and told her I would think about it because I frankly had no idea who those ladies were. I'm dating myself, but the internet was not as easily accessible in those days, so it took me a little time to uncover the fullness of what she was saying to me. After some research, I came up with the answer, and I'll interpret it for you here:

"Amber, I see you. I see you standing alone in a sea of white faces and spaces, coming to the end of your education in this community. I see you about to embark on an academic adventure in a new place, and you have likely never studied the thoughts and lives of any Black person beyond those in bondage or struggling to keep their head above water. And maybe, just maybe, you'll allow me to slide a small gift across the desk before you leave my classroom." Those were not her exact words, but that's what she meant. And for that, I will be forever grateful.

This perceptive teacher handed me an idea and a hall pass to the school library. While there, I discovered literary mirrors for the first time since I had read *Roll of Thunder, Hear My Cry* by Mildred D. Taylor in fourth grade and written it off as a remarkable anomaly—something I had hungered for ever since. I checked out *The Bluest Eye* and *Beloved* by Morrison, *The Color Purple* by Walker, and *Their Eyes Were Watching God* by Hurston. I then proceeded to write the only research paper I ever cared about in my entire academic career.

I came alive while getting lost in those books. I followed familiar reveries, and my senses were shocked by worlds that hinted at things I had seen or heard during visits with grandmothers and great-aunts but could not fully comprehend. I read about experiences I could easily relate to, set right next to some that were foreign to me—even more so than the white stories I had been reading all along. But what I took away more than anything were the voices of Black women.

Fast-forward two decades, and I began to understand that in the flood of ensuing textbooks, term papers, and job interviews, the seeds my teacher had dropped didn't have time to take root before being swept away by the wind. And by the time I became a mother, I had been swimming in someone else's pool for so long that all I knew how to do was invite my daughter in for a dip.

But thank goodness she had not yet learned how to smile and wave mechanically. She didn't inherit my disease to please, and she was not having it. The water was frigid when she plunged in, and she refused to get used to it. She balked and complained, flailed her arms, and demanded that I hear her cries for liberation.

WHERE ARE THE MIRRORS?

My child was determined to be seen, and her insistence revealed that I was perpetuating the same cultural emptiness I had experienced as a schoolgirl. I began seriously studying the concept of books as mirrors, and the more I researched, the more sense it all made. A mirror is a book that reflects a child's own culture or personhood and helps build their identity. In literary mirrors, children can find themselves, their families, and their communities reflected and valued. When reading books where they see characters like themselves moving through the world, they feel belonging.

Nancy Larrick, former president of the International Reading Association, wrote an article highlighting that millions of "nonwhite children are learning to read and to understand the American way of life in books which either omit them entirely or scarcely mention them. There is no need to elaborate upon the damage—much of it irreparable—to the [Black] child's personality."[1] This is a spot-on assessment of what's happening in most public, private, and home-based learning environments today, so imagine my surprise when I looked at the bottom of the page and saw that the article I was reading was published in 1965.

Over a decade before I was born, experts raised the alarm that something was terribly broken in our children's literary world, yet I grew up with few books as mirrors. Twenty-five years later, Bishop sounded an identical alarm, but my daughter still lived without substantial mirrors.

And now today, new voices are ringing cowbells, laying on the horn, screaming into the mic, and banging their heads against the wall while children carry on searching for their reflections in vain.

Each year, the Cooperative Children's Book Center (CCBC) releases the number of children's and young adult books by and about BIPOC (Black, Indigenous, and People of Color).[2] Of the 3,716 total books received from U.S. publishers in 2019, these numbers show the percentage of total books that had at least one primary character identified as belonging to one of the following groups:

WHITE	41.8%
ANIMAL/OTHER	29.2%
BLACK/AFRICAN	11.9%
ASIAN/ASIAN AMERICAN	8.7%
LATINX	5.3%
DISABILITY	3.4%
LGBTQIAP+:	3.1%
FIRST/NATIVE NATIONS	1%
PACIFIC ISLANDER	0.05%
BROWN SKIN (NONSPECIFIC)	9.2%

There has been some small progress, but as the CCBC report points out, "Taken together, books about white children, talking bears, trucks, monsters, potatoes, etc. represent nearly three quarters (71%) of children's and young adult books published in 2019."

I would take this a step further and point out that, within the small subset of books featuring BIPOC characters, many of the stories revolve around brokenness. Author and illustrator Christopher Myers aptly named this landscape an "apartheid of literature." He describes this as a place where characters of color are "limited to the townships of occasional historical books that concern themselves with the legacies of civil rights and slavery but are never given a pass card to traverse the lands of adventure, curiosity, imagination or personal growth."[3] Myers challenges us to broaden our assumption that children need mirrors merely for the sake of reflection, suggesting that books integrated into children's worldview aren't merely mirrors, but also become maps. And if we follow his premise of books as maps, what path are our children led down when every road leads to enslavement, strife, prejudice, and poverty?

DEFINING SUCCESS

What I've just shared may feel discouraging, but rest assured that the path forward is not a dead end; it's an open door. It's an invitation for intentional parents to regain their agency and curate an extraordinary home library that rivals the reflective potential of the Hall of Mirrors in the royal Palace of Versailles.

This library need not be an actual room, but can consist of bookshelves, baskets, carts, or crates creatively tucked here and there throughout a home, wherever space and ingenuity allow. If I could focus my attention on only one aspect of home culture, it would be developing an intentional, literature-rich space with an abundance of mirrors reflecting each child who calls that place home.

One responsibility of an intentional parent is to "become a dedicated promoter of books in your family," as Clay and Sally Clarkson put it in their book *Educating the WholeHearted Child*. They go on to write, "It is not too strong to say that to the degree you fail to enrich your children's lives and spirits with good books, you run the risk of leaving them spiritually impoverished for life."[4]

This is serious business, yet it's not something to be tackled by school boards alone. It's best addressed in the lap of a parent or loved one, at the kitchen table, in a snug bed, or a backyard hammock. In those intimate spaces, children absorb the messages "I belong" and "I am valuable." And as those ideas begin to take hold, they're more prepared to confidently traverse life with detailed maps outlining their place in the world and the myriad roads they can wander.

Author and illustrator Grace Lin won the Newbery Honor award with her book *Where the Mountain Meets the Moon*. The book has been hailed as a "Chinese *Wizard of Oz*," and Lin calls her main character, Minli, an Asian Dorothy. It was while watching Lin's TEDx Talk that I solidified my understanding of the critical need for mirrors. In it, she said, "It seemed like there was nobody who looked like me anywhere. There was nobody that looked like me in school, there was nobody that looked like me in the movies, there was nobody that looked like me on TV or in the magazines. And most important, there was nobody that looked like me in the books that I loved. . . . How could I create any vision to share with the world when I had never even looked at myself? . . . My books are the books I'd wished I had when I was a child."[5]

After wading through a river of my daughter's tears, I realized that books are some of the most powerful tools in a home; they have an almost magical ability to express values, convey meaning, and transmit emotion. When selected with thoughtfulness and care, books can be brilliant life-giving mirrors that reflect a child's self-image while validating and valorizing their lived experience. Alternatively, books can be instruments to magnify the experiences of others to the point that our children no longer see any evidence of their own existence in the margins.

When I understood the importance of books as mirrors, I filled our shelves with literary looking glasses, and I immediately witnessed my little girl perk up like a thirsty plant after an early morning rainfall. Every new book that crossed our threshold became an opportunity to fortify my children—not because magnifying others is inherently bad, but because our shelves were so unbalanced that my kids needed to bask in their reflections for a while.

Adding the right books to our library is an ongoing activity because reading abilities, interests, and maturity levels constantly change. What remains consistent are the changes I've witnessed in my daughter since I began prioritizing reflective books in our home. Nina's exuberance, wit, and cheer returned so quickly after integrating mirrors into our home that it felt miraculous. One of the early indicators that we were on the right path was when she began incorporating her Black baby dolls—the ones that had been relegated to the back of the closet—into her imaginative play. Once she felt known and seen through her books, that feeling of self-love and worth permeated all aspects of her play. Those mirrors turned into road maps, and she's now an avid reader and artist who maneuvers in the world while being rooted in a strong sense of self as well as curiosity and openness toward people of all colors.

FROM COLORBLIND TO COLORFUL

Some people don't believe that children need to see themselves in books. They think great literature supersedes diversity by speaking to the human condition and that we shouldn't take skin color or ethnicity into consideration. Instead, they say, children should immerse themselves in stories and glean whatever lessons the author is trying to impart by imagining themselves in the characters' place. However, this sentiment is based on flawed assumptions. Offering children of color stories with characters who reflect them in no way restricts the opportunity to use their imagination. If that were the case, we could argue that white children reading books about white people never use their imaginations while reading, which is obviously not true.

This argument also assumes that children who have access to literary mirrors will read them exclusively without regard to any other titles, including the traditional classics that are so often held up to the light during these discussions. This assumption is also misguided. Children must encounter a wide range of books across genre, style, time, and more. My children read and enjoy many classic and contemporary books with an array of protagonists without regard to race. The books I bring into our home as mirrors do not supplant or erase titles hailed as universally representative of the human experience. Mine is not an either-or proposition. It's a call for expansion.

Insisting that children of color continue to read *only* the historically prescribed canon is limiting. That argument is no better than that of someone who insists that children only be given mirrors, which is equally shortsighted. But when people list examples of universally good books, they inevitably rattle off titles where people of color are suffering through life's circumstances, subjected to subservient roles, or nonexistent. Ignoring this fact and insisting on a narrow view of what constitutes a good book diminishes the idea that a book can be both a mirror and quality literature. Mirrors can hold universal stories that include and transcend ethnicity. To think otherwise threatens to pull us back to the days of "white is right," and we've fought too hard to rid ourselves of that mentality.

While well-intentioned, the idea of a colorblind library, in which race is not a consideration when selecting books, exposes children to the outdated theory that race-based differences don't matter. This ignores the realities of cultural differences and racism, leaving some children to feel unseen and unvalidated while others are left without the vocabulary to examine and discuss their thoughts on race. Silence does two things, depending on the child: it breeds ignorance or feeds shame.

The way to raise children who appreciate, but are not overly focused on, the race of the characters and people they read about is to have colorful shelves. Bookshelves full of color. On these shelves, diverse books are the norm. That is the exact opposite of a colorblind selection strategy. It's necessary because children are intelligent and absorb messages from the world around them at an incredible pace. Colorblind shelves are usually homogenous, and children can interpret that lack of diversity as a lack of importance regarding the absent voices. Intentionally curated shelves communicate that inclusive stories are mainstream stories, and listening to a symphony of voices is just what we do.

Colorful curation is the parent's responsibility, and young children don't need a front-row seat to our adult library-cultivation conversations. I never sat my daughter down and said, "Honey, I am going to start buying more books with Black girls in them because you need to have literary mirrors. You're Black, so you'll appreciate those books more than the many white books on our shelves." Rather, the books were simply placed on our shelves and tables alongside books of all sorts with little fanfare. There is no "Black book" section in our schoolroom, and my children are not privy to the many late-night hours I spend researching and selecting the books they see every day.

Most of the resistance to books as mirrors comes from parents whose children don't have to make as many leaps while reading. As with many aspects of parenthood, the situation becomes direr when you're the parent of a child in need. When you witness your child in pain or in the throes of confusion, you can see more clearly how suggesting that they try harder to imagine themselves in all their books doesn't feel like a loving approach.

Sometimes the argument against books as mirrors comes from people of color. Most often, I hear that their parents provided books without ever considering race, and therefore they're doing the same with their children. Or that they didn't have mirrors growing up, and they turned out fine. I find this argument troubling, as it reminds me of people who say they drive under the influence or never wear a seat belt and nothing bad ever happens. It seems like such an unnecessary gamble. Providing children with mirrors—books where they see themselves represented and reflected—is an undertaking with no downside, whereas the potential upside is considerable. Why not try offering children a plethora of good mirrors and see what happens?

When curating your home library, it's wise to keep the following things in mind.

LOOK BEYOND SKIN COLOR AND ETHNICITY

When choosing mirrors, parents must not lose sight of narrative. Not every book featuring a child who looks like your child is the right book for your home. You still must consider the messages the book sends, the maturity level of the writing or storyline, and the connections your child can draw from the author's words.

After intentionally curating picture book mirrors, I began looking for elementary chapter books to add to our home library. A quick search pulled up multiple options featuring young Black kids, and I purchased most of them. After receiving them and pre-reading for appropriateness, I realized that while these books did feature brown-skinned children, many had lives that in no way mirrored my children's lived experiences. The fathers were gone or rarely around; the mothers worked hard to care for kids alone. The children wandered around the city, hanging out with friends confronting scenarios and using language beyond their years.

I don't have a problem with my children reading those books. In fact, I want them to be read. These stories often reflect authentic scenarios within communities of color and our broader society, and they're essential mirrors for some. Still, they didn't encompass the fullness of what I was seeking.

I kept wondering, "Where are the well-written chapter books with young BIPOC children who like to go swimming and play with puppies? What about girls sitting at the table giggling over silly dance moves while Mommy and Daddy put the finishing touches on dinner? And how about bike riding, camping, visits with Grandma, pet fish, and gymnastics?" My children enjoy traveling, solving mysteries, and getting lost in museums, too. Are those everyday experiences with loving, intact families only believable within the realm of white stories?

Fantasy, sci-fi, and epic adventures of all sorts resonate with my older children. Yet, the domain of wildly imaginative books featuring diverse characters is a barely perceptible sliver of the market. I've had to search long and hard to find chapter books and middle-grade fiction that come closer to reflecting those positive and creative aspects of the Black lives in my home, and you may have to do the same.

One question I've received when discussing books as mirrors is "What about white children? Do they need mirrors?" And to that, I say, "Absolutely." *All* children need mirrors. Generally, there's no need to focus on white children needing to see more white people in their books, as those mirrors are abundant. The odds are that nearly every book they pick up will somehow reflect the images, stories, or experiences of people like them.

However, mirrors are not only skin-deep. I give many examples of mirrors reflecting race or ethnicity because it's a critical void in so many homes and schools, and that's how the need for books as mirrors first manifested in my house. But other aspects of a child's personhood may need to be reflected, especially the parts of their lives that threaten their sense of self and security with their place in the world. Some of these include:

- Physical, developmental, behavioral, and emotional disabilities or special needs

- Religious differences or approaches to spiritual practices

- Varying types of family structures or living situations

- Significant life changes or experiences such as divorce, remarriage, or death

- Foster care, custodial changes, surrogacy, or adoption

Any of these situations can warrant a need for literary mirrors, and as the designated purveyors of culture in our homes, we have sway over what constitutes the perfect library. We're charged with working diligently and choosing wisely as we select our children's books. Booklists and bloggers can provide fantastic ideas to dig into, and savvy librarians are a source for great suggestions. A good friend can certainly make recommendations, but only you can determine the mix and flavor that best reflects the family you're loving and leading.

WHAT TO LOOK FOR IN A MIRROR

In our home, bookshelves and baskets include a variety of mirrors, with a particular focus on these categories:

- Pictures and stories of melanated children having fun, playing, and interacting with their families and environments in positive ways

- Biographies showcasing women and people of color who have lived exciting lives or made impactful contributions to our communities

- Historical fiction that shares the viewpoints and authentic experiences of Black people across various time periods and throughout major historical events

- Stories that include cultural signals—elements that give a head nod to the African American experience—through illustrations, photographs, and descriptions of food, music, language, and interactions that children recognize as familiar

- Contemporary novels that feature Black characters but are not about *being* Black

- Nonfiction books by or about women and people of color highlighting subject matter expertise in various fields of study and avocation, including entrepreneurship, visual and performance arts, activism, business, science, writing, technology, leadership, and travel

- Poetry books that reflect our culture and voices through verse and imagery

- Books of all kinds that transform tragedy into triumph

Some of the questions I ask myself when selecting books to add or remove from our home library include:

- How is this story reflecting my children? In which ways is it a mirror, and which aspects are not part of my child's experience? Be sure to dig deeper than skin color alone.

- Is there a balance between hard historical truths and uplifting stories that offer hope and highlight beauty, even if found among ashes?

- Are there enough books showing people like us thriving and having *fun*?

- What has my child been gravitating toward and why? Do I need to provide more of what she loves or balance the shelves with books that challenge her with a new perspective?

- Is there an aspect of our culture he's struggling with? Does he need to see a specific trait or experience normalized?

- Is this book worthy of passing on to future generations? If not, what's its purpose? Certainly, not every book has to be worthy of this calling. Most will not, but I want to clearly define our books' roles on the shelf.

While literary mirrors are essential for *all* children, some need them more than others, and children of color are certainly the ones most impacted by the shortage. However, books that serve as mirrors for some are windows to the world for others. In the next chapter, we'll look at how everyone suffers when children lack access to books featuring different people.

5

......

PULL BACK THE CURTAINS

Uncovering Books as Windows to the World

> It is limiting and inaccurate to only educate our children provincially
> when they must live their lives in a global context, facing vast differ-
> ences and awesome similarities. They must learn early and often
> about the valid framing of both windows and mirrors for a balanced,
> ecological sense of their place(s) in the world.
>
> —Emily Style, *Curriculum as Window and Mirror*

CHILDREN WHO SPEND ALL THEIR TIME GAZING AT THEMSELVES
in the mirror risk entering adulthood with an incomplete view of the
world and an overdeveloped sense of self. Even when they manage to escape these likely scenarios, they often lack nuanced relational depth. When
it comes to navigating diverse environments, they have 2D experiences in
a 4D world. They can hear and see all that's going on around them, but
they often miss out on the adventure.

When I encounter someone who has never been in relationship with
or learned anything about Black people, their discomfort is palpable. Our
interaction is awkward, and I'm frequently left with complicated feelings
of confusion, irritation, pity, or sadness. Sometimes I want to break the
uncomfortable silence by asking, "Well, did you at least watch *The Cosby
Show*?"

My children also face the sting of repeated encounters with other children who have no concept of my family's Blackness. I suspect that their

playmates are products of either oblivious parenting or well-meaning but off-target attempts at colorblindness. In either case, my children bear the burden of education that should have been birthed in their companions' homes.

"Does that brown stuff rub off?"

"What does it feel like to have color on your skin?"

"Why don't you ever wear your hair down?"

"Do you guys have the same dad?"

"Why is your sister a different color than you?"

"Did you like living in Africa?"

"Black people can't have freckles."

"Why do *you* have to wear sunblock?"

"I counted, and there are six of you brownies in this building right now. That's a lot!"

"You can't be a princess because princesses don't have braids."

"We're not going to watch that movie because my mom said the Little Mermaid can't be Black."

"My grandpa is in the bathroom, but when he comes out, we have to stop playing because I'm not allowed to play with Black kids."

"Hurry up at the water fountain! If you keep taking so long, I'm going to put you back into slavery."

These were said directly to my children except for the last statement, delivered to my friend's daughter in the hallway of her elite performing arts studio. And this is just the tip of the iceberg. I could fill pages of this book with more of the same statements from children who don't have a clue.

Some of these interactions are inevitable because kids are prone to saying whatever crosses their minds, and parents can't anticipate and counteract their every thought. I, too, have been in situations where my children are the ones trying to figure out the world around them in loud, uncomfortable ways. Children are children, and to expect them to be otherwise is unjust. I'm not suggesting that we aim for perfection, but there's much room for progress. White children need models for how to understand and communicate with communities of color.

Real-world relationships are the most valuable tools for cultural competency, but finding and forming authentic cross-cultural connections is not always a simple task, as we'll see later in this book. Even children who have the advantage of diverse environments may only be privy to certain aspects of another's culture, especially if their cross-racial interactions only occur when their friends are away from the primary cultural influences of home and family.

A LIBRARY OF WINDOWS

Home and family are where differences are celebrated, particularly for children who aren't part of the majority culture. Books are often the best or only avenue available for kids to see inside the homes of others and begin to fill in the soft outlines of their understanding of how other people see the world. Providing books that give honest and varied views of different people's lives is like pulling back the curtains of a darkened room, allowing light to pour in through the windows.

Children who grow up seeing a wide variety of skin colors splashed across the pages of their picture books won't be surprised when they see the same rainbow of colors at the playground. Those who have read books about Black girls getting their hair done and all that entails will appreciate their curly or braided styles but will not gawk or dismiss them as unfit for royalty. Kids taught about melanin and ethnicity will know that skin just feels like skin no matter who you are. And children who eat dinner at tables where honest conversations about race are the norm will never threaten to make someone a slave. Books are by no means panaceas, but the more children read about the reality of lives lived outside their bubbles, the richer their relationships and experiences will be.

Books as windows are more complex than books as mirrors. Windows provide a realistic view of how others live while simultaneously situating children within the context of a wider world. This framing is important for all children, regardless of background, but it's critical for white children because so much of what they read, watch, listen to, and see is created in their image.

Many white children have little to no meaningful interaction with communities of color. The reasons for this may be geographical or economic and may or may not be intentional. Regardless of the explanations, it's safe to say that white children have a significant need for literary windows to fill the gaps that can so easily widen between themselves and people of color. And boys specifically need to be offered windows that highlight the fullness of the lives of girls and women, as we'll explore later in this chapter.

Emily Style is the former codirector of the National SEED (Seeking Educational Equity and Diversity) Project and the educator who first developed the mirrors and windows concept. She writes, "White males find, in the house of curriculum, many mirrors to look in, and few windows which frame others' lives. Women and men of color, on the other hand, find almost no mirrors of themselves in the house of curriculum; for them it is often all windows. White males are thereby encouraged to be solipsistic [self-centered], and the rest of us to feel uncertain that we truly exist. In Western education, the gendered perspective of the white male has presented itself as 'universal' for so long that the limitations of this curriculum are often still invisible."[1]

An intentional home library of windows is a first step to bringing balance to an otherwise colorless curriculum, and it's a creative way to raise children who operate with humility and confidence.

WHAT IS A WINDOW?

There's no strict prescription for what constitutes a window because priorities and perspectives vary across households and backgrounds. But generally, I've found that many of the best selections fall into the following categories:

- **A DAY IN THE LIFE:** Books that show how children in other countries, regions of our own country, and even our neighbors who look different live their daily lives today are invaluable. It's easy for this category of books to become trite, so seek authentic voices when possible and choose dignity over tokenism and stereotypes in every case.

- **FAMILY IS EVERYTHING:** Family-focused stories offer ample opportunity for children to see the many similarities between their loved ones and others. This dynamic is just as important as embracing differences. Family-centered books are also where we can most easily witness joy expressed through food, music, clothing, rhythms, and traditions, giving children a vivid sense of our common humanity and shared values.

- **A PICTURE IS WORTH A THOUSAND WORDS:** Photographs and illustrations communicate things that authors often leave unsaid. They can show the variety of dress, skin color, hairstyles, home decor, food, leisure, transportation, and more. Books featuring quality pictures are perfect for strewing around the house for children to happen upon and flip through.

- **FOLKTALES:** Legends or myths passed down through generations of people within a culture or cross-culturally are unique ways to understand the core beliefs of a people's ancestors. The storytelling traditions of many groups hold a rich heritage of experiences on which some of their modern views may rest.

- **BIOGRAPHIES, AUTOBIOGRAPHIES, AND MEMOIRS:** It's nearly impossible to write about a person's life without including details on the world around them. Biographies and autobiographies often shed light on how people lived and what they received and gave to those around them, providing day-in-the-life glimpses contextualized within a broader historical perspective. They're gold mines for learning about people and the spaces in which they operate.

- **POETRY:** I'm not sure that any other art form so quickly and thoroughly communicates the beliefs, customs, and dreams of a person or group of people. Thoughts shared in verse explore what the poet may find familiar, what she loves, the beauty or pain she sees in her world, and even her opinions on real-life occurrences. Poetry is a near-perfect window.

- **HISTORICAL FICTION:** Rooted in reality but not hemmed in by factual occurrence, historical fiction often brings humanity to the triumph and credibly redeems tragedy. Some of these books are a gentle way to introduce tough topics, while others spur children to emulate heroes and ensure that some parts of history don't repeat themselves on their watch.

- **FANTASY AND SCIENCE FICTION:** Characters of color are vastly underrepresented in fantasy, sci-fi, and speculative fiction, a genre that comprises books in other worlds involving magical, futuristic, or other imagined features. These highly creative stories rarely contain BIPOC voices, and when they do, the characters are most often relegated to minor roles or killed off early in the story. But seeing people of color playing a role in imaginative work, especially when an author is also a person of color, erodes the stereotypes surrounding this type of literature and other aspects of creative life. And these books are FUN!

- **PASSION PROJECTS:** Exposing children early and often to BIPOC leaders and historical figures who are passionate about their chosen vocation is a way to connect windows to your child's natural interests. A child interested in the work of architect Frank Lloyd Wright, as I was as a child, would be intrigued by books about Maya Lin, Zaha Hadid, or Philip Freelon—Chinese American, British Iraqi, and African American architects whose work can be seen in iconic spaces around the world. Children who enjoy fashion design or first ladies could read about Ann Cole Lowe, a Black fashion designer who made Jacqueline Kennedy's wedding dress, among other classic pieces. Whatever our children's passions, we can help expand their worldview by showing them that talent and determination thrive across all colors and cultures.

- **PRIMARY SOURCES:** Books containing copies of primary sources such as speeches, interviews, documents, and letters are often windows that speak entirely for themselves. Resources such as these can provide more truthful and accurate accounts of people's perspectives during a particular time.

- **BEYOND CULTURE:** In addition to books highlighting the lives of different ethnicities and cultures, titles that give voice to other less-explored perspectives are critical. Windows transcend race and should be broad enough to uncover more than our limited interpretations of personhood. Stories of refugees, immigrants, people living in poverty, and individuals with differing abilities are examples of stories that often go unheard. Books on each of these offer innumerable opportunities to experience life through the eyes of another.

All these window categories are valuable and worthwhile. But we need to be thoughtful about introducing them to our children because without context and life experience, some of the messages can be missed or misinterpreted.

THE EARLY YEARS (AGES 2-4)

In the early years, the goal is to introduce toddlers and preschoolers to a range of characters from diverse backgrounds. Much of what they assimilate will come from illustrations in picture books, including books featuring characters with various skin tones and hair textures. Validate and discuss observations your child may make about appearance, whether they're communicated as similarities ("She has big hair like me!") or differences ("That boy has very dark skin").

Children at this age enjoy hearing the same stories repeatedly and may even begin to "read" along as they memorize the words, so be sure that diverse books are as readily available as those featuring white children, animals, and inanimate objects. Look for books that visually show racial diversity and differing abilities without overtly being the book's topic. And find books that acknowledge and celebrate differences with no judgment. For this age, avoid books that introduce racial tension, discomfort, and enmity.

Key message: Not everyone looks like me, and that's cool!

EARLY ELEMENTARY (GRADES K–3)

The books read during these years should progress as your children mature. Now is not the time to burden them with every historical truth. Allow them the opportunity to journey through their books and develop an understanding of harsh realities over time. But be sure not to let fear or the desire to protect your child's innocence prevent you from sharing hard stories or initiating difficult conversations when appropriate. Keep in mind that younger siblings often move along faster than firstborns because they're generally exposed to more at an earlier age.

When children become school-age, they can continue with the books they've enjoyed as you begin to layer on four additional types of books.

1. **FOLKTALES, FAIRY TALES, AND TALL TALES FEATURING CHARACTERS OF COLOR FROM VARIOUS CULTURES.** Fairy tales can be diverse retellings of favorites from Hans Christian Andersen and the Brothers Grimm, but be sure to include original African, Latino, Asian, aboriginal, and First Nations folktales along with those reflecting your family's particular heritage. Bring in contemporary stories alongside those passed along through generations and across oceans to settle in today's homes and schoolrooms. These magical tales involve intrigue, friendship, justification for the inexplicable, big truths, bold exaggerations, supernatural happenings, and enchanted adventures. But no matter the subject matter or the storyteller, these books should include faces of color moving through imaginary places and spaces.

    Though they're an excellent way to introduce diverse people and cultures, be careful not to overuse these tales, as they don't reflect how people live today. Hearing stories and seeing images of diverse communities within our contemporary society is essential for building connection, so be sure to offer balance.

2. **PICTURE BOOKS FEATURING MODERN CHILDREN AND FAMILIES FROM DIFFERENT ETHNICITIES, CULTURES, AND COUNTRIES.** Most children savor opportunities to "meet" other kids in their books. Take advantage of this natural curiosity by supplying your children with books that show various aspects of the lives of others. Stories of specific cultural celebrations are fine occasionally, but focus on stories of

everyday life and avoid books that make others seem exotic or "foreign." Be careful not to unconsciously present the idea that all different people live far away or are only visitors. This is an excellent time to introduce engaging geography books about other regions of the world and our own country, increasing your child's sense of place.

Be sure to include a range of books that depict diversity within a specific ethnic group, including physical differences (range of skin color, types of hair, etc.), socioeconomic conditions, geography, living environments, family structures, and more. This helps avoid the oversimplification of cultural norms and lifestyles while supporting the idea that diversity exists within groups as much as without.

3. **HISTORICAL PICTURE BOOKS AND BIOGRAPHIES HIGHLIGHTING THE LIVES OF WOMEN AND PEOPLE OF COLOR.** Choose books that focus on the accomplishments, achievements, and triumphs of women and people of color, rather than only detailed accounts of tragedy or intense struggles. The goal is not to avoid mentioning hardship, as that's not realistic, nor does it help build foundations of admiration and empathy. Instead, we're looking to avoid books with overly mature content or those that may blur the lines between right and wrong, as children this age are often still developing their understanding of human nature.

This is the time to discuss freedom, equality, and equity. Normalize conversations on stereotypes, prejudice, and discrimination, while slowly introducing tougher historical topics such as the genocide of Indigenous peoples and African American enslavement as they come up while reading or when you bring them up if the discussions don't occur naturally. Begin giving your children the tools to resist negative messages about their identities and those of others, and be careful not to demonize or deify historical figures.

4. **CHAPTER BOOKS FEATURING AND INCLUDING BIPOC CHARACTERS.** This will be your biggest challenge for this age group. Many of the most popular early readers and chapter book series, such as Frog and Toad, The Boxcar Children, and Magic Tree House, traditionally recommended for this age group, feature white children or talking animals, so you'll have to deviate from traditional sources while building out

your home library. Blogs, social media accounts, and databases featuring diverse literature will be beneficial, and I've provided ideas for getting started at the end of this chapter.

Key messages: People not only look different, but they live differently, too. Despite our differences, we have a lot in common. People different from me love their families, have hopes and dreams, and like to have fun, as well! Historically, some people treated others differently, unfairly, or maliciously just because of how they looked, and sometimes it still happens today. This is called prejudice or racism, depending on the situation, and both are wrong.

LATE ELEMENTARY (GRADES 4–5)

As children move into late elementary, they're ready to dig into denser texts and stories that give more context to the racial tension introduced in earlier years. During this time, most children shift from learning to read to reading for pleasure. They should have plenty of windows to choose from during their leisure reading, and they should also begin reading more about historical events and people.

Be sure to balance the history books with plenty of modern nonfiction books about people of color and what they're doing today. And don't forget the books featuring children of color just living life, going on adventures, and having fun. Always seek to humanize rather than objectify. Continue to introduce quality inclusive picture books alongside chapter books.

Provide more diverse poetry books, short stories, biographies, and historical fiction. Allow your children greater latitude to select their own books from your curated shelves during their free reading time. If you notice them repeatedly selecting the same type of book, prioritize windows you don't want your children to miss during family read-alouds. Remember, just because a child can read independently doesn't mean you should no longer read aloud to them. Sometimes it helps if you read the first two or three chapters aloud before handing it off for silent reading. Get them hooked on a great story and they'll be more open to reading the rest on their own.

Key messages: Indigenous and African people had a long, rich history of civilization, traditions, and culture well before Europeans came to America, took the land, and established the Atlantic slave trade. I understand racism, how to actively resist it, and how to handle myself when I experience or witness it. I know that people are not all good or all bad, but a mix of both. Differences make us unique, and most people have a lot in common.

MIDDLE SCHOOL (GRADES 6–8)

By the time your children reach middle school, you can relax your vigilance and start permitting them to dig deeply into the joys and tensions framed by powerful windows. Their books will continue opening their eyes to the realities of diverse communities at a much faster rate, which is a good thing. Engage your children in ongoing conversations about everything—this is an age when tough table talk becomes particularly crucial to maintain.

If you have concerns about a book's content or maturity level, and you can't pre-read the entire book, rely on in-depth chapter summaries and book reviews. A little digging will help you ask the right questions and be a worthy sounding board as your children encounter many tough subjects for the first time.

Middle schoolers should regularly read biographies of women and people of color, especially if their school textbooks or nonfiction history books lack diverse perspectives. Historical fiction tends to be especially compelling for this age group. Work hard to find engaging contemporary fiction windows. There's still much work to be done, but these types of titles are being introduced at an increasing rate, making them easier to find than ever before.

Ideally, middle schoolers will begin thinking, "My parents and I speak openly and frequently about many of the issues in our society, and I enjoy learning more about the world around me. I like reading books about kids who are different than me because it helps me understand what life is like for other people, and the stories are just so good! I try to get to know all types of people when I have the opportunity because I genuinely enjoy and appreciate their friendship. I also work to intentionally include other people because I understand what it feels like to be excluded."

If you have a reluctant reader, be sure to do your research and choose high-interest books well within their reading capabilities. Don't abandon family read-alouds. They're still as important as ever.

Key messages: There are vibrant communities of color worldwide, full of inspired, talented people, but the history of colonialism and racism has impacted today's cross-cultural relationships. There's a rich history of the immigrant experience in our country, including the contributions they've made and the hardships they've endured. Today, there are ongoing immigration debates within this country and around the world. The issues affecting BIPOC here impact communities of color in other countries as well.

TEENAGE YEARS (GRADES 9–12)

Teens who have been exposed to mirrors and windows all along will likely be ready for young adult (YA) titles, but take things slowly. Many YA books can test the boundaries of even the most relaxed parents. Some young teens are likely to be best served by higher-level middle-grade titles and less intense YA books.

However, as your teens get older, it's time to expose them to YA and adult titles while they still have you to guide them through the ideas and concepts they'll quickly encounter once they leave your home. Parents who launch young adults who haven't had a chance to fully engage with challenging realities while under their parents' wing are doing their children and their communities a disservice.

Your child should open every type of window during the teen years. They're preparing for adulthood and need to seek out and thrive in diverse environments. Specifically, be sure to provide the following:

- Memoirs and biographies by and about people of color and women

- Controversial, landmark, or historical novels that made a mark on the literary world

- Contemporary fiction that allows your teen to enter the worlds of others

- Nonfiction books on global topics written by passionate authors

- Thematic anthologies and collections of short stories highlighting aspects of diverse experiences

- Nonfiction books written by people of color who have expertise in your teen's areas of interest

- Books written by non-American authors, set in other countries, that highlight the lives and experiences of their people

Take inventory of what your teen is reading and fill in the most vital gaps with family read-alouds. Yes! Keep reading aloud. Even to teenagers. Reading aloud can be cemented as a way of life, something to be enjoyed for years to come.

Key messages: History is complicated, and we're still experiencing the complex legacy of our country's unique freedoms and brutal past today. So many people see and experience the world differently than I do. They often feel unseen, unheard, or misunderstood, and I should listen and learn. I have choices about the kind of person I'm going to be and how I choose to interact with others. Not being part of the problem is not enough; I need to be part of the solution.

QUESTIONS TO ASK WHEN CHOOSING WINDOWS

- Am I introducing my children to accomplished figures in all fields and domains who happen to be BIPOC, or does my booklist focus only on strife, enslavement, and desegregation?

- Am I relegating books on Black and Brown people to limited celebratory times like Black History Month, Hispanic Heritage Month, or Arab American Heritage Month and ignoring them the rest of the year?

- Do our elementary books avoid offensive expressions and pictures, racist teaching, and stereotypical representations? Do our middle-grade and young adult books that contain insensitive or offensive stereotypes use them as teachable moments rather than present them as fact?

- Are my sons reading books with female heroines?

- Are my kids seeing children of color in their literature where their BIPOC status isn't the book's focus?

- Do our books featuring disabled characters perpetuate ableist narratives?

- Do we read books written by authors from various countries and regions of the world?

- How is gender being presented in the books my children read?

- Do the stories we read emphasize the dignity and resilience of people living under oppressive conditions, or do they suggest an overly simple answer to the sociohistorical dilemmas of the cultures represented?

- Am I ensuring that our home library acknowledges the diversity of experiences within a particular cultural group?

RAISING GLOBAL CITIZENS

Before deciding to invest resources in curating an intentional home library, parents need to define their "why." Why go through the trouble of creating a book culture around mirrors and windows, reading aloud, and maintaining ongoing dialogue around tough topics? Without a compelling why, it can be challenging to sustain the emotional energy and time commitment needed to remain enthusiastic about our mission through the years.

For most of us, raising children who find meaning in knowing and being known is at the root of our choices. We want to create a home atmosphere where children value differences and embrace diversity, and we hope to launch informed, compassionate, and engaged global citizens into the world.

Knowledge of others is the only way to impart a global mindset. Children must learn *from* people who are different, not just *about* their differences. This happens through involvement in local diverse communities and travel, but it's also conveyed through books. When speaking of the power of story to help develop compassion, *Give Your Child the World* author Jamie C. Martin states, "[Books] will help your family grasp on a new level that what we have in common with our worldwide neighbors far outweighs what separates us. As children make that connection, it naturally develops compassion for their brothers and sisters around the globe and around the corner—because we all have similar needs, hopes, and desires. Great stories build an empathic foundation that leads to a life of service and concern for others."[2]

This empathic foundation, coupled with curiosity and genuine regard for others, fuels a global mindset. Without it, our children are at risk of being left behind, drowning in their ethnocentrism.

FACING TOUGH CONVERSATIONS

Windows don't exist in a vacuum. The books your kids will be reading address the people's or characters' lived experiences, and life is not always comfortable. People of color have tremendous stories of love, adventure, determination, and fun, but stories of being marginalized while enduring pervasive hardship are also theirs to tell. To gain the fullest possible picture of BIPOC lives, you must be willing to face tough topics like prejudice, racism, exceptionalism, and more.

Racism is tricky. Hateful words and actions easily identify blatant racists, and few people disagree on their motives or intentions. But everyday racism is harder to identify. It stalks, almost imperceptibly, oozing into the nooks and crannies of our shared worlds. It starts with families of origin, extended family, and friends, before meandering into classrooms, courtrooms, offices, churches, neighborhoods, and every other institution or gathering place. Silent racism often goes unchecked as it's perpetuated, socializing children to normalize and accept what they can't name.

Biologically we're all the same, but socially we are not treated as such. Many people agree with this premise but refuse to consider the ramifications. Others cling to their colorblind ideals and insist on parenting for the world we dream of for tomorrow without addressing the realities of today. And some deny the very existence of the insidious nature of racism, allowing it to gain even more power. When we arm children with windows that demonstrate the ways racism shows up in the lives of people of color, children can better assimilate the messages they receive about the value and worth of others as they learn how to help.

Exceptionalism is not as commonly recognized as racism, but the two are inextricable. As a child, I regularly heard negative comments about

Black people without regard to my presence in the room. Bewildered and uncertain of what to say, I would clear my throat to remind my friends or their parents that I was within earshot, only for them to reassure me that they weren't talking about my "kind of Black people."

I was somehow set apart in the minds of white people as exceptional. They viewed the one Black family they knew as fully realized and sympathetic while regarding Black people at large as an undistinguished mass to be feared or disdained. By the time I became an adult, I assumed we had progressed beyond this type of thinking, but some people are still as misinformed in this area as they were decades ago.

This type of warped thinking is born of lack of exposure, among other things. When children only see one kind of Black, Latino, Asian, or Middle Eastern person, for example, they base their perception of the entire group on their limited exposure to a few. And with the negative portrayal of people of color on the news and in film and TV, children may be left with wildly distorted views.

Books can begin to remedy this situation. Children grow their ideas by meeting diverse and positive historical figures, fictional characters, and contemporary individuals in real life and through windows. People of color are varied and nuanced, and lumping them together according to limited notions of who they are and what they bring to the table is small-minded. Well-curated bookshelves help expand our children's minds, preventing them from falling into the trap of a single story.

THE SINGLE STORY

How do we know when we have furnished our home with enough windows? For me, the number of windows illuminating our home library increased as I saw their beneficial effects on my children and my interest in this area grew. But there is no such thing as a perfect library. While I may not have a magic number that constitutes a worthy collection, I know that our aims must be broader than the single story. You can't just read a book about a kid in Thailand and check the Asian box, a girl in Kenya and check the African box, and a boy in a wheelchair and check the disability box. Our commitment involves repeated exposure to various voices and characters, even within the same culture or experience.

"African American experiences are diverse and unique. The black experiences of the South do not necessarily reflect those of the North, nor do inner-city situations parallel rural settings. Make sure your classroom library reflects this diversity, as well as that of blacks living in places such as the Caribbean, Africa, and Great Britain," explained the late children's illustrator Floyd Cooper.[3] The same applies to home libraries. Even within a single culture, there are many stories to be told and explored.

When reading mirror books, it's easy for the reader to recognize authenticity and quickly sniff out stereotypes and tokenism. This is not the case when books are windows. The inherent distance between the reader and the lived experiences of the protagonist or subject can complicate matters. The risk is that our children may not realize what they don't know, and at times, they may mistake a single story for *the* story of a people.

Author Chimamanda Ngozi Adichie describes the problem of the single story. She explains, "The single story creates stereotypes, and the problem with stereotypes is not that they are untrue, but that they are incomplete. They make one story become the only story. . . . The consequence of the single story is this: it robs people of dignity. It makes the recognition of our equal humanity difficult."[4]

The problem of the single story isn't resolved simply by reading multiple books about the same people group. You could read your child ten books about Indigenous peoples, but if all the books focus on a single nation, or worse yet, there's no mention of differences between them or even their existence today, then you may be unintentionally perpetuating the single story. When we expose children to a one-dimensional story about a group of people, it limits their understanding of who people truly are.

VOICES OF WOMEN

The voices of people of color are not the only lost voices in literature and learning. A glance through the titles of the Western canon, the books fueling the Great Conversation, and the reading lists espoused by many community schools and homeschools will reveal how little the thoughts and contributions of women have been valued throughout history.

Our home libraries must remedy that situation.

Parents of boys often tell me that their sons will not read "girl books." I understand this impulse because my sons love digging into books featuring boys, but they also read, hear, and enjoy many stories featuring girls. Within the walls of our home, we don't have girl books and boy books; we only have stories. And just as the books featuring people of color sit alongside their more typical counterparts, books featuring female protagonists and the accomplishments and lives of women share the same space on the bookshelf and during our family read-alouds.

Girls are expected to read books about boys, and no one thinks to question it. But ask a group of boys to read books about girls, and you may end up with a mutiny from the boys and their parents and teachers. I've seen this dynamic play out in my own circles.

I run a book club for children ages eight to ten in our local homeschool support group. When the children read a book starring boys, we have full attendance, but when we discuss books with female protagonists, very few boys attend, if any. I've never had a parent of one of the girls question the book selection, but the boys' parents are generally quite concerned about their sons' exposure to "girl books."

Ironically, my oldest is the only girl in our group's middle school book club, and they read books featuring boys nearly every month. She's noticed the imbalance, yet she still claims book club as her favorite group activity. Once, when the boys forgot to vote for the next book, her single vote landed the group with *Inside Out & Back Again* by Thanhha Lai. Some of the boys immediately expressed their dismay at being forced to read a book about a girl. Inspired by Lai's childhood experience as a refugee fleeing Vietnam and immigrating to Alabama, this Newbery Honor Book is a compelling number one *New York Times* bestseller. But the boys could only see a girl, and they couldn't hide their disdain.

"When a boy is directed to books that reflect only a narrow aspect of the world—often a part he already knows—or he is shamed for any interest in what is considered a 'girl book,' his understanding of girls and of himself is devastatingly incomplete," states Caroline Paul, the author of the *New York Times* bestselling *Gutsy Girl: Escapades for Your Life of Epic*

Adventure.[5] Paul was not permitted to speak about her book at a middle school because the administration felt it would exclude boys. That week, she looked at the *New York Times* children's bestseller list, and of the top ten titles, nine featured white boys. The tenth starred a boy of color and a white girl together in the book adaptation of a *Star Wars* movie. None featured a solo female protagonist.

Devastatingly incomplete.

Paul's is not an isolated experience. Author Shannon Hale has written about boys being excused from school assemblies when she speaks because her books feature female leads. She says, "Stories make us human. We form bonds by swapping personal stories with others, and reading fiction is a deeply immersive exercise in empathy. So, what happens to a culture that encourages girls to read books about boys but shoos boys away from reading books about girls? What happens to a boy who is taught he should be ashamed of reading a book about a girl? For feeling empathy for a girl? For trying to understand how she feels? For caring about her? What kind of man does that boy grow up to be? The bias against boys reading about girls runs so deep, it can feel daunting to try to change it. But change can start with a simple preposition swap: When talking to young readers, we can communicate that a book is *about* girls without prescribing that it's *for* girls."[6]

When so much of their experience validates their existence and supports the notion that society revolves around them, boys should be able to handle books that weren't written directly about or for them. Their manhood depends on it. If we want men to embrace the voices and ideas of the women who show up in myriad ways in this world, we need to keep the hearts and minds of our boys open from the beginning. They need books that validate the existence and worth of women, and they need parents who do the same.

WINDOWS FOR ALL

It's tempting to assume that children of color don't need windows. While it's true that most have an abundance of windows into white worlds, they're often just as underexposed to other cultures as their white counterparts. While BIPOC children crave mirrors, they also need to grapple with expressions of life beyond the borders of their experiences.

Windows can provide a view of how different people experience all aspects of life: race, culture, immigration, religion, regional differences, variations in language and dialects, celebrations, births and deaths, food, music, education, romantic relationships, friendships, parent-child relationships, extended family, home life, work, and play; and those experiences vary across and within peoples and groups.

Building genuine solidarity with others takes effort, and non-white families don't get a pass on doing the work. The goal is that our children will collectively know themselves and others, and the need to celebrate differences and similarities applies to everyone, regardless of background.

WHERE TO FIND WINDOWS

Finding the right books isn't always an easy task, but like-minded authors and organizations are the ideal places to begin your search. Organizations like these offer a multitude of resources to help build your family's library:

- AMightyGirl.com

- ColoursofUs.com

- DisabilityinKidlit.com

- DiverseBookFinder.org

- HereWeeRead.com

- SocialJusticeBooks.org

- StoriesofColor.com

- TheConsciousKid.org

- WeNeedDiverseBooks.org

Many children's booklists only include traditional classic titles alongside older Caldecott and Newbery award winners. My family thoroughly enjoys these established favorites; in fact, our shelves are lined with them, but I also rely heavily on more diverse quality lists featuring the voices of people with different backgrounds and abilities, including:

- American Indian Youth Literature Award

- Arab American Book Award

- Asian/Pacific American Award for Literature

- Carter G. Woodson Book Award (Diverse titles)

- Children's Africana Book Awards

- Coretta Scott King Book Awards (African American experience)

- Ezra Jack Keats Award (Universal qualities of childhood, a strong and supportive family, and the multicultural nature of our world)

- Middle East Book Award

- Pura Belpré Award (Latino/Latina experience)

- Schneider Family Book Award (Disability experience)

- South Asia Book Award

- Sydney Taylor Book Award (Jewish experience)

- Tomás Rivera Book Award (Mexican American experience)

- Walter Dean Myers Award (Diverse main characters)

WHERE DO WE GO FROM HERE?

We have a small window of opportunity, a limited time to focus on the messages we want to instill, override, and supplant in our children. While we have our children at home, these years are the best times to counterprogram any harmful or diminishing beliefs they may begin to internalize. A home library of mirrors and windows is a tool of resistance. By opening our children's literary worlds, we gift them the knowledge of both self and others.

Early twentieth-century British educator Charlotte Mason once said, "Mothers work wonders once they are convinced that wonders are demanded of them," and the same can be said of devoted fathers. But once parents commit to curating a diverse and wide-ranging home library, how do they go about selecting the right books to place on the shelves? What makes a book "good" anyway? In the next chapter, I'll share guidance on what to look for beyond mirrors and windows, books that nourish a child's innate personhood and sense of wonder, books that may not yet have found their place in the historically prescribed canon but that are lifegiving and vital nonetheless.

6

LIFE-GIVING BOOKS

What Makes a Book "Good"?

Good books are good nutrition.

—Gwendolyn Brooks, *To Young Readers*

IN MOST SCHOOLS, A SUPERIOR EDUCATION HINGES ON THE historically prescribed Western canon, a relatively static booklist that combines the previous decades' and centuries' most essential literary works. There's some debate even among the major supporters of this type of required reading, but most agree that certain books deserve a prime spot in the minds of learned students. Examples include:

- *The Iliad* and *The Odyssey* (Homer)

- *The Divine Comedy* (Dante)

- *Hamlet* (William Shakespeare)

- *Paradise Lost* (John Milton)

- *Pride and Prejudice* (Jane Austen)

- *Oliver Twist* (Charles Dickens)

- *The Adventures of Huckleberry Finn* (Mark Twain)

- *The Scarlet Letter* (Nathaniel Hawthorne)

- *Moby-Dick* (Herman Melville)

- *Anna Karenina* (Leo Tolstoy)

- *The Great Gatsby* (F. Scott Fitzgerald)

- *To Kill a Mockingbird* (Harper Lee)

These titles, along with dozens more, are accepted as the best of the best, those highly valued books that have shaped our thinking and achieved the revered status of "classics." They hold timeless, universal truths, and their influential themes and characters are often alluded to in modern culture and conversation.

Alongside these well-established titles sit modern not-yet-classics, such as books that have received the Newbery Medal, an annual award for the most distinguished contribution to American children's literature. As the first and most prestigious award of its kind, the Newbery Medal influences the literary lives of middle-grade readers. Newbery books become instant bestsellers. They're highlighted on special shelves in libraries and bookstores and are often prioritized in classrooms and homes.

But this old and new required reading is not without controversy.

There's a growing grassroots movement, led by teachers, to reevaluate the classic literature taught in classrooms. Known as #DisruptTexts, its supporters look "to challenge the traditional canon in order to create a more inclusive, representative, and equitable language arts curriculum that our students deserve." They believe that "a literary diet that reflects the rich diversity of the human experience is critical to develop empathy and understanding," and these beliefs are reflected in the movement's four core principles:

1. Continuously interrogate our own biases and how they inform our thinking.

2. Center Black, Indigenous, and voices of color in literature.

3. Apply a critical literacy lens to our teaching practices.

4. Work in community with other antiracist educators, especially Black, Indigenous, and other educators of color.[1]

The #DisruptTexts movement has come under fire for promoting censorship and condemning the teaching of canonical texts, though its founders have spoken out against both claims. Some are concerned that their diverse and contemporary recommended titles for reading and teaching—books like *The Round House* by Louise Erdrich, *Salvage the Bones* by Jesmyn Ward, and *Another Brooklyn* by Jacqueline Woodson—are threatening to topple the lists of tried-and-true classic literature.

The movement has a name that's easy to identify and track, but hashtags can't be controlled, so as with many online rallying cries, it's difficult for some to separate the ardent aims of its organizers from the short-sighted or ignorant posts of extremist fans. However, one thing is certain: the #DisruptTexts leaders are not the first or only people to advocate for a broadening of literary diet.

REDEFINING CLASSICS

I'm often asked to comment on the mostly white classics versus more diverse contemporary titles, with the questioner obviously looking for me to take a stance one way or the other. But the answer is complicated. There's much disagreement about what children should be reading, and both sides have salient arguments.

There seems to be a near-obsession in certain educational circles with the need for all children to read as many classics as possible, with some even insisting that they're the *only* books a child needs. On the other hand, it's erroneous to claim that all classics are irrelevant, having no place in the hearts or minds of children. As with most things threatening to divide opposing sides, there are truths on both sides when I consider the arguments.

The books that have long been considered canonical entered the canon for a reason. They often contain beautiful language and foundational ideas that speak profoundly to the human condition. We can't simply label them as outdated titles to be tossed out or relegated to academic research. These books have endured, remaining relevant from one generation to the next. Their writing styles have influenced countless authors, including authors of color like Frederick Douglass, James Baldwin, and Dr. Martin Luther King Jr.

In 1850, French literary critic Charles Augustin Sainte-Beuve was asked to define a classic. He said, "The idea of a classic implies something that has continuance and consistence, and which produces unity and tradition, fashions and transmits itself, and endures. . . . [A]n author who has enriched the human mind, increased its treasure, and caused it to advance a step; who has discovered some moral and not equivocal truth, or revealed some eternal passion in that heart where all seemed known and discovered; who has expressed his thought, observation, or invention, in no matter what form, only provided it be broad and great, refined and sensible, sane and beautiful in itself; who has spoken to all in his own peculiar style, a style which is found to be also that of the whole world, a style new without neologism, new and old, easily contemporary with all time."[2]

It's difficult to deny that books such as those described by Sainte-Beuve should be a part of a child's education. Yet, these same classics sometimes contain traumatic representations of people of color that need to be carefully examined and addressed if they're to be shared with our children. But often, the issue is not in what is said; it's in the silence. Most titles generally accepted as classics entirely lack any representation of diverse voices. Is it right to ask children to spend most of their reading lives in the company of authors and characters diverse in thought and perspective but sorely lacking cultural representation? Surely there is more than one narrow list from which to educate.

Ethnic homogeneity is not the only aspect of modern classic literature being questioned. Some feel that many of the selections are impressive to adults, while leaving children uninspired. When the American Library Association (ALA), the organization responsible for the Newbery Medal, was criticized for selecting books beyond the reach or interest of many children, Pat Scales, the president of a division of the ALA, responded, "The criterion has never been popularity. It is about literary quality. We don't expect every child to like every book. How many adults have read all the Pulitzer Prize–winning books and the National Book Award winners and liked every one?"

On the other hand, children's literature professor Lucy Calkins says, "I can't help but believe that thousands, even millions, more children would grow up reading if the Newbery committee aimed to spotlight books that are deep and beautiful and irresistible to kids."[3]

The seemingly opposite thinking of these two experts gives us space to consider the argument that exposing our children to books of superior literary quality is essential but cannot override the goal of sparking wonder in their hearts. It also points to the inherent subjectivity in determining which books should be required reading for our children.

A focus on literary quality is worthy. Indeed, our children should wrestle with ideas of great thinkers and familiarize themselves with more complex language and themes. But this raises several pressing questions: Is literary quality *all* that matters? Can contemporary voices and diverse books also offer these gifts? And who gets to define "literary quality" anyway? More important, who is to say what is and is not a good book for *your* children, particularly?

In the 1980s, Italian journalist and author Italo Calvino purported that elevating a book to classic status is a personal choice. In his essay collection *Why Read the Classics?*, he states that "*your* classic author is the one you cannot feel indifferent to, who helps you define yourself in relation to him, even in dispute with him." And while he agrees that, among other admirable things, "a classic is a book that has never finished saying what it has to say," he concludes that "there is nothing for it but for all of us to invent our own ideal libraries of classics."[4]

OUR OWN IDEAL LIBRARIES

Many of the books that have fed the Great Conversation are still relevant, but they're not enough. Even the more modern classics alone can't possibly impart all we seek for our children to know, understand, and experience in their reading lives. Our children deserve a widening of the playing field. And while supporters of the typical canon worry about censorship as some of their favorites are being removed from required reading lists, insisting that only traditional classics be given serious attention and discussion is an opposite and equal form of censorship. It's a narrowing of possibilities based on the assumption that children can only find quality writing, universal truths, worthy thoughts, and inspiring ideas between the pages of older traditional texts or even relatively new award-winning books.

I'm not suggesting that we "cancel" the classics. In fact, I've gone so far as to make a case for some of these beloved favorites when I speak to parents about their children's books. I've read many traditional classics to my children and will continue to do so. However, let us question the idolization of a prescribed set of books as *the* right books to the exclusion of all others, including contemporary titles and, by default, most titles featuring people of color. Checking every box on the required reading lists of yesteryear may no longer be as vital to the family cultures we're now trying to create, and updates are necessary. Yet, I do see the risk in abandoning universal booklists entirely.

As a society, we often reference characters or ideas derived from classic literature, sometimes unconsciously. We're able to do this because there's an assumption that most people have read or interacted with specific foundational texts at some point. Without the ability to reference and understand these collective cultural markers, we're not fully participating in the richness of our shared common vernacular.

Sometimes the characters themselves become words that quickly impart meaning in our discourse. The mere names of certain literary characters communicate much. A Pollyanna is an extreme optimist (*Pollyanna* by Eleanor H. Porter), and a Scrooge is immediately understood to be a curmudgeon (*A Christmas Carol* by Charles Dickens).

At other times, authors are credited with inventing words or phrases. Though some of these may have been spoken before William Shakespeare put them in writing, we credit him for introducing us to the following:

"All that glitters isn't gold." (*The Merchant of Venice*)

"As good luck would have it" (*The Merry Wives of Windsor*)

"Break the ice" (*The Taming of the Shrew*)

"Come what come may" ("Come what may") (*Macbeth*)

"Eaten me out of house and home" (*Henry IV, Part 2*)

"In a pickle" (*The Tempest*)

"Pound of flesh" (*The Merchant of Venice*)

"Wear one's heart on one's sleeve" (*Othello*)

"Wild-goose chase" (*Romeo and Juliet*)

And there are even plenty of common adages in today's lexicon that originated in the Bible. For example:

"Fight the good fight" (1 Timothy 6:12)

"A wolf in sheep's clothing" (Matthew 7:15)

"The powers that be" (Romans 13:1)

"Go the extra mile" (Matthew 5:41)

"By the skin of your teeth" (Job 19:20)

"A fly in the ointment" (Ecclesiastes 10:1)

We can usually grasp these sayings without reading the original texts, but encountering them in context enhances comprehension and even provides a little buzz of excitement for being "in the know." These terms first entered our language because enough people understood what they meant without explanation. Without a shared set of foundational readings, we're at risk of losing the ability to absorb literary terms into modern conversations and writing.

Bestselling author Antonio García Martínez says, "We're quickly becoming a culture where there are no common symbols or stories underlying discourse, even among educated elites (at least beyond Netflix shows)."[5]

Abandoning all traces of a generally accepted booklist in favor of entirely individual literary pursuits will further perpetuate this issue. I hope that my children leave home with a set of beloved titles that include those

I grew up on, those that have permeated our culture, so they, too, can understand the "common symbols and stories" of our society. But I would also like them to have a relationship with contemporary titles that add flavor and dimension to their imaginations and sense of wonder. Some of these books will never measure up in literary quality, but hold their own in the ideas they impart. In contrast, others will eventually become classics in their own right as the pool of cultural symbols expands.

While I don't want to burn the classics, I do want to de-elevate some of them and set a few others aside to make room at the table for other voices and perspectives. For this to occur, we must make choices. Our thinking on literary standards has evolved, but the number of hours children can or should devote to sitting and reading has not. We can lovingly offer a finite number of books during childhood, and we cannot aggressively ratchet up this number to stuff our children with too much of a good thing.

Curating our own "ideal libraries" that meld old and new to provide children with diverse, wonder-filled, inspiring ideas is more of an art than a science. Parents play an active role in determining precisely how to meet the call for opening the doors to an irresistible literary life, one that takes kids on a compelling journey and prioritizes passion and connection over blind adoption of a definitive list of must-read books.

LIFE-GIVING BOOKS

By all means, let's fill our homes with good books that reflect our children and others, but an optimal home library is not limited to only mirrors and windows. We need to offer a broad selection of books across genres that incentivize wide and varied reading. *Quality literature matters, but if we want to foster a lifelong love of reading, we should acknowledge that books with more simplistic language or quotidian situations can balance our children's literary "diets" by providing a much-needed dose of levity and fun.* We must curate our bookshelves in the same manner that we curate the rest of our children's media. And when this is done well, we open a world of rich stories for our children to enjoy and grow from throughout childhood.

An increasing number of school and home educators have become adherents to the principles of Charlotte Mason as they look to grow lifelong learners with an internal desire to self-educate. According to the Charlotte Mason Institute director, Dr. Deani Van Pelt, "Charlotte Mason espoused a relational education in a living environment filled with books, experiences, nature, and ideas, where the child is viewed as a person and the educator as one who cooperates with God."

Mason encouraged the use of what she called "living books"—books written by authors passionate about their subject matter that inspire children to explore meaningful ideas through rich narrative rather than dry facts or stale lists of things to be memorized. And she warned against the use of what she called "twaddle."

As with living books, there's no single definition of twaddle, but a working definition from Charlotte Mason curriculum provider and author Sonya Shafer, based on Mason's own writings, lays out its characteristics as:

- Talking down to a child

- Diluted

- Undervaluing the intelligence of a child

- Reading-made-easy

- Second-rate, stale, predictable

- Goody-goody story books or highly spiced adventures of poor quality, titillating

- Scrappy, weak, light reading[6]

Mason wrote, "Even for their earliest reading lessons, it is unnecessary to put twaddle into the hands of children."[7] And "That children like feeble and tedious . . . story books, does not at all prove that these are wholesome food; they like lollipops but cannot live upon them."[8] If good books are good nutrition, then twaddle would be the cheap, sugary, store-bought dessert. It's not that our children should never encounter light reading (a nutritious snack), but twaddle should not make up a significant part of their literary diet.

In her third volume, titled *School Education*, Mason said, "We are all capable of liking mental food of a poor quality and a titillating nature; and possibly such food is good for us when our minds are in need of an elbow-chair; but our spiritual life is sustained on other stuff, whether we be boys or girls, men or women."[9]

It seems that Mason was suggesting that we primarily present living books to our children as the main course with some light reading, or even occasional twaddle, as needed. A great deal of flexibility exists when subjectively determining what is and is not a living book. However, within Charlotte Mason circles, the moniker of "living books" has often been assigned to older books filled with rich language, compelling stories, and enduring ideas. In other words, the terms "living books" and "classics" are often used interchangeably.

Because of this unfortunate conceptual yoking of living books and classic literature, living books have become nearly synonymous with "white books," as well as those wherein people of color endure oppressive or impossibly difficult circumstances. But Mason wrote, "A book may be long or short, old or new, easy or hard, written by a great man or a lesser man, and yet be the living book which finds its way to the mind of a young reader. . . . The master must have it in him to distinguish between twaddle and simplicity, and between vivacity and life."[10] Clearly, living books include classics *and* other books that inspire and ignite interest and wonder, even if new or written in a different literary style or voice. But rather than fight against dogma, I began looking for a way to describe the types of books that I'm suggesting children need.

I couldn't find anything that adequately illustrated what I had in mind, so I coined the term "life-giving books" and have since expanded my original definition beyond the realm of just mirrors and windows. My reason for developing new language for this type of book is to allow room for writing that doesn't always fit the traditional mold of superior literary quality. Recent books that are life-giving to some children build interest and invigorate their unique hearts without necessarily meeting the standards of what some have come to expect from a living book.

Life-giving books are those that build a child's sense of self by providing real and imagined heroes of all kinds along with common folk who look like them and experience the world through the similar lens of a

shared or recognizable culture. These unique works add wonder and interest to a child's literary life and provide additional ballast to a young person's
construction of their self-perception and worldview. While they may not
always rise to the unequivocal literary beauty and inspiration of traditional
classics, life-giving books touch a child's soul, and it would be shameful to
dismiss them as mere twaddle. Life-giving books may share some characteristics of classics, twaddle, or both, but they stand alone as a necessary
adjunct to the carefully fashioned atmosphere of an intentional and inclusive home.

As parents, we have the power to define "good" books as we stock and
refresh our home libraries, transforming them into mainstays of diverse
and delectable reads. And we can make these decisions with confidence.
Pioneering research scientist Thornton T. Munger said, "I distrust the man
of one book, or of one class of books. . . . The men who think and read in
various directions are the better entitled to their opinions. Read variously,
and you will find after a time that one of the chief delights of reading is
substantiating what you find in one department by what you find in another. One thus follows the hidden threads which bind the creation into a
unity."[11] Munger mainly referred to the narrow culture of those who only
read books related to their profession, but the concept holds true in a
broader sense—it's essential to read widely on a diversity of topics and
perspectives.

The canon of universal classics shifts slowly and carefully over time.
But life-giving books reflect personal family values and ideas—sometimes
based on cultural needs and at other times rooted in familial preferences—
and can be updated and incorporated within our homes at will. There is
strength and security in conventional booklists, but there is beauty to be
discovered between the covers of profound newer stories that speak to our
children as well. And in the words of bestselling author Haruki Murakami,
"If you only read the books that everyone else is reading, you can only
think what everyone else is thinking."

As we look to expand our libraries with life-giving books, additional
factors to consider include the background and experience of the author,
the need to balance difficult narratives with more lighthearted fare, and
respect for a child's personhood.

INCLUDE OWN VOICES

Writer Corinne Duyvis popularized the hashtag #OwnVoices, which describes an author from a marginalized or underrepresented group writing about their own experiences from their point of view, instead of somebody else writing as a character from a group to which they do not belong. The term is nuanced, and Duyvis herself has made it clear that claiming the #OwnVoices label does not place a book or its author above criticism because the designation is not an automatic seal of approval, authenticity, or quality.

Kayla Whaley from Disability in Kidlit makes a compelling argument for #OwnVoices. She says, "Even when portrayals of diverse characters by majority-group authors are respectfully and accurately done, there's an extra degree of nuance and authority that comes with writing from lived experience. Those books that are #OwnVoices have an added richness to them precisely because the author shares an identity with the character. The author has the deepest possible understanding of the intricacies, the joys, the difficulties, the pride, the frustration, and every other possible facet of that particular life—because the author has actually lived it."[12]

Grasping hold of #OwnVoices books is essential, and I try to add great ones to our home collection whenever possible. "Books by cultural insiders most reliably provide rich, subtle material that can be enjoyed purely for entertainment or to gain insight into another realm of experience. Because the authors are well-rounded people whose ethnic or racial background is simply one facet of their being, they create characters who likewise go far beyond caricature and tokenism," states Laura Simeon, school librarian and member of the Coretta Scott King Book Award Committee.[13]

Some parents insist on *only* #OwnVoices books on their shelves, and though I understand their perspective, I haven't made it an absolute rule in my own home. Cultural outsiders have penned several of my children's favorite books, and I would never remove those from our shelves. But I prioritize books written by authors who share the same racial identity as their characters or the people they're writing about. I remain flexible while always keeping the end goal in mind: cultivating inspiring and healthy ideas for my children. I also strive to help create positive change in the world of children's books—a world where marginalized authors have traditionally struggled to get the same "pay, promotion, and praise," as Whaley so aptly once described.

BALANCE THE "STRUGGLE"

Books are some of our most critical tools for building a socially conscious home because they show us things about ourselves and others that we typically don't encounter in the same way elsewhere, but we must use these books with care. There's a shortage of quality books, particularly chapter books, featuring Black characters who are not enslaved (or formerly so), fighting for civil rights, struggling through urban poverty, or coming to age among broken families and even more broken spirits.

We established in previous chapters that it's incredibly unhealthy for children to read solely about the lives of white fictional characters and the contributions of white historical figures. But even as more parents become aware of this and seek to make changes, when they look to add colorful titles to their home library, they immediately gravitate toward books highlighting the struggles and triumphs of the poor, oppressed, ignorant, or downtrodden.

There are dangers with feeding children a mostly white literary feast speckled only with morsels of slavery, Jim Crow, and "the struggle." In this situation, children of color may, among other things:

- Rarely experience the delight of getting "lost" in a book.

- Be left feeling insignificant and one-dimensional as the offspring of former slaves, struggling "minorities," and nothing more.

- Miss out on the benefits of seeing themselves as players in an engaging plot.

- Begin to feel ignored or invisible.

- Buy into harmful stereotypes in children's literature.

- Set off in life thinking that people of color have never contributed anything worthy of serious study and examination.

- Be unfamiliar with the origins of various forms of art that comprise current BIPOC cultures.

- Begin to identify with white children and adults as the purveyors of correctness.

- Erroneously believe that all people of color in the world have required "saving" from white people before becoming whole.

- Lack the opportunity to see imaginative characters who reflect their life experiences (because even the illustrations in otherwise race-neutral books remind them that the characters were intended to be white).

And white children may develop these very same thoughts about people of color. That doesn't mean that books about the struggle aren't necessary. Historical fiction centered on Black experiences is my daughter Sasha's most beloved genre. I've shared many of my favorite Black history biographies and nonfiction books highlighting trials and triumph on my HeritageMom.com website. But I don't believe that these books should comprise all of what children read about Black people.

And the same applies to books featuring other underrepresented groups. As you look to expand your home library beyond the traditional fare, be sure that your shelves tell the stories and experiences of other people of color beyond just Black people. People living in less wealthy countries, immigrants, people with disabilities, women, and others shouldn't have their stories relegated to pain, sorrow, ableism, or a pervasive need for rescue from their circumstances either.

HONOR YOUR CHILD

As parents, we have a responsibility to guide our kids toward what we know to be best. Our maturity and experience afford us wisdom that their limited worldviews don't allow, but children are not empty vessels. They are ours, and they are also their own people. As any experienced parent will tell you, children are born with personalities, hang-ups, and gifts.

They can be molded but not altogether changed. This acknowledgment of unique personhood matters in various aspects of child-rearing, and our children's literary lives are no different.

When selecting books for your home library, the most elegant approach takes your child's individuality and autonomy into consideration. This doesn't mean that you only provide books that your child deems relevant, but it does mean that those titles are not completely ignored, assuming that they're not harmful.

As a child, I was an avid reader. Essentially raised as an only child (my siblings are much older), I happily filled my solitary hours with books of all sorts. I had assigned reading for school and excellent books provided by my educator parents, but I also had the freedom to choose other books based on my interests and desires. My mom and dad were always aware of what I was reading, and they offered guidance, but they didn't interfere with my choices.

I naturally gravitated toward classics and life-giving books, but sometimes I chose plain old twaddle. Just the kind of titillating books that Ms. Mason said is good for us when "our minds are in need of an elbow-chair." And they didn't ruin me. Whether I curled up with The Baby-Sitters Club, Sweet Valley Twins, or a Nancy Drew mystery (diverse fun reads were not a thing in the eighties!), my time spent reading lighthearted fare was not wasted. I logged hours of light leisure reading right alongside more profound texts, and those drops in the bucket of my ocean of lifetime reading were delightful moments—nothing more and nothing less.

We can stretch our children to expand their exposure, imagination, and tastes, but we shouldn't continuously force-feed them books they find dreary and uninspiring. With some children, finding the right mix can lead to a battle of wills, so it's best to aim for balance, compromise, and unified purpose rather than pitting parent against child with a winner versus loser mentality. Sometimes parents may even be required to mourn what they once thought was the perfect book selection in favor of supporting and honoring their children.

Growing up, I adored *Anne of Green Gables* by L. M. Montgomery. The Avonlea adventures and misadventures of Anne Shirley and her bosom friend and kindred spirit, Diana Barry, captured my imagination from the first chapter through the very last. I read and reread every book and watched the 1985 television miniseries on VHS so many times that I could mouth the words along with the actors. I reenacted scenes with my BFFs on the playground during recess, taking turns being auburn Anne, dark-haired Diana, and the loving Marilla. This book series was a part of me, and I couldn't wait until my children were old enough to enjoy it as thoroughly as I had.

The first night that I sat them down to read aloud from my beloved book, my kids just stared at me with complete disinterest. I could tell that they weren't immediately taken, but I figured that a few more nights would hook them. After we were a hundred-plus pages in and they were begging me to stop, I had to process my disappointment before putting the book back on the shelf. Honestly, I still hope that they'll be inspired to give Anne with an *e* another shot one day, but until then, I have to accept that what sets my heart on fire will not always be the same thing that inspires my kids.

Our kids may sometimes become co-curators as they seek to take on a more significant role in selecting their own books. I enjoy poring over book reviews and perusing back covers alongside my children while we chat about the pros and cons of various titles. And I don't mind taking a back seat to become more of a procurement agent, chauffeuring children to the library or indie bookstores, or helping them process purchases on-line. Much like the whimsical bookplates and ex libris stamps my kids love to add to our books, having a say in what ends up in their reading baskets gives them a sense of ownership over their literary lives. It helps them identify as readers and people who value thinking through the books and characters they choose to spend time with.

Guide your children as you see fit, but leave room for the machinations of their own stories to unfold. Without judgment, let them meander through books that call to them. Honor who they are as they seek pleasure and comfort inside the pages of a beloved book. Build freedom into your home library. Allow room for your child to experience what Pamela Paul and Maria Russo, the authors of *How to Raise a Reader,* call the "natural, timeless, time-stopping joys of reading."[14]

As you work to fill your home library with good books, ask yourself these questions:

- Do I, as an adult, believe that this is a good book, or am I only considering it because I think I should?

- Will this book complement other titles my child encounters at school, home, or in the community (Grandma's house, church, co-op, library storytime)?

- Does this book feed or build upon my child's interests and passions?

- Will this story spark my child's imagination or give her something new to think about?

- What other books could I offer my child based on titles he has connected with in the past?

- Is the plot accessible and interesting to my child?

- Are the characters well-developed and memorable?

- Is this book appropriate for my child's developmental level?

- Do any elements of this story speak to my child's world: setting, characters, events, language, illustrations?

- Is this the type of book my kids will remember for years to come?

- Has my child developed an excellent reading relationship with this author?

- Can I see this book becoming a classic or required reading someday?

- Is there something in this story igniting my enthusiasm and making me look forward to sharing the reading experience with my children?

- Will my kids want to read this book more than once?

- Is reading this book a good use of my child's limited reading time?

- Does this book spark joy in my child? Is it FUN?!

Thinking back to Pulitzer Prize–winning poet Gwendolyn Brooks's ode to young readers in the opening of this chapter, a home library curated with irresistibly good books, thoughtfully selected in a spirit of freedom, allows our children to feel "nourished by the riches of the feast." And this, in my opinion, is the greatest and most desirable reward for our loving labor.

The home library is the first area I shook up in my quest to redefine my home environment, but I quickly learned that I couldn't stop there. We'll explore other aspects of our home atmosphere to support a colorful and inclusive family culture in the following chapters.

PART 3

Shaping the Home Atmosphere

WHEN OUR CHILDREN WERE YOUNG, WE MOVED AROUND A LOT as we dealt with juggling tenants, selling rental properties, and satisfying our desire for more space amid the aftermath of the 2008 financial crisis. After one particularly tough move when my pregnancy and the Georgia humidity weren't getting along, I was relieved to finally settle in a lovely house that fit our family. I'd wanted my children to have a comfortable home to grow into, and I had an insatiable urge to nest. This house seemed like the perfect opportunity to check all the boxes.

After our first night in the new place, I awakened to the sound of tiny, muffled sobs. I hopped out of bed to find my youngest daughter silently crying on the steps. I scooped her up and inquired about why she was upset. She said, "I want to go back to our old house. I don't like this one because I couldn't find you." As I sat there rocking her in my arms, I considered how happy I'd been to give her all the accoutrements of middle-class suburbia when all she wanted was me. To us, home was a house. But to our kids, home was wherever we were.

When I first heard the term "houseless" used to describe people who have traditionally been considered homeless, the terminology sounded strange to my ears, but I didn't need an explanation. I immediately thought of my daughter crying on the steps and knew what the term communicated. A house is a place, but people and connections make it a home. A person can be unhoused but still have local ties, community, and roots in a particular place and among familiar people. A houseless person may not feel that they lack a sense of home. On the other hand, someone can have shelter and still harbor an internal state of homelessness. A sense of home denotes infinitely more than just physical space.

I've seen many definitions of home, but none have provided as much clarity for me as that of the Dalai Lama: "Home is where you feel at home and are treated well." I often instruct my kids not to define a word by using the same word, but in this case, there's beauty in his circular reasoning. He solidifies that there's no single right way to experience home. We can't otherwise fully explain it because home is not comprised of standardized components that you can see and replicate. It's simply a personal impression based on a sense of belonging. It involves how you're treated and how you feel when you're in a space alone or living communally with others who value you.

Our job is to make a home for our children. Not just shelter, but a place of refuge and covering where they feel safe to become. Within our homes, our children should be treated well. We should provide mental sustenance and feed them ideas that will help them think critically and speak confidently. Affection and direction should flow abundantly. Our kids should have space to grow and move while simultaneously feeling cocooned. And while maneuvering through childhood, they should *feel* at home.

Home is the place where children receive context. They can undoubtedly receive guidance elsewhere, but there's an Albanian proverb that says, "The sun at home warms better than the sun elsewhere," and it's true. It's at home that kids gain an explicit understanding of where they fit within their family and implicit clues on how their identity will impact them for better or worse within the broader community. As we consider what creating an inclusive and colorful family culture means, we can start by "collecting" our children.

In *Hold On to Your Kids: Why Parents Matter*, authors Gordon Neufeld and Gabor Maté write, "At the very top of our parenting agenda we must place the task of *collecting* our children—of drawing them under our wing, making them want to belong to us and *with* us." After building a case for why this matters, he goes on to describe four steps for collecting children from infancy through adolescence:

1. **GET IN THE CHILD'S FACE—OR SPACE—IN A FRIENDLY WAY.** The most effective methods will vary by child and by the various ages and stages within childhood, but the goal is to nurture relationships. Much of this nurturing occurs in my family as we work on projects and share experiences, but it's looked different through the years. As children mature, we have to experiment with ways to maintain attachment points, but the end goal is always to provide the necessary attachment for as long as our children need it.

2. **PROVIDE EMOTIONAL SECURITY FOR THE CHILD TO HOLD ON TO.** This step involves letting our children know that we love, accept, and enjoy them, and we can practice it through emotional warmth, physical affection, and attention, among other things. In this case, we're reminding our kids that we see them and that we like what we see.

3. **INVITE DEPENDENCE.** Based on the idea that our "preoccupation with independence gets in the way of cultivating connection," this step invites our children to rest as we meet their needs with the understanding that true independence is birthed from healthy dependence.

4. **ACT AS THE CHILD'S COMPASS POINT.** "We have to remember that children are in need of being oriented and we are their best resource, whether they know it or not. The more we orient them in terms of time and space, people and happenings, meanings and circumstances, uniqueness and significance, the more inclined they are to keep us close. We must not wait for their confused look but assume our position in their life as guide and interpreter."[1]

In the following chapters, we'll travel through our homes, spotlighting occasions to collect our children. I'll highlight touchpoints and opportunities for us to leave an imprint on our children's hearts and minds. While embracing our role of guide and interpreter, we'll explore the messages permeating our homes with an eye toward these questions:

- What do our children know about themselves and people who look like them or experience life in similar ways?

- What do they believe about people who look different or live differently than them?

- How can I, as a parent, give shape to the story woven into the fabric of my home?

We'll start with leaning into family culture to connect kids to the past, give them perspective for today, and hope for the future. Then we'll move on to the messages entering our home from the outside via various forms of media and pop culture. And finally, we'll discuss how honest history paired with the redeeming power of culturally rich learning can fill the space within our homes with beauty, contentment, and hope.

7

DEEPLY ROOTED

Leaning into Family Culture and History

I am not suggesting a collection of warring cultures, just clear ones,
for it is out of the clarity of one's own culture that life within another,
near another, in juxtaposition to another is healthily possible.
—Toni Morrison, *The Source of Self-Regard*

I'M A NOVICE GARDENER, AND WHILE PERUSING AN ONLINE
growing guide, I read that we should water our plants deeply. Light watering encourages roots to concentrate closer to the soil's surface, where sudden drying is a problem, while deep watering fosters deeper and stronger root systems.[1] Neither plants nor children will become firmly rooted within our homes by happenstance. They must be nourished. How do we build a deep-watering family culture that supports the growth of a robust root system?

There's no single correct answer to this question, as it will look different for each of us, but the idea is that, within our homes, our kids should develop a strong sense of connectedness. By embracing their heritage, they'll learn what it means to come from a line of people with communal experiences and a shared culture. When children feel rooted in their own narrative, they don't feel threatened by the differences they encounter in other people. They can branch out to others as they develop an understanding that everyone they encounter has a story as unique as their own that deserves to be heard, respected, and celebrated.

Relish your role as a purveyor of culture within your home. Take the reins and lead your children down a path of discovery through creative family projects. Not as an assignment but as a way of life. Engaging your kids' heads, hearts, and hands to create tangible reflections of who they are and where they come from increases their engagement and interest in family and cultural history and, in turn, the broader community. It also simply helps our children remember.

In her 1949 book *The Need for Roots,* Simone Weil wrote, "To be rooted is perhaps the most important and least recognized need of the human soul. It is one of the hardest to define. A human being has roots by virtue of his real, active and natural participation in the life of a community which preserves in living shape certain particular treasures of the past and certain particular expectations of the future. . . . Every human being needs to have multiple roots. It is necessary for him to draw wellnigh the whole of his moral, intellectual and spiritual life by way of the environment of which he forms a natural part."[2]

Digging into the past feeds the roots and makes our branches grow. In this chapter, I share some of the ongoing projects my family has pursued in our home to stay rooted in our heritage and family culture.

CONDUCT FAMILY INTERVIEWS

This sounds straightforward, but children can gain so much by just conversing with various family members. This never-ending project can take on all sorts of shapes depending on how much your children enjoy the process. At the very least, your kids can develop a list of questions and simply interview family members about their childhoods, careers, hobbies, relationships, and more. Most people enjoy talking about themselves, and I've found that older generations especially relish sharing stories of their past with people who care.

My kids often align their interviews with their interests. Some use audio recordings to later write their findings as a short story or article, while others have pretended to be news reporters as they recorded interviews on video. At our family reunion this summer, my oldest will interview her great-great-aunts and -uncles to find out as much as possible about her great-grandmother, their oldest sister, who passed away before my kids could know her. This is just one element of an ongoing project, which also involves Nina determining how to preserve the information she gathers.

Don't forget that this is just as much about the process as the information. If your children don't have family members to interview, have them interview you and each other. Old family friends can also be fabulous stand-ins. I know that I have stories galore about my childhood besties, and I would love to fill in the blanks for their grandchildren someday. Even if your kids don't have ties to anyone who knew their family members, there's value in talking to someone who grew up in a similar place or during the same time as their grandparents or other relatives. For example, decades from now, any one of us will be able to tell a child about life during the COVID-19 pandemic.

DEVELOP A FAMILY RECIPE BOOK

I grew up amid swirls of meal planning for large-scale family events where people came from near and far to grab a heaping spoonful of my aunt Charlotte's mac and cheese chased down by her famous peach cobbler. And to this day, we argue about who can best replicate Mama Susie's buttermilk waffles and chocolate pie because both were nothing short of pure perfection. My paternal grandfather was a chef in a hotel restaurant by day and the owner of his spot, O'Neal's Place, by night. He's known for cooking food that was so good that the very taste of it is etched in the minds of family and friends forevermore.

With a history this entwined with food, creating a family recipe book was a no-brainer. But just like I lean into slow cooking and living, I've embraced the slow development of our book. It's not something we sat down and put together like a jigsaw puzzle or Lego set. We add to it over time, slowly, as we become better at capturing the essence of a recipe or get our hands on an old copy.

I love reading cookbooks. Not just the recipes, though they're nice, too, but more the stories behind the recipes and the people who made them. One of my favorite cookbooks right now is *A Good Meal Is Hard to Find: Storied Recipes from the Deep South* by Amy C. Evans and Martha Hall Foose. As Martha describes her attraction to the language of flavor, she writes, "The essence of a dish tells a story. Some can be comfortingly intimate, and others are surprisingly new. Stringing together words, like seasoning a dish, should be done with care. . . . Sweet words to one held dear like apricot jam can be cloying if not tempered with a bit of saltiness to keep things real."

She goes on to say, "I am drawn to the gratifying ritual of day-to-day meals and have a reverence for passed-along recipes. The superstitions of cooks and the strong-held beliefs of diners never cease to amaze me. The recital of anecdotes while pots are bubbling, the narration of instruction when recipes are passed along, and how the quality of ingredients should be as high as the sincerity of words will keep me in the kitchen."[3]

Oh, how I can relate to this! A touching family recipe book, recognized as a treasure by all who behold it, is not only about the recipes. It must include good stories. And that's why it takes time to create. Find a system that works for your family and begin capturing the directions for making your people's famous and infamous dishes. Take pictures of the food, the table setting, your kids in their aprons, and anything else that brings out the story. And be sure to jot down as many notes as you can about what makes each dish special.

It's a very real possibility that you don't have any old family recipes, or no one who is still around can remember them, but that's okay. Start documenting the recipes that are carrying your family through this year's traditions, celebrations, and Friday nights. Take photos and include stories about where the recipes came from and why they're in your family's rotation. Let each child pick their favorites or tell how their mouth waters every time you pull out a particular pan. Claim these small details as your own and help your children build their stories.

WORK YOUR WAY THROUGH A HERITAGE COOKBOOK

If the idea of developing your own recipe book sounds daunting, you and your children can also work your way through a cookbook written by someone who shares some aspect of your children's heritage. Choose books that have excellent photography and a good storytelling element to entice your kids' eyes and ears. These are some of my family's favorites:

- *The Taste of Country Cooking* is a seasonal cookbook by chef Edna Lewis, who grew up in a small farming community settled by freed slaves. Her stories are as delicious as her recipes, and she inspires us to preserve the beauty and bounty of country cooking. One of my favorite parts of the book is when she says, "Ham held the same rating as the basic black dress. If you had a ham in the meat house, any situation could be faced."[4] How can you not love a woman who breaks things down like that?

- *In Bibi's Kitchen: The Recipes and Stories of Grandmothers from the Eight African Countries that Touch the Indian Ocean* by Hawa Hassan with Julia Turshen is a unique collection of recipes from home cooks, not professional chefs, in South Africa, Mozambique, Madagascar, Comoros, Tanzania, Kenya, Somalia, and Eritrea. I don't know exactly where my ancestors were on the African continent, but it probably wasn't one of these countries. Even so, when I share this cookbook with my kids, we imagine that each Bibi (grandmother) is our own.

- *Afro-Vegan: Farm-Fresh African, Caribbean & Southern Flavors Remixed* by Bryant Terry is a treat because we're vegetarian, and it's nice to have a book that we can fully enjoy without substitutions. Everything about this book sings to us. The author even refers to artist Romare Bearden, someone my children spent months studying in our school lessons, saying, "Bearden's stunning collages are a major inspiration for *Afro-Vegan.* Just as he fused paint, magazine clippings, old paper, and fabric to visually reflect the African-American experience, I have blended vegetables, grains, legumes, fruits, nuts, and seeds to delve into the food history of the African diaspora."[5]

- *The Cooking Gene: A Journey Through African American Culinary History in the Old South* by renowned culinary historian Michael W. Twitty is another personal favorite. It's a "memoir of Southern cuisine and food culture that traces his ancestry—both black and white—through food, from Africa to America and slavery to freedom."[6] Though it has recipes sprinkled throughout, it isn't a traditional cookbook. I share parts of this book with my kids because we once had the pleasure of meeting Twitty at a local history museum, and we became enamored with his words, presence, and of course, his food.

We don't sit down and read straight through these books. They live with us like old friends, and we pull them out and peruse, read aloud, and flip through as we decide what to dabble in and make our own. The cookbooks that work best for your family may not be like these at all. Find what speaks to you and what will nourish your children as they learn how their shared heritage has influenced others.

MAINTAIN A KEEPSAKE CHEST

When I was a young girl, a family friend introduced me to the idea of a hope chest, a large decorative box usually made of carved wood and used to store linens or other special items that a young woman would need when beginning her household upon marriage. I didn't have one, but it always seemed like such a romantic idea, and I've grabbed onto an updated version of the concept in my home.

My husband and I keep a wooden trunk that my mom passed down to us at the foot of our bed and, in it, we store things that we've decided as a family we want to preserve for future generations. I also collect small items that I think will be meaningful to our children, including our sons, when they become adults and start their own families. I'm pretty committed to not extending the project beyond what can be held by this single chest, so we make the decisions about what to put inside with care.

When my children were young, this activity didn't concern them, but now that they're older, they enjoy helping the family decide which things should make their way to the keepsake chest. Occasionally, I even find a random quirky item thrown in by an overzealous child, and I resist the urge to toss it out by acknowledging that "one man's trash is another man's treasure."

In addition to a quilt and an incomplete afghan, our chest contains various items: sweet notes the children have written, special pictures they've drawn, favorite clothing items or shoes long outgrown, loose photos with messages on the back, and handmade items that were given to us or created in our home. The contents have little monetary value but are of great importance to my family, and the process of determining what to keep provides continual opportunities for legacy-building conversations with our children. It helps them recognize that they're part of something bigger than themselves and that their daily comings and goings have significance now and will be savored by others later.

CURATE AN EXHIBIT OF FAMILY ARTIFACTS

During dinner, my family will often play word games while we're eating. One that they all enjoy is Say It in Five. We go around the table, and each person has to describe something (the person next to them, the last movie we watched, our favorite vacation, etc.) using exactly five words. No more and no less. It's fun to see how creative everyone gets when they have to ponder every word.

The Atlanta History Center, my children's favorite local museum, offers a virtual field trip experience based on the same concept as Say It in Five but with a twist. The museum shares *Atlanta in 50 Objects*, a collection of objects related to important stories and themes suggested by members of our community, and then asks children to create their own exhibit using five stories that make their home special and five correlating objects that tell those stories best.[7]

Kids are encouraged to photograph the objects, label them (name of the object, where it came from, year it was made or became part of your home, etc.), and write down the story about why each object was chosen.

One of my daughters worked on this project over our last school break, and her observations and selections were so poignant. I loved hearing what she felt were the most important stories of our home and family life, and the things around our house that she thought best brought the stories to life. Among other noteworthy items, she selected her guinea pigs and shared the story of how she gained our trust before she was permitted to have them. I would never have chosen that story or our pets as significant markers of our home, which highlights part of this project's value. We get to see how our children view home and family, and that insight is priceless.

CREATE FAMILY PHOTO BOOKS

Growing up, I always teased my mom because my siblings' baby books are adorable and complete, while mine is entirely blank after the page that includes my name and the next page with a gift list from her baby shower. I famously vowed to do better by all my children, and I was on a roll until I got to kid number three, and then I completely fell off with the fourth one.

Despite my baby book woes, I've consistently managed to create an annual family photo book. In my dreams, they'd be beautiful scrapbooks with themed pages and über-creative baubles and cutouts, but in reality, they're just Shutterfly books created with clicks and typed text. But what matters most is that they're complete, and they're ours.

What motivates me to pour hours into this project is my children's delight in our collection of photo books that sits on the living room shelf next to the fireplace. I'm not exaggerating when I say that they're looked through and talked about every week by at least one of my kids. Through these books, they've gotten to know loved ones who have since passed, and they've seen how we spent our days when they were "knee-high to a grasshopper," as my husband likes to say. Now that they're old enough to help create the books, they always tell me to "save that one!" when we take what they know is a book-worthy photo. In an age when everything is increasingly digital, my kids' ability to hold family stories in their hands is especially meaningful.

DEVELOP A COMMONPLACE HABIT

A cross between a scrapbook and a journal, commonplace books are filled with all types of material, including recipes, poems, quotes, and references. Strongly guided by the unique interests of the creator, no two commonplaces are exactly alike. These books have been around for centuries, but recent years have seen a rise in their use by people of all walks of life who want to give space to their thoughts or preserve ideas that speak to them.

Traditionally, commonplace books have been meant for purely personal use, but years ago, I saw a mom online refer to her family commonplace, and I grasped onto the idea. A shared commonplace allows our family to capture compelling passages or thoughts from the books we read, along with funny vacation stories, explanations of beloved family activities, important lists, and inspiring ideas.

Some people choose to maintain a digital version of a commonplace book for the search capabilities because a frequently used hard copy can become unwieldy over time. While I see the value of easy searching, there's something compelling about a book filled with our handwriting, smudges, and crooked lines of text. It feels more intimate and valuable to me, and it's more tangible for my children.

Choose a format that works best for your family based on what you value most. If you decide to go with a physical book, include your children in the purchase process if they're old enough to understand. Help them see how special it is and the care you're putting into selecting just the right book for your family. Your enthusiasm is infectious.

ENJOY CULTURAL HANDICRAFTS AND LIFE SKILLS

Handicrafts, or handcrafts, are practical or decorative objects made by hand. Often pursued today simply for personal enjoyment, many handicrafts are rooted in cultural activities born of necessity. Learning to enjoy them can be another way for our children to connect with the past and find purpose in using their hands to create beautiful things.

I don't consider myself a talented artist, but I've always enjoyed making things. Even as a child, I was intrigued by the process of taking raw materials and turning them into something desirable, and I enjoy passing that mindset on to my children. Every few months, we choose a new handicraft or life skill to pursue. I didn't grow up doing many of the things my children now consider second nature. Still, I know that I'm only a generation or two removed from intimate knowledge of these types of activities, and I love helping my kids reclaim that part of their past.

Occasionally, we pick up new skills from a local artisan, family friend, or by trial and error, but we typically rely on self-paced instruction at home. You can find ideas and detailed videos for creating or learning anything online, but I often become overwhelmed by the analysis. I don't have time for endless internet searches, so I've come to appreciate having just one good book to get us started. I prefer books that inspire my children with quality photographs and clear instructions using supplies that we can source at a reasonable price. Here are some books we've enjoyed:

- Sewing School books by Amie Petronis Plumley and Andria Lisle. We've collected their books on hand sewing, machine sewing, fashion design, and quilting, and we've gotten years of ideas and instruction from them.

- *Crochet for Beginners: A Complete Step-by-Step Guide with Picture illustrations to Learn Crocheting the Quick & Easy Way* by Nancy Gordon. We have quite a few crochet books, but I like this one best for getting a child quickly up and running. Early success defines my kids' relationship with our handicrafts, so I value books that help them make something nice right away.

- *Herbal Adventures: Backyard Excursions and Kitchen Creations for Kids and Their Families* by Rachel Jepson Wolf. The introduction to this book says it all: "When our great-great-grandmothers were tending to their families' needs, they looked no further than their own backyards for remedies to bring comfort and healing. Here they found the herbs they needed to treat a cough, soothe a sore throat, calm a diaper rash, or quiet a fussy baby. They knew which plants were appropriate for which conditions, and this knowledge was fine-tuned to suit their region and to their families' needs. Like favorite family recipes, this wisdom was passed down generation after generation."[8] Yes, to all of that!

- *The Beginner's Guide to Raising Goats: How to Keep a Happy Herd* by Amber Bradshaw. We don't own goats, so this one may seem a little odd, but my oldest is a farmhand three days a week at a local homestead. While there, she's responsible for feeding seven adult goats and a bunch of kids along with other animals. She loves her job and wants to learn as much as possible about caring for goats, as she's hoping to have her own someday.

- *The Natural Soapmaking Book for Beginners* by Kelly Cable. My youngest daughter is into DIY cleaners, fragrances, and natural dyes, so this book is right up her alley. She teamed up with her sister to get goat's milk from the farm and went to work making wonderful soap that our entire family has enjoyed.

- *Easy Wood Carving for Children: Fun Whittling Projects for Adventurous Kids* by Frank Egholm. Initially purchased for my oldest son, this book quickly became a go-to resource for all of us as we learned to whittle. Explicit instructions, including the type of wood recommended for each project along with photographs and diagrams, make this one a winner.

Over the years, we've pursued these activities along with embroidery, beading, clay modeling, cross-stitch, latch hook, weaving, leather stamping, papermaking, wool felting, origami, paper sloyd, doll making, papier-mâché, press flower craft, gardening, and more. I plan our handicrafts in advance (so I have time to pull the supplies together), and our next ones will be wood burning (pyrography), macramé, and basket weaving.

We build time into our weekly schedule to work on creative pursuits as part of our family rhythm. I typically purchase small starter kits that contain the basics we'll need to dive into a new activity. And though I encourage my children to create for personal enjoyment, we also prioritize gift-giving as a foundational "why" behind our work.

I never know what will capture the attention of one child or another, and every time I try to guess, I'm proven wrong. Who can ever really understand the inclinations of a child's heart? All I ask is that they heartily engage with the family for a few months, and if they never want to pick up the activity again, that's fine by me. However, what typically happens is that the materials are put away after a time, only to be drawn out again weeks or months later by a child whose interest reignites after hearing a story, having a related experience, or out of sheer boredom.

I usually research a little about our activity and share stories of the people who used the skills passed down through the generations.

Sometimes I can connect a handicraft directly to a specific family member because I recall seeing them do it. But more often, I'm relying on the cultural *idea* behind the process. In other words, it could be something I know our people did or just something I think they may have done based on things I've heard and read. It's not a science for me. It's truly a matter of the heart.

For example, we explored the work of quilting guilds by reading about the Gee's Bend quilts made by a group of women and their ancestors in Gee's Bend, Alabama. We then visited a folk art exhibit at our local history museum featuring exquisite quilts that, once ignored, are now recognized as some of our country's artistic treasures. Shortly after, we attended the Atlanta Quilt Festival, where my children could speak with women whose work was displayed.

Through these experiences, quilting has become a family interest. My oldest just completed the top of her first piece, an ambitious queen-size quilt for her grandmother, that took her nine months to finish. As I recently shared a *Boston Globe* article with my kids about the "centuries-long tradition of narrative and social commentary quilts" within the African American community, new ideas sprouted. The journalist explored the idea that "narrative quilts are like historic documents,"[9] and I couldn't agree more. That idea connects my kids and what they're creating to other people who still make the same things, further watering their roots.

MAKE FAMILY PORTRAITS AND WRITE ABOUT THEM

In elementary school, I remember my teacher turning off the lights and shining a lamp toward a piece of paper on the wall. She directed us to stand sideways between the lamp and the paper while she traced the silhouette of our face onto the paper. From there, she instructed us to decorate the picture in a way that represented who we were.

As someone who has never been able to draw well, I valued that project because it was an artistic rendering that relied more on my thoughts than my drawing skill. I remember going home and replicating the project on my parents and anyone else who would give me the opportunity. Silhouettes became my artistic expression du jour, and when my grandmother died twenty-three years later, she still had the profile I'd drawn of her on her bedside table.

Portraits are powerful. They generously allow the artist to represent aspects of a subject that may not otherwise be immediately noticeable, but the bounds of the art form require that the artist remain true to the essence of their subject. Self-portraits are even more telling because they communicate things that only the artist herself will know. Having your child create family portraits in their preferred medium (paint, colored pencil, clay, charcoal, punch needle, collage, fabric, etc.) can be an empowering and beautiful way to collect memories.

When finished, ask your children to write a few notes about themselves or the portrait subject, if it's not a self-portrait, on the back of the piece. Allow younger children to dictate their thoughts while you write. Add the date and their signature, and that artwork becomes a permanent part of your family story.

PRODUCE A FAMILY NEWSLETTER

When I was a kid, I published a quarterly family newsletter to my grandparents, their siblings, and a slew of cousins and aunts and uncles. Every publication included birthday celebrations, birth announcements, anniversary highlights, and words of remembrance about anyone who may have passed away. I wrote articles about exciting things happening to various family members across the country and included photos and little anecdotes shared by people I interviewed.

The newsletter wasn't a school project or something my parents required, but they did encourage me to pursue it and funded the long-distance phone calls (remember those?), supplies, and postage. I was stuck with an archaic version of Print Shop and stacks of hard copies to collate, staple, and send off through snail mail. But our kids have access to lots of great programs that can help create sleek digital newsletters while managing family email subscriptions and more.

For this type of project, I think less is more. I'd suggest starting with brief quarterly or biannual newsletters until you see how committed your kids are to the endeavor. My children love using technology, and this is just the type of thing that I like for them to spend their time on. In addition to creative record-keeping of family history, it's meaningful work, a sweet way of remaining in touch with extended family, and a gift to loved ones.

COMMISSION AN HEIRLOOM

Technically, a keepsake doesn't become an heirloom until it's passed down for generations, but in today's era of Ikea furniture and digital files, having something meaningful to pass along often requires forward-thinking intention. If you have master artisans within your family or social circle, you may already have multiple things in mind that could one day become heirlooms. But for the rest of us, an art commission can be a way of acquiring a one-of-a-kind piece.

To help instill a legacy mindset in my children, I wanted to include them in commissioning art that could become a part of our family's history. I first considered furniture because nothing sets my heart aflutter like beautiful pieces of woodwork, but I ultimately decided on a small piece of art because of future portability. I've seen family members scramble to keep furniture in the family as everyone tried to contend with the cost and logistics of moving and storing it. I don't want to put that burden on anyone, nor do I assume that future generations will remain committed enough to tough it out with a huge armoire.

Ultimately, we settled on family sculptures for our first "heirloom" pieces. Our family worked with clay a lot this year, and the children feel drawn to the work of Edmonia Lewis and Augusta Savage, revered Black sculptors born in the mid- and late-nineteenth century, respectively. Realistic sculptures capture the movement and essence of a person at a particular moment in time, and my family appreciates their lifelike nature.

Of all the ideas presented in this chapter, this one can be the most limiting because it typically requires a significant financial investment. If a piece of professionally commissioned art, which can range from hundreds to thousands of dollars, is not feasible for your family budget, consider these ideas:

- Keep your eyes open for novice or up-and-coming artists whose work speaks to you. I've followed the careers of a few online, primarily through Instagram, where I met our sculptor, and I've seen how the prices of their work increase over time. In the beginning, many artists charge lower rates that your family may be able to swing.

- Ask the artist if there's anything you can do that would allow them to discount the commission. For example, our artist offered a lower rate in exchange for permission to sell copies of the originals. That was an easy yes for me because it was a way for my family to afford the pieces while honoring her work and legitimate need for fair compensation for her time and talents.

If pursuing projects like these doesn't come naturally to your family, I want to assure you that it hasn't always been a part of mine either. However, if you desire, this is the type of thing that can become a way of life in your home. It only requires intention. Don't look at these projects as short-term endeavors to stress about as you frantically check them off your family's to-do list. Instead, take the long view and see them as occupations to pursue leisurely and with purpose, at a natural pace, throughout childhood.

In their book, *The Lifegiving Home*, Sally and Sarah Clarkson echo the foundational ideas of this chapter by supporting the cultivation of a home environment that our children will cherish their entire lives. They write, "All people need a place where their roots can grow deep and they always feel like they belong and have a loving refuge. And all people need a place that gives wings to their dreams, nurturing possibilities of who they might become."[10] Though they cover different aspects of creating a place to belong, they, too, focus on nurturing an environment where celebration permeates every part of a home, all year long, year after year.

We've established that our children must claim their own identities and that home is where they become rooted in who they are. For some, having deeply rooted children is reason enough to pursue an intentional childhood, but many of us are hoping for more. Confucius said, "The strength of a nation derives from the integrity of the home." Families build nations that spill out into the world. We're hoping to grow families that make the world a better place for all. Not a perfect place or a place without suffering, but a place where burdens are shared, and purpose and progress are infectious. It's a tall order, but our homes are up for it. Our children are worth it.

The vitality of a tree resides in its root system, but what attracts us to majestic trees are their full branches reaching up and out and the fruit they bear. While you're watering those deep roots in your child's rich heritage soil, go ahead and sneak under the fence and spend some time in your neighbor's garden. As you talk to your kids about who they are, take the time to infuse your conversations with the beauty of other people. Often.

Our influence on our children's lives and their developing values is a weighty responsibility and a dazzling gift all in one. Much of what we've discussed so far involves conversations, books, and activities to introduce within our homes. In the next chapter, we're going to talk about how ideas presented from the outside, through media, can support or threaten the home atmosphere we're working to cultivate, and we'll explore the power of media literacy.

8

REPRESENTATION MATTERS

Navigating the Ups and Downs of
Media and Pop Culture

Invisibility can be good as a superpower. But psychiatry reveals
people don't like it very much.

—Joyce Rachelle, author of *The Language of Angels*

I WAS DELIGHTED WHEN ONE OF MY CLOSE FRIENDS SENT A
text about a movie that she knew my kids would love. She linked to an
article about Disney casting nineteen-year-old Halle Bailey as the star of
their live-action *Little Mermaid* movie. The picture accompanying the report revealed that Halle is a beautiful young lady who happens to be Black.
The director quoted in the article said, "After an extensive search, it was
abundantly clear that Halle possesses that rare combination of spirit, heart,
youth, innocence, and substance—plus a glorious singing voice—all in-
trinsic qualities necessary to play this iconic role."[1]

When I read this, I was beyond excited, just as my friend Jen knew I
would be. I can't even begin to tell you how meaningful this casting was
for my family and thousands of others. Children of color are starving for
validation in mainstream media, and the opportunity for them to enter a
fantasy world featuring an iconic character who looks like them is epic!

Armed with the exciting news, I gathered my children around me that
evening to share a picture of Halle and discuss the upcoming movie. Rather

than going back to Jen's text and pulling up the original innocuous article, I naively did a quick Google search in front of my girls, and that turned out to be a big mistake. As soon as the first headline registered with me, I quickly turned my phone over, but not before my oldest daughter read it:[2]

#NotMyAriel White Twitter Is Big Mad About Disney Casting a Black Little Mermaid

She then turned to me with a twisted look on her face and asked, "Why are white people mad about Ariel being Black? She looks like me." And in a mere second, all the joy we were just about to share was stamped out by the selfishness and contempt of strangers. Before I tell you how I answered my precious girl, I'll share the questions that immediately came to my mind as I tried to pace my breathing so I wouldn't cry:

- Why would it bother someone who already receives validation every day for someone else to have one small, relatively insignificant moment to feel special?

- Why did "White Twitter" go bonkers over a Black woman being cast as an *imaginary* character?

- Why is white always the default?

- Who would rob all the little brown-skinned girls across the country, even the world, of the chance to finally see themselves reflected in a seafaring princess?

- Why does the nostalgia of the original Ariel's pale skin override the concept of inclusion across children's media?

- Why can't I enjoy this one moment in time with my children while they relish being seen?

- Why does this even have to be a thing?

The pathetic headline blindsided me. Had I even an inkling that the casting was contentious, I would never have searched in front of my girls. My guard was down, and my children's hearts paid the price. When my daughter posed her question, I felt vulnerable because I hadn't had time to craft the proper response. But seeing her cheeks flush, I knew I couldn't put her off until I had a chance to choose the perfect words, so I opened my mouth, and here's what came out:

"Honey, you do look like Halle, and I'm glad you recognize that because you're both gorgeous. I want you to know that I didn't intend for you to see that headline. I'm sorry this happened because my job is to protect you, and it hurts me when you're hurting.

"I also want you to know that Ms. Jen is the one who told me about the movie. She knew how much you'd enjoy it and how important it would be to our family. [Jen is white, and at that moment, it felt important for me to let my daughter immediately experience love from someone who looks like the people fighting against a Black Ariel. I needed to break up the monolith of "white people" so she could see the diversity of character within the group.]

"We're not even going to read the comments about Ariel being Black because we don't want our hearts pulled down by people who don't matter. Some people are selfish and self-centered; they want everything to be about them. They feel angry or threatened when someone who looks different than them is celebrated. They want things to remain the same because it's what feels best to them.

"We hold our heads high and enjoy all that we can despite their negativity, but I know it hurts. I can't fix this for you, but I can remind you not to base your self-image on others' opinions. Please don't let ignorant or mean-spirited people define you. Your life is full of amazing people of all backgrounds who know your value and adore every bit of you. Lean into that, smile your bright smile, and keep your head up. Shake the haters off. Stand tall and move forward, knowing who you are. And whenever you have the chance to represent us and others amazingly, be brave and do the right thing. No matter what."

I wish I could say this was the only conversation I've had with my children about media and how people of color are represented, but it's not. This is a recurring theme in my home, and it will continue to be relevant for the foreseeable future. We can't neglect to acknowledge the lack of color on our children's screens. As tough as these conversations may be, we don't have the luxury of avoiding them because our kids are receiving inputs on diversity, stereotypes, positive representations, and misrepresentations at an ever-increasing rate.

MEDIA USAGE AND REPRESENTATION

Although estimates of media usage vary, the American Psychological Association states that children between two and eight spend an average of two hours per day on screens. Tweens between eight and twelve spend an average of four to six hours per day on screens.[3] With this much time devoted to online and digital media, the lack of diversity within the advertising, film, television, digital, and gaming industries should be a point of concern for all parents. Conversely, we can use the power of positive media imagery to our advantage.

Representation matters.

Books are invaluable, but a picture is worth a thousand words. The visual storytelling found across media platforms communicates volumes about our children's self-worth and how others view them. In her book, *Reel to Real,* late author bell hooks says that although we know that movies are not real life, "no matter how sophisticated our strategies of critique and intervention, [we] are usually seduced, at least for a time, by the images we see on the screen. They have power over us and we have no power over them."[4] If this is the case for adults, imagine how much more influence film and television have on our kids.

Positive, diverse screen experiences are critical for children of color and others whose identities are rarely explored. Healthy media encourages underrepresented children to see realistic expressions of themselves and their families rather than distorted images of the group or communities they identify with. Positive representation builds self-awareness and confidence during childhood and adolescence as kids work out who they are and will be.

When children see people who look like them playing roles that authentically characterize crucial aspects of their lived experiences, it signals that society sees them and that they matter. Watching people of color, women, or people with disabilities on-screen doing things that spark interest inspires children to believe that they can do the same. Yes, they can and do gain inspiration from seeing others do those same things, but the visual of someone who looks like them offers a powerful and nuanced sense of belonging.

For me, that kind of inspiration came from *The Cosby Show* and its spin-off, *A Different World*. Their creator's incomprehensible acts have since marred the reputation of both, but these shows breathed life into the homes of kids growing up in the eighties. For Black kids, *The Cosby Show* validated the idea that we can have intact families with funny and loving, well-educated parents and adoring grandparents who show affection and value their children for who they are. And *A Different World* gave a glimpse into college life at an HBCU, something I vowed then to experience, and I did. The show featured wise older men and women within the Black community, brilliant and silly girls, clever and immature boys, jocks, creatives, academics, and free spirits. Never had I seen people like me explored on television with that level of multifaceted complexity and variety.

Diverse representation matters for kids from underrepresented groups, but it matters just as much for white, middle-class, able-bodied, straight, neurotypical kids in the suburbs, who need to see authentic representations of other people and how they experience life. *The Cosby Show* and *A Different World* let the white kids I grew up around know that my family was not an anomaly. Those kids were able to peek inside the home, albeit fictional, of a Black family that was like theirs but with its own flavor. They got a chance to see one version of what life can be for families who are American and also Black.

Due to various circumstances, most notably social segregation, many children have to build their perceptions of others on what they see on-screen. When our kids watch shows and movies featuring positive images of people they don't spend time with in real life, it builds understanding. It helps pave the way for smoother interactions as their exposure to others (hopefully) increases with time.

There are myriad benefits of positive screen time, but there are adverse psychological outcomes associated with homogenous and misrepresentative images for children of color and their white counterparts. With kids spending more time than ever in front of screens, the stakes are high, and we can undo much of our intentional work curating an inclusive home culture if we're not careful. As parents, we're the gatekeepers to our children's digital world, and we can't take that responsibility lightly.

It may feel daunting at first, but I'm proof that parents can quickly become more discerning about what their children are watching by educating themselves and paying attention. With practice, the differences between positive, mediocre, and negative representation are easier to sort out, and we can learn to recognize and resist invisibility, distortion, and tokenism in our children's media.

INVISIBILITY, DISTORTION, AND TOKENISM

Screen time is not evil. TV shows and movies can be enjoyable tools that support culturally conscious family ways when used appropriately. But when misused, they can hinder our children's ability to be healthy members of varied and colorful communities. Invisibility in media and elsewhere breeds disconnectedness.

In Ralph Ellison's landmark novel, *Invisible Man,* the narrator explains, "I am invisible, understand, simply because people refuse to see me. . . . [I]t is as though I have been surrounded by mirrors of hard, distorting glass. When they approach me they see only my surroundings, themselves, or figments of their imagination—indeed, everything and anything except me."[5] This experience of feeling unseen is traumatic because it shows children that they don't belong in the stories they watch or forces them to imagine themselves in those stories, all the time. A home where children consume a steady stream of inputs that communicate their irrelevance is not a nurturing space for becoming.

With approximately 60 percent of the U.S. population being white, we can reasonably expect that at least four in every ten characters on television, in movies, video games, or advertisements would be non-white. But despite the recent increase in culturally diverse programming, the children's entertainment and edutainment industries still fall far short of even this baseline expectation. In most cases, children learn that white is "normal" and always in stock, while everyone else is just a specialty item to be thrown in as able. A defective specialty item, at that, since so much of the representation offered resides somewhere between average and awful.

While invisibility is a telltale sign of unhealthy media, researchers have also shown that distortion has a lasting effect on our children. Distortion occurs when media misrepresents people groups or exaggerates common traits to make a character fit a particular trope or stereotype. Consistently presenting one-dimensional and often derogatory images of underrepresented groups inflicts cultural harm by perpetuating stereotypes and biases around ethnicity, gender, ability, age, sexual orientation, and other identities. According to a Stanford University article on the portrayal of people of color in film, "When images and ideas presented at a young age take hold, and are reinforced over years of viewing, these images become reality and once these stereotypes and misconceptions become ingrained in the psyche of American children, they become self-perpetuating."[6]

There are innumerable ethnic, racial, and cultural misrepresentations that abound across media platforms, some more subtle than others, but here are examples of common stereotypes:

- Heavily accented South Asians used for comic relief or playing taxi drivers or convenience store workers

- Radicalized Arabs plotting terrorist acts against innocent white people

- Docile Muslim women forced into submission by husbands and other male relatives

- Uneducated and accented Latinos dealing with urban poverty and street life or threats of deportation

- Brilliant or emotionally distant East Asians who play the violin and have overbearing mothers

- Indigenous people living in tepees, carrying bows and arrows, and walking around in animal skins

- Sad and suffering disabled people to pity and save

- Neck-rolling, angry, loudly opinionated, or hyper-sexualized Black women

- Incarcerated, poor, thug, pimp, gangbanging, or drug-dealing Black men

- Black athletes who value sports over education and relationships

In addition to these glaring ethnic, religious, and cultural stereotypes, other concerning themes proliferate across children's media. For example, we often find:

- The promotion and popularity of lighter-skinned people of color and racially ambiguous characters over people with darker skin.

- Diverse characters dropped into white-centered stories.

- People of color (or accented characters) consistently shown as villains or dying off early in the adventure.

- Girls achieving success and favor through magic or supernatural means while boys rely on brainpower, wits, brawn, or science.

- Female characters commonly dressed in provocative clothing.

- A lack of economic, social, intellectual, and geographic diversity.

As decision-makers begin to see that their brands are at risk of being left behind, many are scrambling to throw in a token non-white kid to quell PR nightmares. These attempts are easy to spot because the cast ends up looking like a United Colors of Benetton ad, but the BIPOC kids are never central to the storyline, and the more complex aspects of their identities are missing from the script. This tokenism, the practice of making only a perfunctory or symbolic effort to give screen time and voice to those who are often unseen and unheard, gives the appearance of equity without needing to change much. It's a veiled attempt to placate, but it falls flat for parents who know what to look for.

College student Natachi Onwuamaegbu shared this observation in an opinion piece for the *Stanford Daily* student newspaper: "Representation isn't just a nice way to appease complaining minorities. The media is a reflection of who America is and isn't. America isn't just white, and it never has been. When America looks into a mirror, the reflection is white, Christian, financially well-off. . . . The complexity awarded to white Americans in the media is not seen in minority characters. . . . The media is a way to bring stories to life. The complexities of different races are not realized by most Americans because they are not visible to most Americans."[7]

In the article, Natachi, who is Black, shares that she enjoyed creative writing while she was growing up, but all her characters were white because she was scared to write about things she didn't know. Sit with that for a minute. It gives a glimpse into how deep-seated and complex the issues of invisibility and misrepresentation can be for a child.

Occasional exposure to negative images and messages is inevitable and can be overcome, but the long-term effects of invisibility, distorted media, and tokenism are the antithesis of belonging. They threaten to taint our children's beliefs and hurt our efforts to build inclusive homes. And when that happens, all our children lose. Children of color lose. White kids lose. Disabled and able-bodied kids lose. Boys and girls lose. Muslim, Christian, and Jewish kids lose. Kids with different or no faith backgrounds lose. My kids lose, and so do yours. There are no winners. Children are drawn to media, and they'll make do with whatever we present, but knowing how imbalanced the landscape is, how can we navigate our children's media consumption without exhausting ourselves or creating unrealistic hurdles? There isn't a perfect answer because we're trying to build healthy narratives within a broken framework. However, we don't have to idly sit by, lamenting the lack of inclusive programming. We can actively make progress.

HELP ACCELERATE INDUSTRY CHANGES

The entertainment industry is and always has been overwhelmingly white and male. The repeated cycle of excluding diverse voices and ignoring or even promoting misrepresentations within film and television highlights the importance of having diverse animators, writers, actors, directors, producers, and executives involved both on-screen and behind the scenes. A reckoning is occurring within the industry, but progress will continue to lag until women, people of color, people with disabilities, and all other underrepresented groups are included as decision-makers at every touchpoint. We could sit back and wait for what inevitably will be, but our children are growing up now, and their needs are urgent. Here are a few things we can do today to help make progress:

Conduct a home media audit. Create a list of the TV shows, movies, and video channels your children regularly watch and the websites they inter-act with. If you have no idea, now is an excellent time to become inti-mately familiar with what they're consuming. Research what you find and look for reviews and commentary from various sources.

Then, most important, sit down and watch these shows for yourself. What messages are overtly shared? Are there subtle undertones that could give your children the wrong idea about other people? About themselves? Talk to your kids about what you watch. What do they think about the people in the show? Do your kids feel like anyone is missing? Do they think that's strange or normal? Do they believe what the characters say about [fill in the blank]? Research a few options together that you think would be good additions to their usual rotation or replacements for any you choose to remove.

Keep in mind that nothing is too innocent for the audit. My oldest fol-lows the world of customized ball-jointed dolls (BJDs). Etsy is her favorite place to search for and learn about these dolls as she tracks new releases by independent creators. I encouraged her to spend time on that site, and I didn't monitor it because I felt like looking at dolls on a craft site was a zero-risk activity. But ignorance lurks everywhere.

Little did I know that some of the BJD doll creators list white dolls as "normal" in the skin color drop-down box along with options like "tan" and "caramel," if they even offer those alternatives. Why on earth would anyone list skin tones in that way: *normal*, tan, and caramel? It bothered my daughter enough to show me as she wondered why her skin tone wasn't considered normal. I learned then that 100 percent prevention is impossi-ble, so 100 percent preparation better be our goal.

Recognize the power of your family's dollar. How your family engages with media can help or hurt, so be thoughtful about what your family consumes. Direct your streams, downloads, tickets, and views (i.e., money) toward what you want to see more of in your home. Don't fund things that do not align with your family values.

Support organizations that are pushing for industry change. Various leaders have taken up the charge and are applying pressure to media compa-nies from all sides. They're advocating for inclusion of underrepresented groups in all aspects of content creation, identifying racism and racial or cultural stereotypes in Motion Picture Association (MPA) ratings, and more. Donate your time, money, signatures, and voice to these kinds of efforts.

Watch and promote media featuring counter-stereotypes. Look for shows, movies, and images where the cultures and talents of different people or groups are emphasized and shown in a positive or atypical fashion.

Promote media literacy. Understanding the messages within and behind different types of media is an essential skill for our children to have. We can help by becoming media literate ourselves, teaching our kids, and providing practice opportunities. Key questions to ask when teaching kids media literacy include:

- Who created and financed the project?

- Do you think it was created in response to a current event, societal conversation, pop culture trend, or for some other reason?

- Is the creator hoping to change your opinion or behavior in some way? Why do you feel this way?

- Who is the target audience and why do you think that's the case?

- Is the prevailing message based on opinion or fact? How can you tell?

- Are balanced messages being communicated? Is there evidence of bias in the material?

- How did watching this make you feel? How do you think it may make others feel?[8]

Teaching our children to think critically about what they see and hear empowers them to enjoy media without being used by it.

ESTABLISH RULES OF ENGAGEMENT

In the past, when I've talked about the need for representation and the importance of parental vigilance as we help our children navigate screen time, I've heard things like "This sounds exhausting. Can't my kids ever just enjoy their entertainment without all of the analysis?" My short answer is "Yes, but not at someone else's expense, even if the someone is your own child."

I believe that there's a place for fun and lighthearted media consumption, but find the right thing for your child to veg out on. Suppose our kids begin to associate fun, relaxing recreation with white-centered media just because we're tired and don't feel like monitoring their screen time. In that case, we're only perpetuating the very thing that we're trying to overcome.

Rather than question whether we must always put in the hard work to vet the media our children absorb, we should question why all of this is so hard in the first place, because it shouldn't be. Finding age-appropriate shows with positive representation for kids who are beyond *Sesame Street* and *Molly of Denali* but not ready for *Black Panther* or *Crazy Rich Asians* (two wonderful PG-13 movies that everyone holds up as examples of diverse box office success as though the industry's problem has been solved) feels like an Olympic event at times.

The degree to which parents are willing to responsibly oversee their children's engagement with media varies. Screen time guidelines reflect the parents' priorities, values, and preferences, and there isn't a one-size-fits-all plan. Each family must balance restricting access to unhealthy media with educating and talking through the tough stuff.

Scott and I have experimented over time, and our rules of engagement evolve as our children mature, but our overall strategies have remained consistent. We curate the media content our children are permitted to consume, just as we do our bookshelves. We primarily rely on detailed quality reviews, recommendations from trusted friends, and previewing options ourselves to develop a list of approved shows and movies. Our children can request to have things added to our family list any time, and we take their requests seriously, saying yes as often as we responsibly can.

As we approve shows for our family list, we look for healthy representations of people of color and other underrepresented groups, along with authentic, multiethnic storylines. This isn't too much to ask for, but most children's shows—especially ones for older kids and tweens—don't make the cut. We're not overly strict on other aspects of content, but we do seek out movies that match our children's maturity levels and offer some form of positive or redemptive storytelling.

To be honest, there aren't many shows and movies that match our criteria, so our six- and eight-year-olds don't get to watch as much as we wish they could. Our older ones have more opportunities to view things that fall short of our expectations because we're training them to be discerning. And when something extraordinary comes around, our entire family rallies behind it. One example is *Jingle Jangle: A Christmas Journey* (2020). This imaginative musical is a beautiful illustration of whimsy and fantasy with a diverse cast representing complex characters, a combination rarely ever seen, and we all adore it.

Our television is kept in the basement and only used for streaming or playing DVDs. This adds a level of intentionality to our television time because no one just flips on the TV and starts watching. We also have tablets that are stored together on the main floor of the house. They're password-protected and set up with safe-listed websites. We find it easier to opt in on what we want the children to view rather than attempt to keep other things out.

Friday night is "TV night" in our home, and it's an exciting time! We order pizza, make popcorn, and either grab space on the sectional for a family movie or give the children time on the tablets for curated shows they like to watch. This is the only time of the week that our kids consume TV episodes or movies, and it works well because they know and trust the plan.

We originally made this choice many years ago because I got so tired of my oldest constantly asking to watch something. We've stuck with it because we see how our kids fill their free time with outdoor play, reading, baking, biking, creating, writing, fort building, and exploring, and we don't want them to lose the margin they have for those activities. The added benefit of limited and scheduled media consumption is not needing to constantly monitor what they're watching because we only need to approve enough content for one experience a week.

But not all screen time is considered equal in our home. Our kids watch various documentaries and period pieces and enjoy time on educational apps and websites like Skybrary, DreamBox Learning, Duolingo, Generation Genius, Khan Academy, and BrainPOP, along with YouTube channels like Crash Course Kids and TED-Ed. While our children's time with media consumption is limited, the older kids are given as much time as they need for media creation and self-directed digital learning.

They enjoy using YouTube instructional videos and online tutorials found on Craftsy and offered through Teachable to learn new skills or initiate projects. In addition to making digital art and videos, they spend time editing photography, writing blogs, animating, and much more. Media creation puts our children at the center of the programming and completely removes our need to check for balanced messaging.

Our kids also follow inspiring and diverse content creators (historians, creatives, storytellers, authors, chefs, musicians, artists, makers) on YouTube and elsewhere on the web who share ideas and offer innovative tools in an engaging way. It's easy for children to follow multiethnic and varied creators on user-generated digital platforms because the format allows creators to bypass the entertainment industry's red tape. If you're interested in engaging your children with this type of content, I recommend that you invest in a YouTube Premium family plan that allows ad-free viewing. Then work with your kids to identify their interests and help them develop a list of preapproved channels they can watch freely.

Without accurate representation, we tragically erase the extraordinary multilayered diversity found within our communities. We need to provide our children plenty of healthy exposure to positive media by sharing things we find that are done well and support our family culture. Rather than focusing on what our kids are not allowed to watch, we like to talk about what we're adding to our family list. And instead of demeaning all forms of electronic entertainment, we support the regular use of digital educational resources and strongly encourage media creation over media consumption. Even with this intention, our kids are still occasionally exposed to things we wouldn't have chosen for them. Still, we learn and maintain a constant dialogue about the intersection of beauty, neutrality, and negativity found within the entire media and pop culture landscape.

Your family's rules of engagement may be similar or look incredibly different than ours. That's a good thing! Rigidity and conformity don't serve our children well. Take what resonates with you and add in what you know to be best for your family. The requirements are few, but be sure that you land on something that encourages inclusivity while actively rejecting the notion that invisibility, misrepresentation, stereotyping, and tokenism are normal or acceptable.

9

....

FROM TRAGEDY TO TRIUMPH

Bringing Hard History into the Home

History is not the past. It is the present. We carry our history with us.
We are our history.

—James Baldwin, "Black English: A Dishonest Argument"

SEVERAL YEARS AGO, WE HAD THE OPPORTUNITY TO VISIT TWO
historic homes in our area. Built in the 1840s and only twenty-five miles
apart, they're the ancestral homes of local founding families. Both houses
sit on former plantations that flourished on a foundation of chattel slavery.
Each family had its own story, but with the details largely forgotten after
all these years, I assumed that the experience of touring the homes would
be similar. I couldn't have been more wrong.

In the first home, most of the guide's discussion focused on the plantation owners. She described details of the enslavers' family history and daily
lives as we toured the property: the main home, kitchen house, corn crib,
sweet potato house, storage barn, and the original smokehouse. The guide
mentioned the Black people who'd spent their entire lives helping make
the plantation all that it was exactly three times during our visit.

The first was when the tour guide told the children that "unpaid workers" lived on the land with the family, and I made a mental note to remind
my kids that unpaid workers should be used to describe volunteers, not

enslaved people. As we moved to another part of the home, she talked about how much nicer this family was to their "workers" than other slave-holding families of the time. She even recounted a story where one of the enslaved boys on the property reportedly shot at Union soldiers from the roof to protect the white family from harm. I made another mental note to make sure my children know, without a shadow of a doubt, that nobody enjoys having their lives claimed ("owned") by another, under any cir-cumstances. And finally, we learned that the white people "cared so much about their workers that they buried them in the family cemetery with the other family members." But she left off the part about the white family members being buried in marked graves while the enslaved men and women were dumped in an unmarked space, their identities forever lost to time.

By the time that tour ended, I was distressed by my children's exposure to shallow and biased teaching. The facility's desire to present a pretty picture overrode the need to integrate hard history into the stories of what this white family left behind. They choked out and covered over Black voices, so to this day, I can't explain why I was willing to endure another such tour at the same type of facility. But sometime later, we traveled across town to visit a second historic home, and the experience was vastly different. At this home, known locally as the Smith Plantation, we heard countless stories of people who lived and lost on the land, both Black and white, and it felt oh so good.

The tour guide chronicled various aspects of the Smith family, includ-ing where and how the thirty enslaved people who came to the property with them lived and how they contributed to the family's success. He in-termingled their stories with that of the white family. The first story found on the historic home's website describes the nineteenth-century enslaved labor force from the perspective of Clarinda Richardson, a woman the family enslaved before the Civil War.

We learned about the lives of the white children who grew up in the home and how they spent their time on musical and artistic pursuits with which my children can relate. We heard of the sons who went to war as Confederate soldiers and how one returned home alive, only to succumb to disease less than a month later. And a good chunk of the tour paid hom-age to a Black woman named Mamie Cotton, who worked for the Smith family for fifty-four years during the 1900s. After the last of the Smiths died, the city eventually purchased the home with the stipulation that Ms. Cotton would be able to live out the rest of her life there. The guide showed us pictures of Mamie and her family, her favorite place to sit in the home, and a glimpse of her bedroom containing some of her personal artifacts that remained behind after her death.

None of us were ready for this tour to end. The docent took the time to weave in the voices of multiple generations of colorful people across a series of brutal and beautiful experiences. He brought humanity to the white people's story by presenting touching parts of their lives, but did not shy away from their involvement and reliance on enslavement. And at the same time, he celebrated the resilience and ingenuity of multiple Black people who touched the home, some because they found much-needed employment within and others because they had no choice.

Though the houses share a nearly identical history and culture, the atmosphere cultivated within made us want to run away from the first and lean into the second. The sanitized, one-dimensional, colorblind home seemed synthetic and contrived, despite its comfortable narrative. And it wasn't lost on me that the property that embraced brutal history intertwined with tragic and heartwarming stories from a cast of colorful people was a safer and more comfortable space. The empathetic and diverse atmosphere of the second home was cloaked in authenticity, making it feel like a place to belong.

Someone consciously chose to cultivate the colorful atmosphere of the Smith home. They selected whose images to show and how to present each group and individual. They told their stories with equal doses of honesty and dignity. They made choices about what people would learn and experience while there, and they thoughtfully wove that learning into every aspect of the home in a natural way. None of this just happened. It was the result of intentional forethought and effort, and all of the decision-making mattered.

The disparity between the two properties drew my attention to the power of honesty, inclusivity, and storytelling while building a home culture. I want an authentic home for my children. A place where we don't shy away from real history or try to make the past seem simpler, sweeter, or whiter than it was. Somewhere intimate where we can safely sit with truthful stories that may lead to tears, laughter, and back again within moments. A home that honors and makes space for colorful overlooked voices and a more realistic picture of humanity. I want to balance the bitter with the sweet in the name of hope, and I want to do it around the fireplace. And at the kitchen table and the back porch. When we wake up and when we go to bed. Wherever or whenever the mood hits us.

This vision requires me to release the idea of history as a mere academic subject. It's more expansive than that, and the reframe is crucial. History is a family treasure to be woven into the fabric of our days.

CONFRONTING HARD HISTORY

Many parents take a passive role in their children's history education. They expect the school to facilitate academic learning, and teachers armed with curriculum are tasked with making kids conversant in people, places, and things. But hard history isn't necessarily being tackled at school, and home is the place to address this oversight.

Intentional parents are more motivated now than ever to have meaningful conversations with their children about our country's complicated past and the forces that shaped the society we live in today. But most of us never learned about the tough topics at home or in school, so it isn't always easy to approach complex history in our homes with honesty and compassion in an age-appropriate way.

Recent events in our society have polarized everything, including education. We have parents who believe that patriotism and white-centered history are synonymous, with some going so far as to suggest that the inclusion of Black and Brown voices in history lessons will lead to the complete unraveling of their beloved Americana. These parents don't want to deal with real history, and they're not going to. They're angry and resentful about the reckoning occurring across our nation and much of the world. They've decided that they're going to resist by raising their kids in the good ol' days of our great-grandparents before everybody was "woke and complaining about racism."

We also have parents in our communities who believe that every book and lesson our children are exposed to is overtly whitewashed and utterly devoid of value in the face of injustice and systemic racism. They're ready to publicly call out anyone who doesn't instantly lay down everything they hold dear for the cause. And they've deemed it okay to police and shame individuals who aren't in complete agreement with a symbolic book burning as they rid the Earth of anything that isn't wholly and immediately representative of our diverse communities. And while I understand the frustration behind this all-or-nothing approach, primarily because I've felt it myself, I don't believe that it's a wise position or prudent path.

These two extremes, those who resent all mentions of the stains in our nation's past and those who insist it be shared exactly their way or the highway, impact our homes. Communities of engaged parents are simply microcosms of society and have been affected by the polarization. I've seen lines drawn in the sand and positions staked within our own ranks, just as much as I've seen these things outside the realm of purposeful parenting. But there is another space. Not between, but entirely outside of the two opposing sides. A space that prioritizes authentic community over divisive ideology, even if we don't agree on everything.

Previous generations could get away with siloed thinking and perspectives, but that way of living is outdated, and if we don't prepare our children to thrive in diverse spaces, they will be left behind. If our kids are going to have a shot at authentic cross-cultural relationships and camaraderie, they need to be willing to get to know people who think and believe differently. Not just know them in passing but know their stories and the stories of their people. The stories that have torn us apart and the stories that bind us together.

We must ready our children to be active participants in a diverse democracy. That means that our kids need to grow together in real life, in their books, and across their lessons, including and especially their history lessons. Even when those lessons are hard.

HISTORY AS AN EPIC STORY

I'm not an academic, researcher, or historian. History was the least inspiring class I took in school and the only Advanced Placement exam for which I received no credit. Dates, battles, generals, and another round of dates—all to be memorized and regurgitated on command. I was thankful to leave all of that behind as I progressed into adulthood.

"No more history for me" was my mantra, and having convinced myself that my disdain and indifference were justified, I indeed avoided all forays into historical events and figures that were featured in film, literature, or landmarks. I remained silent when I found myself in conversations laced with historical blather, smiling on the outside but tuned out on the inside. And in my ignorance, I relegated history museums to a pile of places reserved for the elderly and unwitting schoolchildren arriving in packed yellow buses.

But all of this changed when I began to homeschool. As I read aloud from the books on our schedule, something slowly shifted. I didn't immediately recognize the sensation, but eventually, I had to label it for what it was: enjoyment. I was enjoying the history lessons. In spite of myself, I was intrigued with learning how the world we know today came to be and was especially delighted by the stories of people who lived, loved, and lost in another time.

I began to see history as an ongoing inquiry of an epic story. And when I progressed from history as a subject to be tolerated to history as an opportunity to provide windows through which my children could know mankind, my energy and efforts grew. I decided to approach history simply as an opportunity to know people.

I began asking not which events were missing from our timeline but whose voices longed to be heard. I saw that diverse perspectives were missing, but I felt stuck between knowing I wanted more and feeling inadequate to provide it. It became clear that I'd prioritized my efforts to teach my children about all the wildflowers and beautiful birds at the expense of all the wild spirits and beautiful people. And from that point, change came easily.

If we're truly to approach history as an opportunity to know people, we need stories. The power of story draws us into the sights, sounds, motivations, and thoughts of the age, and isn't that what history is all about? History contains hard stories. They are hard to read and hard to hear. And yet, the stories are still worth being told.

Approaching conversations about today's complicated societal issues through the lens of history can help our children understand the causes and inherent difficulties or complexities of today's racial conflicts. It also provides some safe distance from which our kids can explore human behavior in the past while making connections to our world today. Not only can history give context to what our children are seeing and experiencing, but it can also help them make choices about how they engage with others going forward.

We have a unique opportunity to guide our children through this learning in ways that extend beyond the bounds of formal academics. Regardless of the general foundation they receive through traditional schooling or the scope and sequence of popular homeschool curricula, we can help our children dig in. We get to be by their side as they grapple with and make sense of their world. In fact, we can join them on an incredible exploration of our collective epic story right smack-dab in the middle of the living room.

INCLUSIVITY IS NOT A UNIT STUDY

I'm talking about inclusivity as part of a lifestyle. If you decide to integrate honest history into your home and family culture, do so with the understanding that inclusive storytelling and diverse voices aren't something to be incorporated for a season or a year. This way of living requires an ongoing commitment to expanding your child's world *so that* he will find solidarity easy to come by.

There's certainly ample room for studies on the history of specific people groups and cultures. I use them regularly. But the overarching message can't separate people of color by making white the default and everything else a special study. And this message is not just for white parents because, when it comes to education, white is inadvertently the default in many BIPOC homes as well. Ask me how I know. Historically, it has been difficult to find quality resources highlighting the experiences and perspectives of people of color, so many families, including my own, resorted to using what was readily accessible despite its lack of diversity. Availability is steadily improving, but even so, now that I'm aware of how important representation is for my children, I'm often compelled to create my own materials.

Approach your integration of colorful voices and history from a place of immersion and connection rather than analysis and pure academic study. We don't want our children to be controlled by their feelings, but we also don't want to sanitize and rationalize so much of what they're learning that they begin to approach others with a perfunctory expression of sterile togetherness. Relationships rely on informed understanding, but they're also issues of the heart.

Compartmentalizing history is an ever-present temptation. It's easy to remain shallow and rely solely on school lessons and book learning, but playing it safe doesn't bring people together. It doesn't help us raise children with a nuanced understanding of where we are and how we got here. Inclusive history will come alive for our kids when we intentionally allow it to flow into the natural rhythms of our home life.

MAKING HISTORY COME ALIVE

For much of our bedtime reading, I've made a point of using fictional stories in real-life historical settings to impart truth and make history come alive for my children. Fiction can clear away the clutter to reveal how resilient people have balanced great joys with life's seemingly unbearable trials. Well-researched historical fiction gets at the heart of history. It helps build out how different societies functioned by telling us:

- What they likely said and how they may have said it.

- Where they went and with whom.

- How they got there and what was likely to happen along the way.

- The value of money and how it was won and lost.

- How the news media, neighbors, and politics influenced life.

- Which societal values governed the behaviors and misbehaviors of its people.

Historical fiction explores the complexity of the blurred line between right and wrong in a way that most nonfiction books cannot or will not.

The genre is an excellent avenue for delving into tough topics because it brings humanity to triumph and authentically redeems tragedy. It's also a fun way to hear different voices, including those belonging to people who look like my children. While nonfiction satisfies my children's minds, it's fiction that makes their hearts sing.

Sprinkling in a healthy dose of historical fiction certainly sparks interest in my children, but it's not the only way we explore history. Each year, my entire family chooses a historical time period to dive into. That means that we read books about what was happening during that time, watch movies, learn about the people and how they lived, integrate activities and outings, and travel to important historical sites. We listen to music, enjoy art, and read poetry from diverse creators of that era, and generally immerse ourselves in what it was like for all types of people in our country and around the world during those years. This family-style learning brings incredible richness to our conversations and shared experiences as we casually explore the grand story of the world and its people together.

To ground us in the time period, I look for engrossing, nonfiction books explaining the significant events that shaped the years we're studying. These are not dull textbooks. They're interesting topical history books written by people with a great interest in the stories they're sharing. They're the kind of books my children want me to keep reading even when I'm done for the day. The type *you* would choose to read even if you didn't have to because they draw you in.

Since most traditional history books don't include much, if anything, about the experiences and contributions of people of color, I can't rely on a single text. I always pull together a collection of books, some chapter books and some picture books (even for my older kids), that help present a more balanced and honest look at history.

I also love a good biography. Biographies help us explore specific people's concrete comings and goings as we glance inside the thoughts of well-known leaders and everyday people. This is an accessible way to add in incredible amounts of diversity. You can dial up or down any voices based on what your children need to hear more of. I like using both picture book and chapter book biographies because picture books offer beautifully illustrated, compelling stories, and their short format allows us to hear about a broad range of people and the worlds they lived in. Chapter books are lovely because we can "live" with someone for a long time. We can get into the details of their lives and the richness of the time during which they lived. Whichever route you choose, try to select biographies of people that will enthrall your children. And don't pepper them with questions or make them write a book report. Think of this as historical enrichment. Let them ponder it and talk about it. Make it fun!

Outings and rabbit trails are also an integral part of our lifestyle. Performances, cultural festivals, special events, demonstrations, reenactments, visits to landmarks and museums, and historical films are part of the regular rotation. I treat these opportunities as part of the main course, not just nice-to-have extras, because these are the things that pique my children's interest and breathe life into our inclusive historical explorations throughout the year. We've made many lasting memories while chasing these little adventures, and all my kids look forward to them.

To identify great opportunities, I have set up a specific email address that I use to sign up for the newsletters and mailing lists of our local historical societies, museums, cultural arts centers, community centers, ethnic organizations, special interest groups, libraries, historic sites, national parks, state parks, and travel websites. Periodically, I go through the relevant emails and note dates for activities and excursions I know my family will enjoy. I'm open to all sorts of engaging opportunities, but I pay special attention to things that give my children the opportunity to learn from people of color because those are harder to come by.

If your family enjoys traveling, consider taking a road trip to discover a different facet of history. Over the years, we've enjoyed exploring the complexities of American history while visiting the former homes and plantations of past presidents and other prominent families throughout history. Some of my friends have questioned the wisdom of our road trips to places like George Washington's Mount Vernon and Thomas Jefferson's Monticello. I think there's a fear that by visiting these estates where some of our country's leaders held humans captive against their will, I'll be perpetuating the message of heroism without facing the realities of how these men and their families lived. But that can't be further from the truth.

I don't shy away from human complexities with my children, and there's no better place to explore the nature of man than on the porch of a slave cabin resting on the property of some of our country's most esteemed leaders. My children are learning to grapple with the idea that history doesn't fit into neat boxes because people are messy. And the organizations running these properties have, quite frankly, done a better job than I ever could of giving an honest portrayal of flawed humans.

I especially recommend signing up ahead of time for specialty tours that focus on the lives of the enslaved and other specific aspects of the properties. I appreciate the rich conversations these tours ignite in my family and how they bring our books to life in an incredible way. And be sure to make time for the incredible gift shops at these historic sites. They always contain exquisitely curated diverse book collections filled with titles I've never seen elsewhere.

To prepare children for visits to one of these properties, you can introduce them to some of the complexities through books like:

- *My Name Is James Madison Hemings* by Jonah Winter (Picture book)

- *Never Caught, the Story of Ona Judge: George and Martha Washington's Courageous Slave Who Dared to Run Away* (Young Readers Edition) by Erica Armstrong Dunbar and Kathleen Van Cleve (Middle grade)

- *In the Shadow of Liberty: The Hidden History of Slavery, Four Presidents, and Five Black Lives* by Kenneth C. Davis (Young adult)

Be sure to include visits to places that specialize in telling the stories of people of color in their own words. Smaller history museums like the African American Panoramic Experience (APEX) Museum in Atlanta, Georgia; the Pocahontas Island Black History Museum in Petersburg, Virginia; the DuSable Museum of African American History in Chicago; and similar facilities are often staffed by passionate historians who work hard to preserve the stories of their people. And more prominent museums like the Smithsonian's National Museum of African American History and Culture in Washington, D.C., provide unique opportunities to see a wider breadth of Black experiences across centuries.

Whenever you travel, be sure to check the National Register of Historic Places to find out about intriguing sites that may be nearby. Not far from this Smithsonian museum is the Charlotte Forten Grimké

House. Born free to activist parents in 1837, Charlotte Forten was part of Philadelphia's elite Black community. Forten was a prominent abolitionist and women's rights advocate who battled racial and gender inequality.

Books that pair well with visiting places such as these include:

- *Dream Builder: The Story of Architect Philip Freelon* by Kelly Starling Lyons (Picture book)

- *Ruth and the Green Book* by Calvin Alexander Ramsey (Picture book)

- *Freedom on the Menu: The Greensboro Sit-ins* by Carole Boston Weatherford (Picture book)

- *Rhythm Ride: A Road Trip Through the Motown Sound* by Andrea Davis Pinkney (Middle grade)

- *Diary of Charlotte Forten: A Free Black Girl Before the Civil War* by Charlotte Forten (Elementary)

- *Carved in Ebony: Lessons from the Black Women Who Shape Us* by Jasmine L. Holmes (Middle grade, young adult)

Other landmarks like the Fort Mose Historic State Park in St. Augustine, Florida, provide insight into forms of resistance, which is typically ignored or glossed over in traditional history lessons. At the site of the first legally sanctioned free Black settlement in the territory that would become the United States, the small on-site museum houses artifacts and information on the history of the unique property. And of course, there are great books that help build out the rich history of the area:

- *Fort Mose: Colonial America's Black Fortress of Freedom* by Kathleen Deagan and Darcie MacMahon

- *Fort Mose: And the Story of the Man Who Built the First Free Black Settlement in Colonial America* by Glennette Tilley Turner

Whether our children are being taught in school or at home, chances are that their history curriculum is not wrestling with the tough stuff. It's unlikely that our kids will naturally be led down a path that includes the fullness of BIPOC voices and the relationships between various cultures and ethnicities through time. The lack of intention and resources in schools and traditional homeschool programs can be frustrating, but the truth is that our children's growth and character are ultimately our responsibility. Home is a place to initiate learning and build relationships, but it's also a place to correct wrongs and fill gaps. Part of the allure of home lies in its power to provide.

"Those who have no record of what their forebears have accomplished lose the inspiration which comes from the teaching of biography and history." This quote, attributed to historian Carter G. Woodson, warns of the consequences of a limited view of history. By integrating interest-led book learning with real-life experiences, we're able to help make honest history come alive for our children. Hearing multiple perspectives on related and disparate topics lays a foundation of historical context and understanding that our kids can continue to build upon for their entire lives. We're teaching them to seek out and listen to an amalgamation of voices as they study the past and experience life today, and this level of engagement and interest is what invites our children to care.

10

. . . .

CHOOSING JOY

Finding Beauty Through Culturally Rich Learning

Even a wounded world is feeding us. Even a wounded world holds
us, giving us moments of wonder and joy. I choose joy over despair.
Not because I have my head in the sand, but because joy is what the
Earth gives me daily and I must return the gift.

—Robin Wall Kimmerer, *Braiding Sweetgrass*

ALONGSIDE THE CALLING TO SHARE HARD HISTORY WITH OUR
children lies a responsibility to leave them with hope. If our kids walk
away from our homes feeling like things always have been and always will
be hopeless, then we've completely abdicated our role as loving guides.
Honest history is both necessary and heavy, but heavy doesn't have to
mean ugly. There's beauty tucked between the pages of every story, even
if it's difficult to spot right away.

When I share the history of Black people in America and throughout
the world with my kids, I strive to balance our honest discussions with
heavy doses of that beauty. I recognize that there's pervasive background
noise—an ongoing thread of struggle—in the complicated stories of all
people, and the Black community is no different. My drive to search deeply
for another frequency, one of joy and hope, is not an attempt to disown the
pain of my people, but rather an acknowledgment that there are experiences worthy of celebration woven into the unique fabric of every culture.

We are our ancestors' wildest dreams. And though we bear the weight of their tears, we also carry their resilience and laughter inside us. Learning the hard truths about the past doesn't always manifest in outward happiness, but embracing the fullness of our stories can bring lasting inner joy and contentment, and that's what I want most for my children.

In the inevitable juxtaposition of both truths—trial and triumph—rests uplifting stories that remind us that dreams really do come true. The freedoms and opportunities we now hold were likely just whispers of hope that our ancestors somehow held on to. I know that the kind of life I live today existed only in the imaginings of the generations that came before me. Sometimes dreams take a long time to unfold and often don't follow a straightforward path, but our hope rests on the back of progress.

The choice to focus on our beautiful achievements is an opportunity to spark a flame of wonder and pride within our families. We hold in our hands a rich legacy of literature, innovation, creativity, and more. And as a mother of four Black children, I think we should grab hold of the goodness we can find, let it linger in our homes and permeate our minds. People of color around the globe have always actively and passionately shined their talents into every corner of society. Their lives are rich gold mines of inspiration and encouragement. Making space for their beautiful stories is an act of intentional love.

Sometimes my children hear historical stories of triumph and beauty wrapped within our formal homeschool lessons, and other times the stories are casually integrated into our days as they fill our home as seamlessly as laughter at mealtimes. Storytelling is woven into the fabric of our family, and I'm as much a student as I am a teacher, learning alongside my children as we delve into various cultures and explore the history of our people. Though I'm not a degreed expert in history or sociology, my role as a committed mother consistently proves to be more than enough.

As the years of shoulder-to-shoulder learning increase, I've learned not to wait for grand opportunities to teach my kids big ideas; rather, I've embraced the idea of sharing many little insights and experiences over time. I've begun to naturally weave the experiences of people of color into my daily life, and ultimately that's what I hope to gift my children: the ability to see reflections of themselves and others amid the everyday. Beauty in the mundane.

As I've sought to balance tragic history with beauty within our home,

I've colored our days with art, music, and poetry. These are some of the easiest ways to bring culturally rich learning into a colorful home. I use these forms of creative expression to help my kids cultivate an appreciation for the varied ways people tell their stories. I've also incorporated the beauty found in cultural foodways and nature as I teach my children to see truth, goodness, and beauty everywhere.

BEAUTY IN VISUAL ART

Our family consistently enjoys art from people of all backgrounds, relying on a mixture of old and new to give a broader view of the past and present. I also include plenty of Black artistry in our home so my children can see themselves reflected in the pieces we examine and in the artists behind the work. We've spent time studying Black visual artists of the past like Joshua Johnson, Henry Ossawa Tanner, Edmonia Lewis, Horace Pippin, Augusta Savage, Jacob Lawrence, Bill Traylor, Clementine Hunter, and Alma Thomas. We celebrate these older masters alongside modern creatives like fiber artists Faith Ringgold and Bisa Butler, who speak to my children's current interest in textiles and quilting. We've also traveled to see the contemporary work of Kehinde Wiley up close as we join him in examining and reimagining the image of Black men and women in modern culture.

When we study these artists, we start out learning what we can about their lives. If I can find a good book, we begin there. If not, we use online resources to gain perspective on the artist and their chosen medium. Sometimes, we'll systematically study six or so of the artist's pieces, one at a time, over several months. Since some of the diverse art we study is not yet in the public domain, I often print pictures of each piece on high-quality cardstock to display around our home while we're exploring that artist. If I can find one reasonably priced, I'll also purchase a coffee-table book or a calendar featuring their work. And whenever possible, I try to take my children to see some of the artist's work in real life. It's not always practical, but we've taken many detours during vacations or visits with family to catch a glimpse. There's nothing that compares to seeing a beloved piece of original art up close.

At other times, our artist studies are far less formal. We may watch a video about an artist and then pull out our art supplies to create a rendition of their artwork or our own masterpiece in the same medium. Or we may just spend a single afternoon visiting an exhibit at our local art museum with no agenda at all. In these cases, we're simply absorbing and enjoying the work while adding another touchpoint along our colorful journey. This was the case when we toured the *Wonderful World of Ashley Bryan* exhibit featuring the artist's illustrations and puppets. And when my oldest had the opportunity to explore the iconic kaleidoscopic environments of Yayoi Kusama's *Infinity Mirror Rooms*.

When I speak with my kids about how people take ideas and make them their own, I like to include color, spunk, and contemporary interpretations right alongside more traditional manifestations of genius. I don't rank achievements or show favoritism for one genre of innovation or success over another. I want my children to know that a path exists for them and others to achieve in every direction.

A few years ago, I was ecstatic to share with them that Jean-Michel Basquiat's untitled 1982 painting sold for $110.5 million at a Sotheby's auction, becoming one of the most expensive paintings ever purchased. It also set a record high for an American artist at auction. Basquiat, who was of Haitian and Puerto Rican descent, tragically died at the age of twenty-seven in 1988, and his work has become iconic.

At times, I feel society hesitates to honor artistic achievements in what we deem to be "only" pop culture, especially when Black and Brown hands produce the art. Basquiat serves as an example of why we shouldn't allow other people's false boundaries to limit our dreams. He began his record-shattering career as a graffiti artist on the streets of Harlem and in the Bronx, yet his star is shining brightly among the top echelon of the art world. Because some of his story is best suited for a more mature audience, I've continued to share him with my children through picture books like *Radiant Child* and *Life Doesn't Frighten Me*, a treasure that pairs his art with a poem by Maya Angelou.

BEAUTY IN MUSIC

With music, there's typically little fanfare beyond listening and enjoying. When I first introduce a new style of music or a diverse musician to my children, I share whatever background information I'm able to gather, and then we just sit and listen or get up and dance if the mood hits us. I like to do this over breakfast, lunch, or snack time with some sort of yummy treat because my kids are more attentive to the music when they're eating. We also play music quietly every evening during dinner as another way to fill our home with various sounds.

Our musical explorations include Black composers like Chevalier de Saint-Georges, Florence Price, Samuel Coleridge-Taylor, Scott Joplin, George Walker, and William Grant Still. We've also explored the work of more modern musicians like Nina Simone (whom my oldest is named after), Harry Belafonte, Louis Armstrong, Ella Fitzgerald, Bob Marley, Aretha Franklin, Wynton Marsalis, Ladysmith Black Mambazo, Sweet Honey in the Rock, and more.

When we're singing hymns, we like to mix it up with soulful gospel renditions of our favorites alongside less widely known versions featuring bluegrass, country, jazz, or Celtic sounds. Or familiar tunes sung or played with an international flair. We especially enjoy singing folk songs, as the catchy words are so easily absorbed, and the unique voices of Elizabeth Cotten, Odetta, and Rhiannon Giddens show up frequently in our home.

Giddens won a MacArthur Foundation "Genius Grant" in 2017, and the singer/banjoist is known for reclaiming the Black heritage of American folk music. She's a trailblazer focused on the musicality of songs with a painful past rather than the settings in which the songs were birthed. And she echoed the sentiments of many when she said, "I've been living in slavery time for a long time, and where I'm moving now is, 'Look at what we've done.'"[1]

Giddens acknowledges that trial and triumph hold hands. They are life partners, and it only makes sense to make room at the table for both. Her voice is distinctive, and once you've heard it, you'll always recognize it within seconds. My children enjoy watching her strum her banjo with a quick-tempo twang, so when I'm alone, I take advantage of the solitude by slowing things down with her soul-touching performance of "Build a House," featuring renowned cellist Yo-Yo Ma. When the song ends, I often long to hear more deep cello notes. I played the instrument as a child, and though my case is caked with dust, my intense love for the sound has never dissipated. The yearning often leads me straight to the strings of Sheku Kanneh-Mason, and I love sharing his beautiful music with my kids.

Kanneh-Mason became a worldwide household name in May 2018 when nearly two billion people around the globe watched him perform at the wedding of the Duke and Duchess of Sussex (Prince Harry and Princess Meghan) at Windsor Castle. His second album reached number eight on the United Kingdom's Official Albums Chart, making him the youngest classical instrumentalist and the first cellist in history to reach the UK top ten. Some have held him up as an anomaly, so I love pointing out that all six Kanneh-Mason siblings are incredible classically trained musicians. Even though we've listened to it umpteen times, we usually begin with his royal wedding performance followed by a sweet "Redemption Song" rendered by all the siblings together.

Listening to those deep, rich sounds inevitably leads me to consider composer George Walker, the first Black person to win a Pulitzer Prize in music, as he died only two months after Kanneh-Mason's iconic wedding performance. What I would have given to be a fly on the wall when ninety-six-year-old Walker saw the fruition of his trailblazing work manifested in the rising star of Kanneh-Mason.

For every step made in communities of color, there's a recognition that we're standing on the shoulders of named and unknown leaders who innovatively made a way out of no way for others to come behind them and shine. At times, I feel overcome by the selflessness they exhibited in giving everything they had, at times even their very lives, knowing they would never personally see the fruits of their labor. All our children need to know their stories.

BEAUTY IN POETRY

My ignorance about the wonder of poetry at one time threatened to deprive my children of something glorious. Because I speak so frequently of my deep desire to connect my children with their heritage, I find it ironic that I was nearly willing to deny them this link to their culture. It's not that I thought there was something wrong with poetry but that I had no real love of verse, so I couldn't understand its impact or appeal.

I didn't cultivate a taste for poetry in my childhood, and I didn't at all feel that I'd missed out. However, despite having neither interest nor nostalgia to stand on, I committed to at least sampling every bit of the cultural feast before determining that one part or another wouldn't satisfy my tastes or my children's palates. And so, with quiet trepidation, I moved forward with a guarded, yet open, mind.

After a slow ramping up, my family eventually journeyed from one volume of poetry to another. I felt washed with confidence as we comfortably grew to digest verses of both the well-known and more obscure minds of today and yesteryear, especially people of color. At the same time, reverence crept in when least expected. The attachment we've formed with poetry is quite an unexpected development for my family because I never imagined that we'd come to know a body of work well enough for a child to state with confidence that thus and such is a favored poet. Over time, we've discovered a love for many poets: Effie Lee Newsome, Langston Hughes, Claude McKay, Paul Laurence Dunbar, Gwendolyn Brooks (whom my youngest child is named after), Maya Angelou, Alice Walker, Nikki Grimes, Kwame Alexander, Amanda Gorman, Nikki Giovanni, and so many more.

As one of the world's most celebrated African American poets, Giovanni's ever-growing body of work is an enduring legacy of every facet of the Black experience. Her poetry offers us another creative way of merging contemporary culture and creative achievement, and she's shown my kids that poems don't have to be old to be good.

Amid her poignant volumes, Giovanni released a book titled *Hip Hop Speaks to Children: A Celebration of Poetry with a Beat*. This bestseller includes both poems and songs and comes with a CD containing over thirty performances of rhymes and rhythms from powerhouse names like Queen Latifah, Gwendolyn Brooks, Langston Hughes, and A Tribe Called Quest. I use this book to show my children the connection between poetry and hip-hop, to obscure the line between art forms, and to open the door for boundless creativity with radical acceptance of various forms of self-expression.

In his book *What Is Poetry?* author Michael Rosen says, "Poems are a midway point between poets and readers. The poet pours in one set of meanings. The reader picks up the poem and puts in another set of meanings, and the two meet somewhere in the middle. That's what reading a poem is all about. It's a conversation between two sets of thoughts: The poet's and the reader's."[2] By regularly putting our kids in touch with the thoughts of diverse poets, we help them participate in a "conversation" that no one else can have. No other person will hear or interpret the poet's words exactly as our children do.

This open-ended relationship that our kids can develop through verse with someone from another century or today, from a different country or next door, is a special gift. As I've watched my children eagerly rally around a diverse body of poets and poems, both complex and straightforward, I've seen how much poetry has moved them to learn more about various people and their cultural experiences. And perhaps most important, my children have developed a love for this form of self-expression, evidenced by the many jotted notes and verses of poetry they've written to share their views on life and the world around them.

BEAUTY IN CULTURAL FOOD TRADITIONS

I've always been fascinated by the tastes, textures, and creativity found within the kitchen. Not my kitchen, in particular, but collective kitchens around the world. This intrigue even led me to become a registered dietitian nutritionist because I couldn't satiate my desire to know more about the science and psychology behind what and how we eat. I'm sure that my passions fuel my family's interest in how people gather and break bread, but there's also a natural connection at play, as food is known for bringing people together.

As we meander through our days, taking opportunities to soak in beautiful images, sounds, and words across cultures, we inevitably encounter the beauty of cultural foodways. I love integrating the art of food preparation and the stories behind what people eat as we enjoy the art, music, and poetry of those same people. As such, my family recently enjoyed the groundbreaking documentary series, *High on the Hog: How African American Cuisine Transformed America*. Produced by women of color, Karis Jagger and

Fabienne Toback, and hosted by the multitalented Stephen Satterfield, the series is based on the wonderful book of the same name written by food historian Jessica B. Harris.

Each episode celebrates the "delicious and restorative" foods of the African American experience and details how each came to form a valuable part of American culture, history, and identity. Alongside the stories are gorgeous displays of communal feasting. The footage shows Satterfield seated at beautifully appointed tables set in rural villages and in the heart of major cities, sharing food with people around the world as they celebrate its ability to communicate love amid even the worst circumstances. We were moved by the series. These are the kinds of stories that I want my children to breathe in. The beautiful ones.

BEAUTY IN DIVERSITY

Our experiences with art, music, and poetry often begin with expressions of our own culture, but they shouldn't remain exclusive to our own culture. The more my family examines our cultural arts, both American and Black in our case, the more easily we discern beauty manifested in the artistic pursuits of other cultures. Being able to experience and appreciate how other people express their stories is gift enough, but the natural by-product of this recognition is connection. And that's what we're here for.

The arresting beauty of the Ethiopian paintings and elaborate lattice-work crosses that my family saw at the Virginia Museum of Fine Arts during a recent vacation led my kids down a rabbit trail to the Ethiopian coffee ceremony. This slow, daily coffee service (practiced mainly to connect with relatives, neighbors, or other visitors) intrigued us. After reading about it, we watched a couple of videos and then went to lunch at an Ethiopian restaurant, where the waitress was kind enough to walk us through the process, an art form in itself. All of this led to a greater interest in the country and its people, and I'm not sure that our fire for the region will ever die out.

Another instance when our family fell in love with an idea and its people began when we learned that poetry is a cherished part of Afghan culture. Afghanistan has been a cradle of poetic expression for centuries, and one of the world's best-known poets, Jalāl ad-Dīn Muhammad Balkhī, or Rumi, was born there over eight hundred years ago. Now Thursday night is "poetry night" in the western city of Herat, and families gather to share ancient and modern verse, listen to traditional Herati music, and enjoy sweet tea and pastries long into the night.[3] We savor the vision of poets reading off elaborate pages covered in beautiful writing while others scroll on their phones as they give each other feedback and argue points. We learned about the passionate discourse that occurs on these nights through a United Nations article, and it gave us a view into a beautiful slice of life we'd never heard of before.[4]

Though the Ethiopian coffee ceremony and Afghan poetry night were new to us, they felt familiar because of our years of enjoying Poetry Tea-time. *The Brave Learner* author, Julie Bogart, says, "Poetry plus tea and treats equals magical family time and enchanted learning," and she couldn't be more right. Inspired by her PoetryTeatime.com website, we've incorporated this lovely practice into our weekly routine with a goal "to savor language, good food, and a special drink together at a lovely table." This little act of celebration not only provides a chance to create a sweet family tradition, but it also connects my children to people everywhere who take time to pay homage to the beauty found in ritual.

BEAUTY IN OUR LESSONS

I want my kids to look back fondly on their childhood, and I want them to have fun! I try to create multisensory and memorable experiences as we "travel" through the world and regions of our own country. Sometimes, when I pull myself together enough to keep copious notes, I share lesson guides outlining our plans on my website for others to glean from. One example is called *Sweet Tea & Cookies*, which I describe this way:

> *Sweet Tea & Cookies is a family celebration of the American South. But it's not about state flags, birds, flowers, and capital cities. Rather, this guide digs deeply into the soul of the South. You'll hear from all kinds of people because the story of the American South is wrapped up and intermingled with a little bit of this and a little bit of that. There*

are contributions that have been made by Indigenous peoples, Black folks, white folks, and others who have come together to leave their stamp on this part of our country. This enrichment guide includes multicultural stories of family, food, music, art, activism, love, tragedy, hope, resilience, fear, celebration, and fun! The South is complicated. But tucked between all the worn creases of its past are things that bind us together and make us smile.

This is an example of how I'll take an area of our country or world and highlight its beauty. I try to make it compelling for my kids to learn about diverse cultures and regions (even their own!) by combining beautiful stories with recipes, poetry, music, handicrafts, videos, and more. When I planned this enrichment study for my kids, I intentionally spotlighted five specific states, those comprising the Deep South, a term used to describe the American states most dependent on slavery during the United States' early history. I wanted to show my children additional aspects of history by highlighting the positive aspects of today's southern culture that distinguish the South from its abhorrent history of enslavement.

Despite the brutal past of these states, one of them (Georgia) is where I'm raising my family today. Though my husband and I are transplants, our children are *from* here, and I want them to know beautiful stories about their home. Yes, they need to learn the hard history. In fact, it's critically important, but it's not the only thing that matters. I also want them to relish the legacy of positive contributions and heartwarming stories that have helped shape this region. By integrating beautiful cultural learning into our home environment continuously and casually, we're able to balance the bitter with the sweet, so my children learn the truth with joy.

When I speak and write about including beautiful cultural arts and foodways into our children's home life, I'm often asked to clarify which "subject" these lessons cover. I struggle to answer the question because the lessons tied to these explorations include but transcend traditional academics. When I'm sharing these things with my kids, I'm not thinking about future test scores; I'm thinking about the people they're becoming and the vision I have for their future. For the future of all our children.

"It is time for parents to teach young people early on that in diversity there is beauty and there is strength. We all should know that diversity makes for a rich tapestry, and we must understand that all the threads of the tapestry are equal in value no matter their color; equal in importance no matter their texture."[5] What I love most about this quote from Maya Angelou is that she specifically called on parents to teach this lesson. While children may study a little art, music, or poetry in school, they don't have the chance to swim in it. It doesn't envelop their environment. And food traditions are rarely seen as a source of beauty to be incorporated into a rich tapestry. Home is where we cultivate an appreciation for life's beautiful gifts.

BEAUTY IN NATURE

When I was a child, I would bring along small empty bottles when traveling with my family to carry back natural mementos from the places we visited. Along the back edge of the bright yellow desk in my bedroom, I housed samples of clumped soil, white sand, ocean water, red clay, and fragmented granite, among other things. It was a tangible way for me to remember our trips and a free undertaking that I had the agency to pursue on my own.

Today I could line up the contents in mason jars along the living room wall, and they'd be trendy treasures. But back then, I stored my budget souvenirs in clear plastic containers with yellow lids, not unlike the breast milk storage containers that used to settle on my fridge shelf, and they were considered precious to me alone.

I'm not sure what happened to my earthy treasures. I suspect that I grew to the point of indifference and purged them, but my interest in the land resurfaced when I began exploring the natural world with my children. We spent innumerable hours frolicking amid fields and forest, admiring beautiful flowers, peering quizzically at strange-looking fungi, and watching insects and animals move casually through their habitats. We would sometimes stumble upon little pieces of man-made history tucked beneath branches or in the shadows of trees during these times. We mostly ignored them initially, but after a while, I started feeling a pull toward the stories of people's interaction with the land.

One day during a guided hike, we passed a huge stone slab with deep holes carved within, and the naturalist shared that it was a mortar hole that women in the Cherokee Nation once used to grind food. After this quick explanation, the group moved along the path, but I lingered and pulled my children aside. I said, "Can you imagine that, long ago, a mother or daughter sat right where we're standing and worked to prepare food for her family? Now we explore and enjoy this space, but it was once someone's home." When I saw the look of wonder in their eyes, I knew that connecting the land to our other interests would be powerful. From then on, I started spending just a little time researching our favorite haunts along with unexplored places that had been on my list for a while.

Through this research, we stumbled upon the oldest cemetery in our area. The aesthetic forty-eight-acre property is a throwback to the late nineteenth century when families personally tended the plots of loved ones, creating an assortment of lovely gardens. At that time, it was a popular destination for Sunday carriage rides and picnics, something I would never have imagined possible in a cemetery until we visited the land ourselves.

While there, a passionate historian walked a portion of the property with us, highlighting interesting physical distinctions while sharing fantastic stories of prominent and virtually unknown members of the Black community who are buried alongside the intricate paths. Oakland Cemetery was developed when slavery still existed in the United States, and further expansions occurred during segregation, so many African Americans are buried in a separate section. The experience of visiting this site forever changed my thoughts and feelings about old cemeteries, shifting them from utilitarian places of sorrow to lovely spaces of serenity and celebration of life. And I love that this calming essence was my children's first experience with a burial ground.

Some of the places we've learned to appreciate don't have significant structures or artifacts remaining on the land. In those instances, it's only the bare ground that connects us to the lives that were lived or lost on it. A 2,965-acre Civil War battleground, where opposing forces maneuvered and fought for several weeks in 1864, holds some of the most accessible hiking trails near our home. We had been there more times than I can even count before we took a moment to stop and consider just what had occurred in the space where we freely climb, run, learn, and play. Women just like me lost their husbands, sons, brothers, and sometimes all the above in battles that shook the very core of our nation. And yet, here we are, roaming about in the aftermath of peace. There's just so much power in remembering.

We love visiting our closest state park with friends to eat lunch and spend the day splashing in the most beautiful creek I've ever seen. For years, the outing was just a fun way to soak in nature and be coolly refreshed on hot summer days, but as my children grew older, their curiosity regarding the crumbled brick walls in the middle of the woods led us to dig for details. Interestingly, we found that the brick walls were the ruins of an old mill, and along with the pristine area surrounding it, were protected by the state park.

The government forcibly removed Cherokee families from their land, and it eventually became home to the New Manchester Manufacturing Company. In its heyday, the cotton mill supported a town of about one hundred workers living on-site, and their lives revolved around the textile operations. The mill and the general store where the workers shopped, on the land where we now play, were burned down over 150 years ago by the Union Army during the Civil War. All that remains today are partial brick walls and the millrace that leads to the factory's waterwheel.

Aside from cradling diverse stories, the outdoor world gives us a path to meaningful work. In his article on environmentalism's racist past, Columbia Law School professor Jedediah Purdy points out that for many of our most revered environmentalists, "working, consuming, occupying, and admiring American nature was a way for a certain kind of white person to become symbolically native to the continent."[6] The exclusionary politics of nature arising from this era paved the way for the great outdoors to be known as a place of great freedom and fulfillment for all, except those with brown skin.

The mere fact that my family is out and about in nature is a reclaiming of cultural heritage and a form of activism because parks, campsites, climbing spots, bike paths, hiking trails, lakes, swim holes, and the like have been uncomfortable spaces for people of color for a long time. The George Wright Society works to unite people from many different backgrounds around a shared passion for protecting Earth's natural and cultural heritage. One of their reports states, "Discriminatory and exclusionary practices go back generations and have long constrained people of color in their efforts to visit parks or engage in various forms of public recreation."[7] Despite this shady past, many of us are participating in a growing movement of Black joy exhibited in shared outdoor locations.

You now find organizations like Outdoor Afro celebrating and inspiring Black connections and leadership in nature. And individual families, like mine, are working hard to ensure that our children establish relationships with the land, extracting what they can for leisure, sport, enjoyment, and learning, and giving back in equal measure. We want our children to feel comfortable and welcomed in outdoor spaces. We want them to know that they belong.

The land holds many tales. Some are triumphant, and others are tragic, but either way, embracing them has added a compelling dynamic to our time in nature. The acknowledgment that people lived out so many stories in the spaces we consider ours naturally instills reverence for those who came before us and inspires us to care for the land because the lives we're living on it today will be tomorrow's treasured stories.

Soaking in the beauty of the natural world is as easy as stepping outside. Whether you live in the country, suburbs, or the city, there is beauty to be found wherever you're planted. Explore hiking trails, waterfalls, and campgrounds. Enjoy outdoor meals in green spaces. Go outside to walk, run, read, and play. Plan an adventure! Not sure how to get started? Check out *Adventuring Together: How to Create Connections and Make Lasting Memories with Your Kids* by Greta Eskridge.

If your family is interested in finding beauty at the intersection of the land, nature, and history in your area, here are some ideas for getting started:

- **START WITH HOME.** By researching old census records, you may be able to discover the names of people who lived on your land, as well as their ages, birth states, year of immigration, marriage status, occupations, personal belongings, and other interesting information.

- **TAKE IN THE FAMILIAR.** Before researching new places, consider digging into the history of the spots your family already enjoys visiting. Search for information, photographs, newspaper articles, and more in the archives of your local library. Contact your historical society or preservation foundation, tell them what you are looking for, and ask for direction.

- **CHECK PUBLIC SPACES.** Peruse the websites of your national and state parks, as they're typically filled with fascinating history. Better yet, give them a call to arrange for a tour. I've found park rangers, naturalists, and outdoor guides to be absolute treasures. They're typically passionate people who enjoy sharing the secrets of the land with anyone who will listen.

- **VISIT HISTORIC HOMES.** Call ahead and find out when docents are available for tours and note their slowest visiting times. There's nothing like getting a private tour with a historian just because your family happened to show up when there were no distractions. And don't overlook the gift shop! These tiny hyper-local, well-curated gift shops often have books and information that we can't easily access elsewhere.

- **CHECK THE NATIONAL REGISTER OF HISTORIC PLACES.** Scroll through the list to see what may interest your family. Sign up for the email newsletters of those locations so you'll be alerted when something special is happening.

- **REVIEW UNESCO WORLD HERITAGE SITES.** I especially love these for when we're traveling, but the list is also great for discovering (or rediscovering) nearby opportunities.

- **CALL YOUR LOCAL HISTORY MUSEUMS.** In our area, some of the museums themselves are situated on land with unique, rich histories. Most museums will be happy to point you toward other properties with fascinating stories, and some even have adjacent gardens, farmland, and forestland to explore.

Beauty flows from the stories we tell through art, music, and poetry. It can be found in our food traditions and the way we feast. And it exists in abundance throughout the natural world, even in the stories of the land itself.

We can learn to appreciate and be conscious of beauty everywhere.

Henry David Thoreau said, "The question is not what you look at but what you see."[8] When we choose to see beauty, the opportunities and methods for colorful learning and growth are expansive. We can naturally, yet intentionally, allow people of color and other less represented groups to permeate our homes in beautiful ways. Everything doesn't have to be a formal lesson. In fact, it shouldn't be.

In the end, we're simply providing opportunities for our children to live broadly, with curiosity, and in deep connection with themselves and others, but this type of expansive living doesn't happen in a vacuum. Life is not only lived within our four walls, as wonderful as they may be. Our children need opportunities to work out what they're learning in dynamic real-world spaces. It's time for those branches to spread!

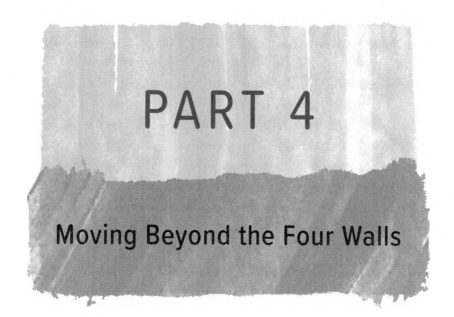

PART 4

Moving Beyond the Four Walls

AS I LOOK BACK OVER THE YEARS AT MY FAMILY'S JOURNEY from colorblind to colorful living, I can't help but smile because it's so clear that what we're doing today is incredibly more meaningful than the choices we made early on. I learned that our children need to feel connected to their roots and the richness of our culture so they'll grow up believing that they matter. That their voices, thoughts, and personhood hold value within their home and out in the world.

Once we understood the importance of supporting them in this way, my husband and I forged ahead on behalf of our children. But in all honesty, I assumed that in building up our own story, we risked creating a divide between our kids and kids from other backgrounds, especially white kids. And this made me hesitant.

Yet, I knew that my children couldn't grow up feeling unnecessary, so I accepted the loss of a certain amount of cross-cultural understanding and relationship as collateral damage. Like a balance scale, I'd planned to strike a fifty-fifty equilibrium between my children seeing themselves and seeing others because I didn't believe that having both in abundance was possible.

But how wrong I was. Ever since we began to cultivate a culturally conscious home atmosphere, our kids have grown closer to people of all backgrounds. Children who lack security and a sense of belonging are distracted by their deficit, leaving them with less emotional bandwidth for pursuing authentic relationships, especially those requiring more effort. But when they aren't forced to expend energy worrying about where they fit into the world, kids can look onward and outward with confidence.

The thing I thought we'd lose while trying to save our children is the very thing that grew abundantly. My daughter's obsession with skin color dissipated, and a quiet noticing grew in its place. My children notice when people look different, speak differently, or have a different story to tell, but they don't feel superior, suspicious, inferior, or resentful of what those differences represent. Instead, they feel hopeful and expectant. They expect to have positive experiences and opportunities for friendship with all types of people, and thankfully, they can pursue those relationships with a healthy sense of their own identity.

I've overtly taught my children that they have a duty to extend their hands across the aisle. But I've also shown them that the attitude with which we fulfill our obligations makes a difference. I have a duty to nurture my children, and it's also one of my life's greatest delights. My children share my duty to pursue cross-cultural relationships, and they find pleasure in doing so for the most part.

But that doesn't mean it's easy. Forging friendships, or even just friendly acquaintances, with people who are different can be challenging. And when you throw in substantial differences like language, religion, socioeconomics, and culture, it can be even harder. What I'm asking of my children, of you and your children, and especially of myself, is that we don't grow weary of trying. That we extend ourselves beyond smooth and easy days to create a new normal for how we see and interact with others.

"Our most deeply held beliefs are not merely shouted publicly. They are lived out among family, friends, and communities. These are the places where doctrines like grace, justice, hope, and perseverance become flesh."[1] These words from Dr. Esau McCaulley have reverberated in my mind for a long time. I refuse to be someone who publicly shouts my beliefs while privately retreating to what's most comfortable. I have no interest in raising kids who always center themselves and their comfort over all else, even if it feels good in the moment.

My vision for being rooted in community, locally and globally, is grand, but the execution has been bumpy. I've struggled mightily with integrating my family's need for safe "villages" where we feel intimately known and understood with my desire to commune with sisters and brothers who look nothing like us. Learning to straddle both worlds without feeling pulled apart is a complicated matter. And working to create and participate in spaces where Black people, other people of color, and white people can do life together in comfort is as much of an uphill battle as it is a joy when I catch glimpses of what can be.

"So let us be about the work to ensure that windows, mirrors, and sliding glass doors are present not only on our shelves but in our personal lives as well, modeling for our students what it means to love our neighbors as we love ourselves—our neighbors both near and far. Our neighbors fleeing persecution and our neighbors that may not act like, think like, and vote like us. Because if our shelves are diverse but our lives are not, we have missed the mark."[2] These compelling words from educator Chad Everett speak to me in every way.

We can't ask our children to love their neighbors as themselves when they don't have a reference point. Children must first understand the feeling of being loved and of loving themselves. Only then will they recognize what it means to love another in the same way. I don't mean that they should idolize themselves while draped in arrogance or think they're better than others. I mean that children should understand what it means to have a cultural and social identity as they recognize and respect the same in others. Their cups should be filled to the brim with plenty of frothy overflow to pour out on others.

The best place for a child to be filled is at home. Therefore, we've dealt primarily with the inner workings of a home that supports belonging and togetherness thus far. But insular living is far from the goal. A good home is a love incubator. A place where children are warmed and prepared for life outside the controlled environment of home and family. Now we'll move beyond the four walls of home and out into the world as we discuss the beauty of global citizenship, the need for community, and the importance of children as changemakers.

11

THEORY TO PRACTICE

Training Through Travel and Language-Learning

We live in a wonderful world that is full of beauty, charm, and adventure. There is no end to the adventures we can have if only we seek them with our eyes open.

—Jawaharlal Nehru, former prime minister of India

WHEN I FIRST SAW A HANDSOME GUY IN THE ART MUSEUM walking toward me, I got excited. He approached me confidently but kindly, and I was immediately attracted to his wit and intelligence. I was impressed that he chose to spend his Friday evening at an art exhibit, and I remember telling my sister that I may have just met "the One." I later learned that he'd never even heard of the artist and was only there to meet women, but the fairy tale lasted long enough for me to meet my prince and share a good laugh. As we continued to get acquainted over a series of increasingly frequent dates, there was one thing that stood out in my mind as incredibly unique: his passport.

I flipped through the pages, saw all the countries Scott had visited, and felt drawn to his sense of adventure. I loved hearing stories about his travels, and when it became clear that "I do" was in our future, we began dreaming of how we'd experience the world together. We talked about where we'd go and what we most wanted to see and do while there.

Children seemed far off at the time (little did we know), but we always included our future kiddos in our imaginary adventures.

We've known from the beginning that we'd travel with our children, but our reasons have morphed and expanded over time. Initially, the idea was simply to enjoy fantastic journeys and explorations. We wanted to have fun!

We planned to expose our kids to new and different places like historic sites and the official and unofficial wonders of the world. We would show them famous cities while experiencing cultural food, music, and art. But as Scott and I learned and grew as individuals and as a parental team, we came to realize that the dreams we hold for our children are wrapped up in global citizenship. We still value the fun cultural experiences, so we haven't revolutionized our plans, but today our number one reason for family travel is people. Not places or things.

In *Parents and Children*, educator Charlotte Mason borrows a quote from F. D. Maurice as she writes that "the family is the unit of the nation." She describes the family as a commune, which is an intentional community of people sharing living spaces, interests, values, beliefs, property, possessions, and resources in common.

She then describes several duties of the family as a commune:

- The family must be social.

- The family must serve neighbors.

- The family must serve the nation.

But then she pauses to let us know that the family's interests aren't limited to those of just its own nation, and this is the part that garnered my attention. She writes, "As it is the part of the nation to maintain wider relations, to be in touch with all the world, to be ever in advance in the great march of human progress, so is this the attitude which is incumbent on each unit of the nation, each family, as an integral part of the whole."[1]

Finally, she goes on to describe what she calls the noble dream of fraternity in which individuals attach to families, which unite to form nations that are then joined together in love and "emulous in virtue." This vision sparked a desire in me to see my family maintaining broader relations, being in touch with all the world, playing our little part to fulfill the noble dream of fraternity.

A global citizen is someone who recognizes that there are no boundaries to our shared humanity and that human rights and civic responsibilities transcend our individual cultures, communities, and countries.[2] Global citizenship requires children to see past themselves and the limits of their finite experiences, broadening their energy and benevolence to encompass others. Children raised this way understand that they're a part of the world, but that the world does not revolve around them.

Some of the most efficient and fulfilling ways to raise global citizens are humbly exposing children to meaningful world travel and teaching them to understand and speak other languages. Our family has sought out practical ways to do both. While researching travel possibilities, we discovered an entire global community of people who learn and live while traveling the world. These families are aptly known as "worldschoolers," and their lifestyles are more varied than you can imagine. From full-time home-schooling nomads to suburbanites who hit the road during extended school breaks and everything in between, there is no limit to the creative arrangements we've seen.

Once exposed to the ethos of worldschooling, we were hooked. Because of our desire to know people and their stories, our strategy shifted from regular short trips to less frequent, prolonged opportunities for slow travel. We still enjoy family vacations, but "vacation" is not a word we ever use to describe our intentional people-knowing trips because it mischaracterizes our intentions.

When we travel, we intend to learn the history, narratives, hardships, and joys of local families as we try our best to build relationships and community. There are bumps and bruises, both physical and emotional, during our stays. There are times when I think about giving up and returning home to Starbucks, Target, a lower altitude, or our comfortable way of life. But we carry on, and I'm so thankful that we do because worldschooling has been life-changing for all of us.

REMAINING FLEXIBLE ON THE GO

Our initial plan was to take our first worldschooling trip once our young-est was weaned and out of diapers, and we almost made it. But after wait-ing for so long, we were itching to get started. Eventually, we stuffed our bags with diapers, wipes, and nursing bras and hopped on a plane to Bo-livia, South America, to settle in for a three-month stay. My husband's job is not location independent (or so his company said before the pandemic), so in the past, he accompanied us on our trips and stayed until he ex-hausted his vacation. Then he returned home to the States while the chil-dren and I stayed on to live and explore.

For that first trip, our kids were eight, six, four, and one when we left, and the little one celebrated his second birthday in La Paz, the city we chose to call home during our stay. On his special day, I couldn't locate a birthday cake for the life of me, so I decided to make one from scratch. Little did I know that inexperienced baking at a high altitude would result in an inedible mess!

Eventually, I made my way to the store, where a kind soul who didn't understand what I was seeking pointed me to the little section of high-priced American imports. I grabbed a box of Pop-Tarts and called it a day. That night, before my kids headed to bed, they FaceTimed with Scott and excitedly informed him that they had celebrated their little brother's birth-day with a scoop of ice cream and the most amazing "Bolivian cookies." And they later shared their love of Bolivian cereal (aka Lucky Charms) with their grandmother. These moments when my American children encounter American goodies for the first time overseas and come to associ-ate them with our host culture have delighted me. And I'm reminded that hidden in every corner of the globe are opportunities for little joys, family stories, and memory-making.

When we returned from that initial trip, we sat down and roughly mapped out a plan that would allow us to visit other continents: Europe, Asia, Africa, and Australia, before our oldest, Nina, graduates from our homeschool. Then we started saving money and researching cities.

A year later, we began studying the culture of the places we planned to visit next. We continued to dive in deeper through books, videos, and conversations with people who know things we'd never find through a

Google search. We booked plane tickets, a bit of ground transportation, and accommodations, and we set out on yet another adventure. Eventually, our worldschooling plans led us across the Atlantic, and we were partway through a three-month European adventure when COVID-19 brought our experience to a screeching halt.

When we first started planning the trip, I thought of the many things that could go wrong and how I would resolve them. After anticipating as many scenarios as possible, I made a packing list that would help me combat nearly everything and brought emergency cash to buy whatever was needed to fill the gap. In all this planning and maneuvering, I somehow missed the possibility of a global pandemic. As we spent the last few days of our time in Europe watching the rest of our trip circle the drain, I remembered an Emily Dickinson poem my kids once recited because our adventure certainly "ravelled out of reach, like balls upon the floor."[3]

During the time we spent in Greece, we were outsiders. Obvious foreigners. And amid the global madness and panic, the locals began resorting to the temptation of rejecting others in favor of the false security of being with their own kind. When we walked onto the subway or into certain stores, I saw looks of disgust. Some people even made faces or pulled their shirts up over their noses when we walked by or sat down. People would wave us away if I tried to ask for directions, or they simply refused to acknowledge our presence. My kids didn't notice everything, but I did. As the pandemic raged, it was clear that the locals didn't want us there, and the feeling of rejection when we were already under tremendous stress and away from home reminded me of why we'd come in the first place: to know people. But this wasn't what I'd envisioned.

When I thought about traveling with my children and meeting people in other countries, I had projected a rose-colored, one-dimensional quality on all our future encounters. I conjured up images of bright sunny skies and friendly people going about their days as we intermingled and unobtrusively made our way through their communities. But I didn't consider that there would be dark clouds. I didn't make room for imperfection or indifference. For frustration or hate. For ethnocentrism or racism. For being human. For having to choose whether to speak in certain situations as I quickly calculated whether revealing our American accents would be beneficial or detrimental at the moment.

But those are just a few of many miscalculations I've made during our travels. I've come to learn that my family has to trade in control and predictability for flexibility and uncertainty the moment we leave U.S. soil. Or, in the words of the poet Alice Walker, we have to "expect nothing. Live frugally. On surprise."

By streamlining our goals to knowing and being known, we reduce the stress of missed opportunities and disappointments born of unrealistic expectations. This flexible, openhanded approach to world travel allows us to enjoy daily rhythms, relish occasional wonders, soak in the culture, befriend people, and grow from many lessons.

PLAY IS A UNIVERSAL LANGUAGE

For one trip, we chose to travel during our winter because it was summer in the southern hemisphere, and we wanted to be there when the local children would be out of school. That ended up being a great decision. Wherever we went, there were a plethora of kids playing and laughing at any time of the day, making it easy for my kids to join in.

I once read that smiling is a universal language. After watching my kids interact with local children in multiple countries, I would say that play is also universal. Kids run, chase, hide, and giggle everywhere, and speaking the same language is wholly unnecessary.

While walking across the central plaza in an Andean village in the Sacred Valley, I saw my daughter stick out her tongue at someone. I couldn't see the recipient of her rude behavior, but I immediately chastised her and was genuinely surprised. She sheepishly looked at me, embarrassed by my reaction, and said she was making faces at some kids nestled between the bushes along the road. I glanced over and saw the sweet faces of a few Peruvian schoolgirls laughing and exchanging wacky looks. They were waiting for my girl to jump back into the game, and who was I to impede cross-cultural silliness? I told her to carry on, and this across-the-way goofy face exchange led to my daughter's first-ever "conversation" in Spanish. I later apologized for speaking to her so sharply and thinking the worst as she built bridges and made friends in her kid way.

Days later, we walked through Miraflores, an affluent district just south of downtown Lima, Peru, and I wanted the kids to pose for family photos in front of a lighthouse. It was their first time on the shore of the Pacific Ocean, and the view was breathtaking. Getting a fantastic shot for our holiday card and watching them soak in the beauty of their surroundings would've made me so happy, but the kids spotted a playground, and all bets were off.

My oldest son pulled an Incredible Hulk action figure and two Hot Wheels out of his backpack, and he was instantly "in" with the local boys. He rode their scooters while they crashed his cars, and they all spoke through roars, grunts, and sound effects. The girls took a slightly less direct approach. They acted like protecting their baby brother was the most critical thing in the world. They channeled their nervousness from being outsiders into a caretaking role, and it worked. All the other wannabe mama bears joined in, and my little one quickly collected four or five kid mamas on the playground. Playing house in this way soon morphed into full-out running, playing, dancing, and singing in no language in particular.

These girls creatively built an entire fantasy world while each spoke her own language. I encouraged my girls to try using their Spanish, and they said okay, but continued with rough Spanglish. And after little brother lost his usefulness, he was picked up and fawned over by a group of Peruvian nannies who were enamored by his big eyes, curly hair, deep dimple, and infectious smile.

A lot of people have asked me about my kids not having friends on our trips. But the kids make friends everywhere they go because play really is a universal language. Children whose hearts naturally turn toward others don't need the perfect execution of a foreign language to build bridges, but does that mean that we don't need to worry about teaching our children other languages? Not at all.

LEARNING A NEW LANGUAGE

International travel is undoubtedly made more accessible and pleasant through knowing a foreign language. Still, there's also a far more crucial reason foreign language study plays a role in our home. It's not just a wise or impressive academic endeavor.

If we return to *Parents and Children*, a book that has had a profound influence on how I view worldschooling, Mason writes, "Is there one sub-ject that claims our attention more than another? Yes, there is a subject or class of subjects which has an imperative moral claim upon us. It is the duty of the nation to maintain relations of brotherly kindness with other nations; therefore it is the duty of every family, as an integral part of the nation, to be able to hold brotherly speech with the families of other nations as op-portunities arise; therefore to acquire the speech of neighbouring nations is not only to secure an inlet of knowledge and a means of culture, but is a duty of that higher morality (the morality of the family) which aims at uni-versal brotherhood; therefore every family would do well to cultivate two languages besides the mother tongue, even in the nursery."[4]

When I first read that, I felt overwhelmed by the prospect of learning and teaching other languages besides English. It felt impossible, so I disre-garded it as a goal for my children. But I couldn't shake the thought in the back of my head because it just makes so much sense. The truth always has a way of gnawing at us, doesn't it?

"Language learning done right is less about collecting foreign vocabu-lary and more about treasuring another person enough to communicate with them in their own words."[5] I ran across this quote while scrolling on Instagram one night, and it resonated so much. How can my family pos-sibly work to realize the goal of universal brotherhood when we can't even speak to the family at our local mercado or those in a country with which we share a border?

After wrestling with these thoughts for several months, I decided that fear should never be an excuse to withhold the opportunity to do right from my children. And from that point on, I chose to do all that I reason-ably could to help my children learn to speak with people in their lan-guages. We started with Spanish for several reasons:

- We live in a community with many native Spanish speakers, so learning Spanish gives us the most opportunity to begin forging relationships in our backyard.

- Some of our nearest non-English-speaking neighbors on a global level are Mexico, Cuba, Puerto Rico, etc. It makes geographic sense for us to start there.

- I took Spanish in high school, so I feel most confident helping the children with that one first. I don't know any other languages at all. Unless you count African American Vernacular English (AAVE) or what used to be known as Ebonics. Though quite helpful locally, it doesn't offer much use in our travels.

- I identify with many Spanish-speaking immigrants in America because I've heard the behind-the-scenes way so many Americans speak poorly of them for various ugly reasons. As part of another marginalized group of people, I already have a love for them built on mutual hardship and not being accepted. I want to know them better. I want to share their burden, and I want my children to do the same. But we need to be able to speak with them.

To be clear, I can speak some Spanish, but I don't *truly* speak Spanish. I'm painfully reminded of my inferior language abilities daily when traveling to places where no one speaks English. I'd be lying if I didn't admit that it's challenging and stressful at times. We've put in the effort because I know it's essential, but it hasn't been easy. We've got the basics down, and we're continuing to grow.

Along with the regularly scheduled Spanish lessons that I facilitate during our school day and helpful apps like Duolingo, my children have worked with native Spanish-speaking tutors in our home, online, and when we're away. Language tutors are typically much less expensive in a country that officially speaks your target language. I paid $11 an hour for a native-speaking language tutor to come to our home three to four days a week to work with my children while we were in Bolivia. That same service was $45 an hour in the U.S.

These many hours of lessons have resulted in my older kids carrying on rudimentary conversations and stumbling through sentences here and there, while the younger ones freeze and look up at me whenever anyone addresses them in Spanish. And when we're in a Spanish-speaking country, that's every single day. All day. And me? Well, the apps help me speak Spanish quite well when I'm sitting in the comfort of my bed in the USA, but they haven't done as much for me amid our travels because this is real life.

While traveling, we have to think on our feet. We also don't have multiple-choice options from which to choose. We're required to come up with original thoughts and sentences quickly while people are waiting. The server is waiting for our order, the grocery clerk is waiting for accurate payment, the taxi driver is waiting for directions, and the cars behind him are waiting for us to get out of the way. The gardener is waiting to borrow a tool, the bus driver waits for us to declare our stop, and the dance teacher waits for our class schedule. Everyone is waiting. For us. To speak. En español por favor.

Learning a language is hard work, and it can take years. At the same time, my children are growing up quickly, and relatively speaking, we have a short time to worldschool together. How can we balance the time it takes to learn a language with the limited time we have to enjoy unique cultural experiences while our children are still living at home?

After wrestling with that question, Scott and I decided to just take the plunge by simultaneously studying a language and traveling extensively without having mastered the language. I was nervous to head out on our first adventure with such little mastery of the local language, but the basics have proven to absolutely be enough. I'm no language expert, but I've spent months in foreign countries by myself with four young children speaking languages that I don't know well, and we've thrived.

So how do we get along in countries where virtually no one speaks English? That's kind of like asking, "How can I homeschool with a toddler?" In both cases, my answer is that you just do your best because that's all you can do. Don't let your inability to speak the local language stop you from taking an adventure. The basics are essential and will take you far. Focus on that, pick up what you can along the way, and feel inspired to continue learning. I'm trying to raise lifelong learners, and as they say, "The easiest way to raise one is to be one."

Are there times when miscommunication causes issues? Absolutely. All the time. But it's also gratifying when we have a brief conversation in another language with a stranger who becomes a new friend, and the more time we spend in a place, the more quickly the local language begins to roll off our tongues.

LEVERAGING "GOOD ENOUGH" LANGUAGE SKILLS

If you're considering international travel with children when a language barrier is likely to exist, do all you can to learn the basics in your target language before leaving home. Prioritize learning a wide variety of valuable nouns and adjectives. Focus your efforts on words you use daily or while on vacation. Look at a children's book, and try to memorize the words that look important. We have *First Thousand Words in Spanish* (with an internet-linked pronunciation guide) by Heather Amery, but there are many resources from which to choose for various languages. Consider your circumstances and focus on learning the words for "eggs" over "eggplant" and "playground" over "buffalo," for example.

Based on my experience, I recommend that you prioritize these:

- Basic foods (vegetables, rice, beans, fruit, cheese, bread, breakfast, lunch, dinner, snack)

- Drinks (bottled water, juice, milk, tea, coffee, latte, cream, sugar)

- Colors (Red, blue, green, yellow, orange, purple, black, and white will be fine.)

- Numbers (1 to 1,000 is excellent if possible, but 1 to 10 is okay if you're short on time because 350 can also be 3-5-0).

- Directions (north, south, east, west, in front of, behind, near, up, down, after, before, right, left, top, bottom, back, front). These words are critical for maneuvering around in unknown places.

- Kid-related gear (high chair, playground, toys, diapers, baby wipes, breastfeeding)

- Household items (bed, computer, shower, appliances, blanket, towel, soap)

- Locations (bathroom, hotel, restaurant, train, bus, taxi, embassy, park, downtown, store)

- People (person, son, daughter, husband, wife, boy, girl, woman, man, baby, family, driver, police)

- Time (hours, minutes, today, tomorrow, days of the week, months)

- General (place, thing, that, this, if, when, why, how, where, who, big, small)

Common verbs. Without knowing some verbs, you're dead upon arrival when trying to speak another language. If you can learn to conjugate these verbs (I go, you go, they go, we go), you'll be even better off. I can conjugate Spanish verbs that follow the basic pattern, but there are many irregular verbs that I haven't conquered. Native speakers generally understand unconjugated verbs, though, so I think it's all good if you know the primary verb. Here are the ten verbs that I find most important, in no particular order:

- To have

- To go

- To want

- To do

- To take

- To put

- To be

- To eat

- To turn

- To say

Do your absolute best to speak in the local language while in another country. Even if you know that you sound horrible, your sheer effort will mean a lot to the people among whom you're living. Americans have an international reputation for being conceited, privileged, and entitled.

Nothing upholds that stereotype more than strolling into a country and insisting on speaking English without even attempting to communicate in their language.

You can successfully communicate with some nouns, adjectives, and a solid set of verbs even if it's not said beautifully. You can always combine the nouns you know with the adjectives and verbs you've learned to describe what you need. Examples:

- When I didn't know the Spanish word for "doll" (la muñeca), I said, "The not real baby for little girls to play," and someone immediately directed me to a stand that sold handmade dolls.

- I had no clue about the word "bridge" (el puente), so I told the taxi driver to turn by the "yellow thing that goes over the water." Is that weird? Totally. Did the driver turn by the bridge? Yes, he did.

- When my little one had a heinous diaper rash, I asked the pharmacy for "a white thing for the red baby bottom because it's not good," and I walked away with some (costly) diaper rash cream.

- And when I needed a one-piece swimsuit, I asked for "the clothes for a woman to use in the water and not a bikini." The store employee showed me where the old maid swimsuits were, and I humbly purchased one.

I could go on and on with examples because this is how I communicate when I don't know how to say something. I match up the few nouns and adjectives I understand with the verbs I've mastered, and I teach my children to do the same. There's so much more to learning another language, but what I value most isn't hinged on perfection. I want my family to play a role in minimizing the cultural divide. The dream is that my children will always grow in their ability to show love and build connection.

I'm not minimizing fluency, but I'm a huge proponent of being "good enough," which ensures that our families don't miss out on life while waiting for our perfectionism to be satisfied. So, grab yourself a little Rosetta Stone, Duolingo, a bilingual friend, a kid's book, or some YouTube videos, and shoot for the basics. Everything else will come with time.

SCHOOLING AWAY FROM HOME

It's not possible to continue with all our formal lessons when we're away. We can't bring the books and supplies we usually use because they're cumbersome for travel. And the whole point of our journeys is being out among the people, which we can't do enough of if we're always in the house doing lessons. Bedtimes slip with jet lag and time zone changes, the environment is entirely different, and I've found that it's much better to flow than to force.

For short-term travel, I recommend that families ditch formal lessons (but keep silent reading and a read-aloud going!) and just absorb natural learning from the local culture and environment. This can also be done during longer trips away, with some families "unschooling" for the duration. The flow will look different for every family, but here's what school looks like for us during longer trips:

1. **SOME LESSONS CONTINUE TRADITIONALLY WITH FEW CHANGES.** We continue as usual in history, math, poetry, and literature while incorporating local history and tales into our formal lessons. Literature is covered by my children's personal and bedtime reading along with our family read-alouds. Poetry is sweet and straightforward, and math is just math.

   Not having access to our home library on the road is a big deal. It requires stellar preplanning, and painfully, I've had to purchase electronic versions of books that we already own. I've also spent a lot of time snapping pictures of pages in books that aren't available electronically. Although I'd had a Kindle for years, I didn't start using it until we began traveling. Everyone in the family has one now. We don't utilize them much at home, but they're lifesavers on the road.

2. **OTHER LESSONS CONTINUE, BUT IN A DIFFERENT WAY.** My children primarily do oral narrations (telling back what they've read) of their readings while we're away, and writing takes the form of regular updates in their travel journals and letter writing to friends and family back home.

   We don't learn new handicrafts while traveling, but we bring supplies to continue ones we already know and enjoy. While abroad, we don't spend every day out and about. There are days for resting at home, doing laundry, or recovering from illness. There are also days when national holidays, the political climate, or local ordinances prevent us from moving about easily. Sometimes it just rains all day.

Whatever the case may be, we need other things to do on days spent indoors because we're not going to sit and read all day. Handicrafts are perfect. They need to be lightweight for travel, and we bring every supply with us because craft stores like Michaels and Hobby Lobby aren't available in the places we travel. On our last trip, I worked on an embroidery project, and the older kids were hand-sewing bags and accessories. Another time, we brought clay and small tools along with art supplies for drawing and nature journaling.

3. **WE DROP A FEW SUBJECTS FROM OUR REGULAR SCHEDULE.** We put aside formal lessons in science, phonics, spelling, and grammar while we're away. My kids pick up a ton of natural history through extensive time spent outdoors, but we don't "study" science beyond making observations and comparisons. The various aspects of language arts are embedded in our reading and writing, but I don't formally teach new concepts in this area.

4. **WE LEARN THE REMAINING SUBJECTS WITHIN THE HOST CULTURE.** Foreign language, geography, art, and music are all encompassed within our daily living. We immerse ourselves in the local community and soak up all we can of the land, its people, and how they express themselves artistically. Sometimes this study is more formal with tours of local museums and places that have cultural, historical, or scientific significance. But most of the time, this learning occurs organically by being with and among the local people.

Essentially, we use a mix of books, videos, and experiential learning for a fully immersive experience when we're away (and when we're home, for that matter). We value clear, unencumbered days where we can walk around and capture the fullness of life wherever we happen to be, so most of our bookwork happens right after breakfast or in the early evening before dinner. Our formal lessons are done regularly but not daily. The pace is uneven because some days we may be gone from sunup to sundown, and other days we're hunkered down at home all day, allowing us to work through more than a single day's lessons. I want my children to develop a deep love of learning, and this is easy to do when we use the world as our classroom.

GETTING KIDS TO CARE

My children are just regular everyday kids. They weren't born with an innate desire to search for cultural significance in ancient ruins or delight in native art found in the center of rural villages. They don't care much for random facts and obscure artifacts. And neither do I, for that matter. This is yet another reason why focusing on people rather than things is so important.

Getting the kids to care involves me, but it's not up to me. The late Stanford University professor Elliot Eisner wrote, "We have come to realize that meaning matters and that it is not something that can be imparted from teacher to student. In a sense, all teachers can do is to 'make noises in the environment.' . . . [W]e have . . . no main line into the brains of our students. We are shapers of the environment, stimulators, motivators, guides, consultants, resources. But in the end, what children make of what we provide is a function of what they construe from what we offer. Meanings are not given, they are made."[6] I guide my kids toward what feels meaningful, and we learn alongside one another, but I cannot *make* them care.

We spend most of our time on everyday living, not tourist attractions. But museums and culturally significant activities are part of some of our days when we're away, just as they are when we're in the U.S. We interact with local people, learn some of their customs, and respect their ways (especially when they're different than ours). We also try to explore their national treasures, the unique things that bring them pride.

There are more historical sites in Athens, Greece, than we could ever see, but of course, one of our first stops was the Acropolis. While there, we visited the Erechtheion, considered the most sacred temple, part of which was dedicated to the Greek goddess Athena. On the south porch of this temple, the roof is supported by six statues of maidens known as the caryatids instead of regular columns. They replaced the originals with reproductions in 1979 to keep the real maidens safe, and those originals are now the star attractions inside the Acropolis Museum.

While reading about the caryatids before our trip, I found that we would only see five of them at the museum because the sixth is installed at the British Museum in London. It was acquired nearly two centuries ago after Lord Elgin, the British ambassador to the Ottoman Empire, had it sawed off the Erechtheion's porch and used it, along with shiploads of adornments from the Parthenon, to decorate his mansion in Scotland before selling the pieces to pay debts.

Whoa. That is an exciting story onto which I knew my kids would grasp. So not only were they intrigued by the empty space from the missing maiden, but when our travels take us to London, where do you think we're going to run? Right. To the British Museum to check out that missing caryatid. And who will be running the fastest? My kids. Something was stolen and hasn't been returned. It's a missing piece, and the people of Greece want it back. We've seen the other originals, and we must see the last one. Now they care.

These are the kinds of stories that my children enjoy. I can't drag them all over the place trying to stuff them with every bit of cultural goodness I can find in every country we visit. Our explorations only skim the surface, but my kids talk about these trips all the time. They remember random details and funny stories. They recall the food and the atmosphere, and more than anything else, they recollect the people. And that's the whole point.

FUNDING INTERNATIONAL TRAVEL

But how do you pay for it all? That's the question on most people's minds when they hear about our worldschooling adventures, and I get it. When we were planning our first trip, we couldn't find a single person who would just flat-out explain how they were making it all work. Whenever we asked, we got responses like:

"Oh, I don't even know. We just make it work."

"Our family of seventeen travels the world on thirty-two dollars a day."

"We sold everything we own and lived off the proceeds for two years."

Interesting answers, but much too vague or unbelievable to be helpful. What people failed to realize was that I wasn't asking out of pure curiosity. I was asking because I wanted to know if we could ever do what they did the way they did it. But no one would provide enough information for me to have even a peripheral idea of how they pulled it off. Because of this, I try to be completely transparent when discussing how we pay for world travel.

Every trip is different, and expenses can vary wildly. We don't incur all of the same costs on every trip, and many expenditures can be reduced or eliminated depending on the size of your family and your preferences. For instance, some countries require visas and immunizations for entry, while many other countries don't have those stipulations. Our plane tickets to South America were expensive, but our cost of daily living was extremely low. The opposite was true for Europe because we used accumulated credit card points to buy the tickets, and accommodations were relatively expensive. Even as I write this today, we're on the lookout for discounted plane tickets to Addis Ababa, Ethiopia, with a plan to stay in my friend's home while her family is away for an extended time. It all just depends.

We're not independently wealthy or extraordinarily well-off. We're just an average family with the desire to connect our children with humanity around the globe, and we rely on frugality and trade-offs to fund our trips. While we're away, we live in working-class neighborhoods among the people. Not in fancy hotels. We aren't galivanting around the countryside on mopeds. We walk almost everywhere and take trains and buses when we need to go farther. We've never once had a rental car. We shop in local markets and cook at home. We pack lunches and water bottles when we're on the go. We aren't enjoying late-night dinners at Michelin-starred restaurants. We're committed to debt-free travel, so we live within the means dictated by the cash on hand. In other words, we live abroad the same way we live at home.

We typically budget $10,000 to $12,000 for a three-month trip. If we were to stay for only two months, the budget would not decrease by a third. Some things (passports, visas, immunizations, plane tickets, ground transportation, etc.) are significant upfront, fixed costs that aren't dependent on how long we stay. This can be frustrating, but it's also another reason to plan for longer, slow travel. Once you get there, you've already expended a lot of your budget, so you might as well settle in and stay awhile.

I wish I could tell you that we do one or two big things that allow us to afford our worldschooling trips, but it's a series of many small things that add up over time. In general, most of the funds have come from these places:

- Using my HeritageMom.com business profits

- Saving our tax refunds

- Selling items on Facebook Marketplace

- Saving monetary gifts from family

- Reducing gasoline expenses with an electric car

- Skipping our annual vacation

- Purchasing less "stuff" by consuming what we have on hand

- Being vegetarian (meat is expensive)

- Eating out less often

- Changing utility companies

- Canceling underutilized services or apps

- Drastically reducing Starbucks visits

- Cutting babysitting expenses

- Going "natural" (Wearing my hair in its natural curl pattern allowed me to eliminate pricey salon visits.)

- Maintaining basic mix-and-match wardrobes

- Using coupons when convenient

- Cutting out several extracurricular activities

- Utilizing the library more often, rather than constantly buying books

- Purchasing annual membership passes to frequently visited places

- Avoiding car payments by sharing a single vehicle

- Changing cell phone plans

- Accumulating credit card points (We put everything we can on a card that we pay off each month.)

- Eliminating or reducing luxury services (valet parking, manicures, dry cleaning)

Some of these money-saving moves are ongoing because they've become second nature. Others are temporary strategies that we use when we've dedicated ourselves to preparing for a specific trip. The ability to afford global travel is partially based on priorities. When I first told one of my good friends what we were planning to do, she thought it was absurd. She said that she couldn't imagine spending all that money on traveling. When I told her that our plane tickets and accommodations for three months cost us less than what her family paid for the Disney cruise they took and the two weeks they spent in Hawaii, she was stunned.

Little by little, bit by bit, we're able to put money away to have these experiences. But most of the time, we're not traveling the world. We're here at home, raising our children, and doing the best we can to give more than lip service to the idea that children deserve a place to belong.

BROADENING THE VISION OF WORLDSCHOOLING

What about the times when we're not traveling around the world? Or when world travel isn't possible? What if you want to raise your children as global citizens but aren't able to provide them opportunities to visit other countries often? Or ever?

According to Eli Gerzon, the unschooling advocate who popularized the term, worldschooling doesn't require world travel. He says, instead, it's when you actively experience and learn from the world around you, including "the home, family, friends, strangers of all backgrounds, libraries, parks, sports, forests, schools, towns, and of course the world and the world wide web."[7] So though worldschooling is casually known as learning while traveling in another country, the truth is that it's just a commitment to intentional community-minded living with a curious, people-focused, global mindset. And that's something everyone can do.

In addition to reading books about different countries and novels set in various cultures or centered on diverse communities, there are numerous ways to connect your children to the world from the comfort of home:

- Learn new languages, and let your children hear you speak positively about people who speak languages other than or in addition to English.

- Study the context in which people from various countries enjoy food and feasting. Experience cultural cuisines in restaurants and through homemade meals with friends from other cultures, or experiment with international recipes while cooking at home.

- Watch movies set in other countries or with different languages (subtitles are great).

- Shop in specialty grocery stores and markets where you can encounter global foods, goods, and people.

- Join a food or grocery co-op. Not only can you often find the best local foods, but these places typically have a communal vibe that you don't encounter in commercial spaces.

- Attend performances honoring the creative gifts of people whose paths you don't usually cross.

- Spend time at library branches in areas of your town (or a town nearby) where people who don't look like you live. Enter these spaces with no agenda. Just hang out and be.

- Sponsor foreign exchange students. Share your culture and make plenty of space for theirs in your home.

- Ask traveling friends to send postcards and bring back small souvenirs for your kids.

- Sign up for subscription boxes like Little Global Citizens, Little Passports, or Universal Yums. If grandparents are looking for a great gift for your kids, try one of these!

- Develop a taste for international music by regularly listening to sounds from around the globe.

- Research visual artists from around the world and incorporate their styles and mediums into your art projects.

- Take live, online workshops with global creatives on websites like Glomado.com.

- Help your kids find pen pals from other countries on sites like ePals.com or Facebook groups like Worldwide Snail Mail Pen Pals.

I'm a mama, teacher, and guide during our travels, but I'm also learning as we go. I don't know exactly what we'll encounter when we're away. I can't control how people respond to us or what they'll think of our American passports or our brown skin. The only thing I can do is show my children that people worldwide are complex—kindhearted and resentful, patient and arrogant, loving and vengeful. Just like us.

Worldschooling has brought my family together in ways I never could have anticipated. There have been incredible highs and tear-streaked lows, but putting ourselves out there, again and again, is what we're committed to doing. The whole point is getting to know people as they show up and not as we want or expect them to be. We bring books and pencils with us wherever we go. We visit gardens and shop in open-air markets. We climb mountains and crawl through caves, literally and figuratively. But make no mistake, practicing love, joy, peace, patience, kindness, goodness, faithfulness, gentleness, and self-control is the real lesson. For my kids and for me.

12

. . . .

SACRED SPACES AND PLACES

Cultivating Safe Villages, Inclusive Community, and Cross-Cultural Kinship

Offering sanctuary is a revolutionary act; it expresses love when others offer scorn or hate. It recognizes humanity when others deny and seek to debase it. Sanctuary says "we" rather than "I." It is belonging—the building block of community.

—Diane Kalen-Sukra

"IT TAKES A VILLAGE TO RAISE A CHILD" IS AN AFRICAN PROV-erb meaning that an entire community of people must interact with children for them to grow in a secure and healthy environment. All children need to have supportive spaces or safe villages to interact with people who look like them or experience the world in similar ways. Time spent around adults and other kids with a similar cultural background fosters a sense of belonging that's different from any other group affiliations children may have. It builds feelings of self-worth and helps form the basis of their racial or social identity.

It took me a while to catch on, but what I've learned is that BIPOC kids need opportunities to find sanctuary within their cultural communities. I refrained from initiating this tender conversation in mixed circles for a long time because I knew that my public admission of this idea would garner attention and pushback. And it has. But mostly, it's been celebrated by families who have lived it and understand the profound nature of ethnic micro-communities. I'm convinced that the time my children spend immersed in the safe village of the Black community is what allows them to emerge as influential cross-cultural bridge builders.

I joined a local support group as soon as Scott and I decided to educate our children at home. I knew that we needed community while embarking on this new adventure, and there was a wonderful group nearby that met regularly for field trips, park dates, enrichment classes, and more. The families in this group are great. The moms are lovely. The children are nice. I enjoy spending time with them, and I miss them when we've gone too long without seeing each other. They've embraced us with open arms since the first day we met. There's nothing wrong with any of them, they're our friends, and that's why we're still in the group today. But everyone else in the group is white.

After being active in the group and the broader homeschooling community for a couple of years, my daughter started exhibiting signs of emotional distress and anxiety. All related to race. She increasingly began to talk about skin color and make frequent comments about being different from everyone else.

As discussed previously, she fell right in line with the 1940s doll experiments that studied Black schoolchildren's attitudes about race by giving them identical white and Black dolls and asking them which one they'd prefer to play with. Sixty-three percent of Black children studied said they'd rather play with the white doll. Seventy-five years later, my daughter was singing that same old tune, and it made me mad.

I related to how journalist Elaine Welteroth felt when she heard a group of young Black men make disparaging comments about dark-skinned Black women: "I was mad because I was waking up to the ways in which society sets up Black people to hate ourselves. I was mad because so many of us are complicit in perpetuating this self-hating cycle of oppression, one designed to make us cling to Whiteness for validation. I was mad because of how insidiously racism works to keep us from claiming our beauty, our worthiness, our power. I was mad to see so many of us operating out of brokenness and shame."[1]

Despite my frustrations, I thought my daughter's obsession with race (or really with skin color, because that's all she understood) was a passing phase. I was concerned, but I assumed she would outgrow it. I focused on similarities with white friends and continued to repeat that we were all the same on the inside. But rather than improving, she only got worse over time.

My husband and I started evaluating our lifestyle and began looking for anomalies that would explain why our child found the world we so swiftly navigated to be crippling. I grew up in a white neighborhood and went to predominantly white schools, but I had a big extended family nearby and spent lots of time at our Black church. Scott's and my families live twelve hours away, and our contemporary nondenominational church was primarily white at the time. Was that the problem? Why wasn't my child around other Black people anyway? We live outside Atlanta, a major metropolitan city, not in rural Georgia.

I had Black friends, of course, but they either lived far away, didn't have children, or worked full-time, making it challenging to coordinate playdates and such. I knew one other Black homeschooling family in our town (make that in our county), and she is a dear friend of mine to this day. But day in and day out, as my family went about the community doing our thing, we were nearly always the only Black people. It never bothered me until it bothered my daughter. When it really bothered her, it *really* bothered me.

We considered moving to an area with more Black people, but quickly ruled that out because the work commute would be horrid for my husband. We decided that changing churches was the low-hanging fruit. So, we stepped away from the church we'd attended since my daughter was a baby and started attending one of the largest Black churches in our immediate area. My husband and I didn't feel connected there, but we did begin to see some improvement with our girl, so we continued for a year, sometimes going to an early service at our home church, followed by a later service at the Black church.

During this time, I studied my daughter and her behavior in every environment. I paid incredibly close attention to what she did and said and how others interacted with her. Not just children, but adults as well. And here's what I came up with: She liked being around our white friends, but she *loved* being around Black people, whether friends or strangers. She beamed when Black teen girls doted on her, when old Black grannies pulled her in close and doled out peppermints from the deep crevices of their pocketbooks, and when other Black moms complimented her on her beautiful curls.

Nina smiled and had a genuinely good time with our white friends, but she was vibrant, chatty, and full of deep-down belly laughter when she tore through the playground with little Black boys and girls. She started requesting more intricate braided hair styles with beads! Yes, folks, this child who months earlier thought she would be the next Elsa from *Frozen* began to ask for one of the most traditionally Black hairstyles I can think of, aside from afros and locs.

The dolls relegated to the back of the closet came out and started having significant roles in her imaginative play. She sought out Black beauties at the store and adoringly spoke of how pretty they were. It was as if she were waking up from a deep fog and starting to live again. It became crystal clear that mere exposure to Black people was a salve for her pain. But this utterly confused me.

How can a young child, my child, raised in a loving, supportive home shielded from racism and negativity already be that impacted by skin color? Where had we gone wrong? I started thinking. Calculating. Wondering. While trying to make sense of this, I began considering how I could set up an IV drip full of this salve so she wouldn't fall ill again. I started questioning whether I was willing to admit publicly that my daughter needed Black people. Not a little, but a lot. I feared what others would think if I did something bold to help her thrive.

It would be enough to find five or so other Black families nearby so we could meet up for activities and playtime during the day. I knew it would be difficult to find that many, but I wasn't greedy. Surely, I could locate just five Black parents who thought this was as important as I did. So I stayed up until 3:00 a.m. three nights in a row (yes, I can be obsessive like that) and created a Facebook group and website to get a local support group for Black homeschooling families up and running. I called it Heritage Homeschoolers and started by organizing a small lineup of upcoming events.

A handful of families showed up at the first event, and I was ecstatic. I couldn't believe it! I found a few families, and I was satisfied. We started meeting up for things here and there, and it went so well. The kids all got along, the moms were getting to know each other, and it was all good.

And then my email started going bonkers.

I was getting daily requests to join the group, and people started paying to become members of the website. Ten families, twenty families, forty-eight families, seventy-five families. And today, five years later, there are over one hundred paying member families in our local support group.

I guess I was wrong. There weren't a few local families looking for Black community. There were a lot of them, and they shared similar stories and experiences. The salve that was soothing my daughter needed to be bottled up and distributed. Black kids need each other, and I had been clueless.

Through this process, I found out that Black moms need each other, too. How surprised I was to find just how quickly I meshed with these mamas! It was like we'd been raising our children together for years. But it had only been weeks.

Months in, they became some of my very best friends. They knew me. They got me. They always knew what to say, and they embraced my quirks and soothed my insecurities. They adored my kids, they loved me, and I felt it. It felt like I had the sweetest thing that I never even knew I wanted.

Oh, how wise my precious daughter was and is. What a gift to be so wide open and perceptive. I'm thankful for her ability to discern what she needed and for her strength to stand up and demand it from a foggy-eyed mom.

So that's what happened. Simple and complicated at the same time. My daughter was broken and lonely and knew it. I was hurt and lonely and didn't know it. A straightforward plan was revealed to me, and it worked. My kids are happier than ever, and so am I.

But the million-dollar question has been "Why does being around other families of color feel so doggone good?" I'm not an expert, so I'm not attempting to give a scientific, peer-reviewed breakdown. I'm only sharing my two cents on why Black folks need each other. I can't speak for people of color everywhere, and I won't attempt to do so. These are my personal thoughts and observations, along with reflections shared with me by other families.

I know that some of what I'm writing will make people uncomfortable. Talking about this stuff can be awkward, but maybe that's why we need to talk about it all the more. I'm speaking from the perspective of educating white people, some well-meaning and others not, who have asked me why

I felt the need to start a Black group when I already had a good (white) group. But it may also be eye-opening for parents raising children of color who haven't actively pursued safe villages for their kids.

For the sake of this discussion, I'm going to focus on our experiences as a Black family, specifically. However, many of my points easily extend to other racial, cultural, and ethnic groups. Various people of color nod their heads knowingly when I talk about these issues because they experience much of the same in their own micro-communities. I've also seen a deep understanding of the need for safe villages across families and children living with mental health, physical, cognitive, or emotional disabilities.

As I share, I won't keep writing "many white people" and "many Black people." I'm just going to say, "white people" and "Black people," so let's agree up front that what I say isn't going to cover every member of those groups. Now we don't have to worry about getting sidetracked over the minutiae while missing the main point. So, [clearing my throat, wiping the sweat from my armpits] here are my thoughts on the necessity of cultural micro-communities:

People of color are bicultural. (Bicultural—having or combining the cultural attitudes and customs of two nations, peoples, or ethnic groups.) We, as Black people, have our own culture, and we're fluent in your culture as well. Controversially, we've assimilated, to varying degrees, and learned how to be more like white people, which makes you more comfortable being around some of us. But you don't know our culture. We have a way of doing things and a way of being that you aren't aware of, and I can barely explain it to you. It's so hard to put into words. We respond to various situations differently. We subconsciously learn and act upon an unwritten code of social behavior that differs from your acceptable behavior code in some instances. In short, when we're with you, sometimes there's a festering feeling of being a visitor in someone else's lovely home. At times, we just want to put our feet up on the couch, let our hair down, and relax.

People of color code-switch. (Code-switch—the practice of alternating between two or more languages or varieties of language in conversation.) This occurs often in bilingual conversations, but it also shows up within variations of the same language. For example, Black people have their own way of communicating beyond what you would call slang or "improper"

English. It's not wrong. It's just different from how you speak. It's characterized by pronunciations (phonology), syntactic patterns (grammar), and morphological features (inflections) that in many instances also occur in other varieties of English, and sometimes we want to use it. It's like your messy bun hairstyle. You know how to do your hair in other styles, but you like the messy bun, even if others think you look undone. When we're with you, we have to talk like you, or you'll be confused, uncomfortable, or judgmental. We can speak however we like with no fear of judgment when we're alone because we all know that we code-switch. I once heard a guy say that he wants a wife he can take to Waffle House or the White House because she's comfortable at both places. That's us. We can mix things up.

BIPOC adults relate differently to children. In our white group, the moms are very friendly to my children, but my kids don't have a relationship with them that extends beyond "You're the mother of my friend." There is kindness but also a sense of formality. I never saw this as a big deal because that's how I related to most of my friends' moms growing up, too. It seemed normal. But in our Black group, the mothers are surrogate mamas who reach out for warm embraces from my kids and serve as sounding boards for their wacky ideas and as recipients of their silly stunts. The relationship includes a heart-melting amount of emotional and physical intimacy that developed in a relatively short time. I can't explain how or why this is, but I suspect it could be cultural because it doesn't appear that the moms in my white group treat my children any differently than they treat each other's kiddos. On the other hand, I've noticed the same intimacy with some white mothers of biracial and adopted BIPOC children. So perhaps parenting a child of color changes people.

Black children behave differently at times. We have hawk-eyes on our children when we (Black moms) are with you (white moms). We feel the intense pressure of representing all Black families. If our kids legitimately misbehave, we think that you'll believe that all Black kids are "bad" or wild, and what you believe matters because, at times, we just want to be accepted.

When Black moms are alone with other Black moms, our children have more freedom to be themselves. Why? Because when children are let alone, they sometimes do little naughty things. We all know that children can and will misbehave at times. We quickly address the misbehavior and then return to our adult conversation without ever once wondering what the other moms are thinking about our little Black kids. That's when they're legitimately misbehaving.

Our children stand out in predominantly white environments, and they're often unfairly singled out for behavior exhibited by plenty of nearby white kids. We can tell that you disapprove because you look aghast, you look uncomfortable, you chastise our children, or you pull your "good" child away from our "bad" child's negative influence. There are also times when our children are not misbehaving, but you think they are, according to your lens. The most straightforward example I can give is volume. Yes, volume. As in how loud something is.

Our kids are often louder and more physically demonstrative than yours. And we're okay with that. They probably learned it from us. White homeschool parties are quiet-ish. Black homeschool parties are not. White homeschool playdates are quiet-ish. Black homeschool playdates are not. White conversations are often calm and quiet. Black conversations are often spirited and loud. Loud Black kids often make white people uncomfortable, and they are constantly telling our kids to "Shhhh! Be quiet," which makes our kids and us uncomfortable.

I had to explain it as being loud so you could understand what I mean, but in reality, we're not loud. That's our normal animated volume. But since many white people don't like it, it has become known as being "too loud" and is often connected to being wild or ignorant. But we're not wild, and we're certainly not ignorant. It's cultural.

Our kids move around a lot—when they're talking and when they're not. It's not ADHD (it could be, but that's not what I'm talking about here). It's not misbehavior. It's normal to us. We are demonstrative and expressive. That's also cultural.

So, being in a Black group is refreshing because our kids can just be kids. The room sounds different, the kids are moving differently, the adults are speaking differently, and the topics of conversation are different. Not always, but often.

We want to do Black stuff. Not occasionally or just in February, but frequently. As in, we do Black things with our kids a lot. And we're pretty sure that you and your kids don't want to do that much Black stuff. The same applies for Latino, Asian, and other families of color wanting to envelop their children in cultural enrichment.

I want to share one tiny example of why representation matters. We attended *The Nutcracker* by the Atlanta Ballet for two or three years with our white group. It was at the beautiful Fox Theatre in downtown Atlanta, it was so lovely, and my girls liked it. When we got in the car, my youngest daughter, Sasha, said, "That was so fun! I love watching those ballerinas!" I felt good about that, and I was pleased that she enjoyed the show.

Fast-forward to after I started Heritage Homeschoolers. Our group took the children to see *Urban Nutcracker*, a stunning performance by a small ballet company at a small community theater. The entire production featured Black ballet dancers. After the show, my girls excitedly climbed into the back seat, and Sasha exclaimed, "That was AMAZING! I want to be a ballerina!"

"I love watching those ballerinas" versus "I want to be a ballerina." Small word change. Critical difference. After watching a stage full of white ballerinas in an elegant theater, my sweet girl wanted to watch them again. After watching Black ballerinas on a little rinky-dink stage, my baby wanted to be a ballerina. And that's why representation matters.

Black moms search high and low for opportunities for their children to see Black people in all types of arenas. We'll drive an hour each way for a Black pediatrician (raising my hand). We'll pay $83 for a discontinued version of a Black Rapunzel Barbie or $56 for a Black GI Joe in a dapper uniform that we know will get trampled and tossed about (raising both hands). We spend hundreds and hundreds of dollars to create home libraries full of so many books with colorful characters that our kids would look at you sideways if you told them that Black books are hard to find. And the list goes on. Our kids hunger for Black stuff, and we'll do anything to provide it.

But we're pretty sure that you don't have that same hunger for providing Black experiences and things for your kids. Are your kids reading diverse books all year long in a book club? Are you going to try to attend every Black cultural performance you can find and afford? Do you teach your kids the role Black people played in every historical period? If not, why would you think my family wants to do all white stuff all the time?

Sure, many things are just neutral. We all enjoy the zoo, the aquarium, and the science museum. But we're not only looking for someone to join field trips or outings. We're also seeking holistic enrichment to help grow our children's minds and hearts in a healthy, truthful, supportive way.

And yes, my white group does do "Black" stuff. I put things on the calendar, and they come. They're good people who want their kids to know about Black history and culture. And they're my friends. So, it's not like my kids can never get that from a white group. However, I plan 100 percent of those activities, and I'm careful not to schedule too many, lest I be seen only as the "Black" mom. With Heritage, the more, the merrier. The families come to our group for the salve, and I don't have to hold back.

Wanting to be around BIPOC doesn't mean that we don't want to be around you. If that were true, I would've quit my white group the day I started the Black group. The two are not mutually exclusive. I can want to be around people of color and white people; I enjoy them both. I like to be around them together, though the opportunity rarely arises. I also don't mind being around white people by myself (I've done it my whole life), but sometimes I want to be around other Black people alone, without you.

One of my white friends told me that she felt that my Black group was an example of reverse racism. She said she would get in trouble if she started a white homeschooling group or a white mom's group. After blinking several times and considering how much I should say, given that I was standing in her kitchen, I calmly explained that there's no need for her to start a white group because she already has multiple white groups.

Almost everything everywhere in our local community is blindingly white. There's no shortage of white anything here. My friend does have white groups, but they don't have to write "white" on the website. They're white by default because they're full of white people doing things in a way that centers their experiences and preferences. The spaces exist with them in mind, and no one ever stops to wonder if or how they can be made more inclusive. Inclusivity isn't just about letting people of color in; it's about including them in the development and growth of thriving communities. Nobody wants to be an afterthought.

My friend said the difference was that she didn't say that Black people couldn't join her group. And therein lies the problem. I never said that white people couldn't join my group either. It's just not for them. They can get in where they fit in, just like I do with my kids. But their kids will be the only ones, and it may be awkward. And it may not fulfill them. And they may not like doing Black stuff and talking about Black things all the time. Just like we don't like doing white stuff and talking about white things all the time.

It's not lost on me that the people who get the most upset about my group spend nearly all their waking hours in white environments. And ironically, my Black group has more diversity (through marriage, adoption, and immigration) than you'll find in any local white group. I'd love to see the biggest complainers modeling cross-cultural togetherness instead of just attacking the attempts people are making to forge a way out of no way.

If you struggle with the idea of cultural micro-communities, I ask you to consider whether there are any instances in your life when you seek out groups where you feel you truly belong, where you feel you can be your most authentic self without the need to explain your preferences or motives. I encourage you to look inside yourself to consider how that sense of belonging and understanding makes you feel. Life is clunky, and the solutions we grasp on to as we try to navigate what the world throws our way aren't always elegant or ideal.

I've noticed that the handful of Americans I meet overseas often get together alone (as in, without any local people). In Bolivia, only Americans were invited to the little expat outings or shared meals, and they specifically stated that sometimes they just wanted to be with other Americans. They said it was so refreshing, and it filled them up. They looked for each other. They set up a Facebook group to help them find other Americans, and when they were together, they spoke English even though they were all perfectly fluent in Spanish. That sounds awfully familiar to me.

Do these Americans living abroad, sitting around eating imported American food, talking in English about American stuff, hate Bolivians? Are they guilty of racism? Does anyone even think to ask them that?

A couple of years ago, one of my friends said, "I'm going to sign my daughters up for ballet so they can be around some other girls. All the neighborhood kids are boys, and all their cousins are boys, too. The girls get along well with their male friends, but sometimes they just want to play baby dolls and be girly."

So, does my friend hate boys? Is she guilty of doing something awful in the name of providing experiences with other girls for her daughter? I don't think so. She observed that her daughters play differently and often have different interests than the boys in their environment. Her daughters miss the type of interaction they get with other little girls, so she's doing what she can to get them that interaction.

And what about my friend whose daughter attends a weekly playtime for children with disabilities? They come together with their families and just hang out without another agenda. My friend told me that her family needs that space because it gives her daughter time to socialize beyond the bounds of otherness. As my friend shared this, I immediately connected with that need and understood her perspective. And so did the people around us.

It seems normal that Americans living in other countries seek each other. No one calls that out as being a bad thing. It's normal for people to orchestrate playtime with other girls for their daughters, and no one bats an eye when my friends seek out safe spaces for their children with disabilities. I see how our community enthusiastically supports the local Jewish community center and honors Saturday morning Chinese heritage classes designed for Chinese children who don't receive cultural education in the local schools. So why have I been challenged and shamed for sharing that my children need interaction with other Black children? It makes you wonder, doesn't it?

We get a break from being politically correct. When we're with our Black group, we don't have to hold back, bite our tongues, or risk offending people. We don't have to endure overhearing hurtful conversations that may or may not be meant for our ears. We don't have to listen to clueless people make excuses for racist behavior. Politics rarely show up at the table.

There is absolutely a zero percent chance that any of the parents in the room have liked racist Facebook pages or racist political memes. None of them belong to Facebook groups of organizations known for hating or marginalizing people of color, even if the groups are hiding behind a curtain of professed religion. No one has Confederate flags on their homes, clothing, or vehicles, and no one wants their children around people who do.

No one cares who sits or stands for the anthem, but it would never even come up because no one sings the national anthem at our events. Not because we lack true patriotism (our group is full of veterans and active-duty military across every branch of the U.S. Armed Forces) but because it's irrelevant as we prioritize living out our country's values over idolizing a display for all to see. In the words of James Baldwin, "I love America more than any other country in the world, and, exactly for this reason, I insist on the right to criticize her perpetually."

Black moms are vigilant about finding affirming resources. We share affirming resources and give a heads-up (or a primal scream) when we encounter materials to be avoided. And you haven't seen anything until you see some Black moms hand-paint or recolor pictures, books, dolls, and other items with brown paint, marker, or digital design programs. We may love the material or can't find anything better, but we refuse to present only images of white people in all our children's studies and playtime. So, the networking among Black parents is vital and full of grassroots information sharing that we can't find elsewhere.

Black women relate differently to other Black women. There are shared experiences that are part of being Black in America, and the other Black moms in our group understand them without me having to explain. They know that I cringe a little every time a white woman coos at my beautiful Black little boys because I wonder whether she'll still find them sweet and attractive when they're fifteen or twenty-two or thirty-five. I don't have to tell her how I feel or how much I want those feelings to go away because she feels it, too. She already knows.

I don't have to tell her that I woke up three hours early to unbraid, wash, condition, detangle, and re-braid my daughter's hair. She can look at her hair and see that for herself. She inherently knows to go out of her way to tell my girls that their hair is beautiful and special. And she knows that I'll do the same with her girls.

She knows that it's taking everything inside of me to bite my tongue and plaster a smile on my face when my daughter tells me that she wants to be on the swim team, where they'll be in the chlorinated pool five mornings a week for six weeks. She knows that I'm sick about the prospect of trying to keep my daughter's hair healthy during this time, but there's no way in the world that I'd ever tell my daughter that she can't do something because of her hair. We grew up in that era, and we're not doing that to our girls, but she still gets that it's hard for me.

She knows that I'm not going to eat or feed my kids before coming to an event at her house because she knows that I know that she'll have a full spread of food, more than we could or would ever eat, and it will be delicious. Good food is a soothing love language in the Black community, and it communicates much more than physical satisfaction. We don't have to tell each other because we already know.

I'm not sure, but maybe it's because of these little things, and many others like them, that the timeline for relational transparency and intimacy between Black women is so much shorter. It's like there's an unspoken sisterhood that forms from thin air.

In *More Than Enough: Claiming Space for Who You Are (No Matter What They Say)*, Elaine Welteroth describes being subjected to a humiliating racist remark while at a party with a group of white friends and a Black friend named Ashley. She writes, "I would have to tell my friends about the incident later and explain to them what that felt like. This is part of the uncomfortable responsibility that comes along with being the only one, the token Black friend. But thankfully this time, I *wasn't* the only one. 'Let's get out of here,' Ashley said, linking her arm in mine. When we locked eyes, I knew there was nothing to explain to her. She understood implicitly the impact of that moment, of that word. Having a Black friend there—even one I had just met—was like having a safety net to catch me, someone who could absorb that pain with me. This unspoken sisterhood was a completely new dynamic for me."[2]

I have a lot of close friendships with white women. This is such a cliché, but some of my best friends are white. I'm not saying that white and Black women can't develop close friendships because that's simply not at all true. What I'm saying is that it usually takes longer. In my experience, Black moms can get extremely close so quickly that it makes your head spin. It reminds me of a meme I once saw that said, "Friendship isn't about who you've known the longest. It's about who walked into your life, said, 'I'm here for you,' and proved it." Three months after starting our Black homeschool group, I felt closer to some of the moms there than I did with any of the moms in my white group after several years of participation. I never saw that coming.

THE CASE FOR SAFE VILLAGES

When I first began considering the value of spending time with people who share the same racial identity, I kept everything to myself because I knew that some would find Black people intentionally seeking each other out and gathering alone to be offensive. Most white people spend tons of time alone with other white people, but for some reason, there is a stigma associated with Black people doing the same. Strangely, it leaves a distaste in the mouths of many, and I was afraid of their unmerited harsh criticism. I also feared being seen as a hypocrite, because I'm known for building bridges. I bring people together, and I've been doing it my whole life.

Like so many others, I'm adept at operating with ease in many environments. I can get down with white people who have only seen Black people on TV (though, admittedly, it's not my preference) and Black people who have never had a real conversation with a white person. I have always been *the* Black girl in the room in many white arenas, and I easily make genuine and loving friendships with white people. I've also always been very aware of being Black, and since my HBCU experience, I'm really comfortable and beautifully at home in a sea of Blackness.

Despite my desire to maintain and build cross-racial relationships, I still get excited when I meet Black homeschoolers, and our group continues to grow. Most of the growth has been via word of mouth because I dare not advertise in traditional spaces. I've watched as others have tried, and it never goes well. I recently witnessed a tense exchange on social media after a Black mom posted that she was looking to meet other Black home-schoolers for her kiddos. Someone shared the post with me because I've been very vocal about how challenging it can be to publicly state that my kids need to be around other Black people.

After the original online inquiry, a white mom responded, "Why does the color of skin matter? This seems like a good example of trying to divide people by ethnicity. Could you imagine the fallout if I was to post a post looking for only white homeschoolers?! . . . I am just so sick of people trying to keep the country divided . . . and make sure people recognize their skin tone instead of who they are. We will never be a UNITED States of America as long as people make post [*sic*] like this. . . ." A white ally tried to explain why the Black mom would need Black community for her children, but the angry mom wouldn't hear of it.

The highly offended white mom failed to offer any solution to the problem faced by children of color who never see themselves reflected in the world around them. She was quick to cast judgment as her white children live their entire lives amid a white community. Her children are blinded by the mirrors reflecting on them every time they step foot out of the house. Yet, she felt comfortable telling someone whose daily experiences look nothing like hers how to navigate life. This type of response demonstrates what I often see when people of color try to find safe villages for their children.

The mom whose Black children were surrounded by white-centered everything was shamed for wanting to find some Black friends for her kids so they could experience the security and peace that comes from not having to think about being different for a few hours a week. While considering the lack of empathy in the white woman's chastisement, I remembered these words from Eugene Cho: "Be careful not to dehumanize those you disagree with. In our self-righteousness, we can become the very things we criticize in others."[3]

This indignant woman basically suggested that the Black mom should forget about her children's well-being, that she should ignore the fact that their "invisible" skin color ensures that they're hated by some and ignored by many and that the pain of being othered is so intense that at times it feels like a crushing weight resulting in emotional atrophy. I know from experience that a mother's love cannot allow her to witness her child in pain and coolly tell her to "hush up and blend in."

In Tembi Locke's memoir, she describes the day her little girl told her that she didn't want to be the only brown girl. Locke writes, "I knew what she meant; being different, being the only one, standing out because of skin color was hard. I suspected it made her feel 'other' or, worse yet, less than. She certainly wouldn't be the first black or brown girl who at some point hadn't wanted to move through the world in a different packaging. Hell, untold numbers of books have been written and award-winning documentaries made delving into the psychological complexities surrounding identity and race for little black girls in predominantly white environments. . . . I knew I had to triage any psychological damage that might be festering. I knew I had to do what black mothers have been doing for centuries: remind my daughter that she is valuable and beautiful in a world that often says otherwise."[4]

The Black mom who posted on social media, a mom with whom I desperately identify, was doing the best she could to find some way to remind her children that they are valuable and beautiful. Rather than empathize with what it must feel like to be in her shoes, the angry mom essentially encouraged her to tell her children to suck up their Blackness, tuck it away, keep their mouths shut, become grayish while blending into the world of white people. Because then the racial issues in our country would be solved by Black people being quiet and alone. And ironically, she said all of this in the name of God.

So yes, I was scared to admit that I could've been that mom, posting on a local homeschooling Facebook page, hoping to find someone Black with whom to sit and "be." I was afraid that someone, or lots of "someones," would think that by creating a safe space for Black children to exhale, I was effectively turning my back on our duty to love without racial bounds.

The misguided mom from the Facebook post thinks reconciliation happens when we turn a blind eye to reality, when some of us (namely people of color) stop trying to meet our needs and start being more like her. Colorblind. But reconciling, restoring friendship or harmony, requires doing. And she is not *doing* anything except breeding resentment. Everyone has a role to play in forging bonds across racial lines. The work looks different depending on the person, but one responsibility is imperative for all: building relationships.

I will always be involved in *ongoing, messy, authentic, inefficient, unprofessional, slow, loving* relationships.[5] These relationships are complex and grace-filled. They require humility and patience. They also need the one commodity that so many of us hold in short supply: time. There's no getting around the fact that it takes time to be intentional. It takes time to develop friendships. It takes time to know and be known. And without that, there is no kinship.

The colorblind mom, and others like her, have rarely taken any time out of their lives to be in genuine relationships with Black people. How do I know? Because if she were in deep fellowship with Black friends, she would intimately understand the fallacy of her argument. She would see that *she* is part of the problem. That her colorblind proselytizing is creating yet another generation of people who just don't get it.

In the article "What White Children Need to Know About Race," the authors suggest that we teach white children to honor and respect racial affinity spaces for people of color. Specifically, the authors write, "Many schools now recognize the efficacy of creating racial affinity spaces for students of color, particularly with regard to countering the effects of stereotype threat and creating a sense of safety and camaraderie within predominantly white spaces. Learning to accept that such spaces can be important resources for peers of color, without feeling threatened or excluded from those dynamics, can be an important step for white students who want to participate in the construction of a healthy multiracial community. Racially competent white students would understand such a gathering of students of color as ultimately supportive of interracial relationships, rather than in opposition to them."[6]

My family shares a precious commodity in our relationships with white people: our time. We learn from them, and we share our truth. We explain how we're different, but we also show them (many for the first time) how similar we all are. Sometimes the relationships flow naturally. They're fluid and easy. Fun and carefree. But at other times, it feels like work, and I get tired. My children get tired.

Being in a Black community gives us a break from being Black representatives. A break from teaching, showing, explaining, and ignoring. A break from having to be brave and from being othered or misunderstood. It gives us a chance to kick back and just be plain old Johnstons.

I know that race does not biologically exist, that we are all part of the same human family and have a responsibility to grow together. Our Black homeschool group isn't a weapon against cross-racial friendships or relational restoration. Nor is it a plea for separatism. It's simply a survival mechanism.

Building bridges can be exhausting, frustrating, and discouraging. And when my love tank is empty, and my resolve weakens, I want and need to be around Black people. That's how I rest. That's how I refuel so I can keep going. My village holds space for me and keeps me from giving up.

If I need this support as an adult, how can I ignore my children's longing for safe villages? Communing with others who share the same racial identity does not negate any responsibility or opportunity people of color have to live well with others. In *Nepantla Familias: An Anthology of Mexican-American Literature on Families in between Worlds,* Sergio Troncoso writes, "The either/or proposition that forces you to choose between your community and, say, your country has never been true. The very skills we learn to cross borders within ourselves help us to cross borders toward others outside our community."[7] My children need to be with other Black people. At the same time, we're living out authentic relationships that demonstrate genuine love and reciprocal sacrifice for people who are different than us. We can have both in abundance.

THE CASE FOR INCLUSIVE COMMUNITY

Some people have called the controlled environment of home education a "bubble." They mean this in a derogatory way, referencing the lack of freedom and exposure they assume homeschooled children are forced to endure. However, I choose to reframe that narrow thinking by celebrating home as a place for safe growth and tender loving care. And my crew of family friends whose children attend school have created similar atmospheres in their homes. But whether schooled or homeschooled, children need the time and space to interact with their broader communities.

Our children need to intermingle with diverse people and experience cross-cultural learning as a natural part of childhood. Intentionally seek opportunities for your children to learn from teachers, coaches, guides, and instructors of color as you sign them up for extracurricular community activities. Look for environments where your child can connect with racially, ethnically, and socioeconomically varied people, as well as people who may be different in other ways.

I often see white parents attempt to do this by taking their children to volunteer in underserved or underprivileged Black and Brown communities. Helping others is a nice thing to do. Still, kids also need plenty of diverse peer-based or reciprocal socialization where they're not "saving" people of color. Through their interactions and observations of the world around them, they should naturally assimilate the idea that white people and people of color have varying degrees of financial stability, education, and living situations. And they all have intersecting identities and can show up in myriad ways depending on the environment or even the day.

Another misstep I see is parents attempting to insert themselves in some of the few intentional safe villages that people of color have created or maintained. In most cases, people of color welcome others into the fold, but sometimes they've carved out a unique space and time to gather alone as they relax and refuel. Recognizing the difference between these scenarios takes time and requires nuanced thinking, but being in close relationship with people of color provides opportunities for discussing these things. Tread lightly and spend time asking questions and gaining understanding before signing up or jumping into a racial affinity space. And when all else fails, and you're in doubt, just ask. And be supportive and at peace regardless of the answer.

Organized enrichment and extracurriculars also provide opportunities for children to move beyond stereotypical gender-based interests. Author bell hooks writes, "Racism has always been a divisive force separating Black men and White men, and sexism has been a force that unites the two groups."[8] Raise your children to resist societal norms that create hostility between the sexes.

Encourage your daughter to try a sport she'd enjoy but may assume is reserved only for boys, or sign your son up for cooking classes if he likes preparing meals for the family. Look for a male dance instructor or a female scientist to guide your children as they explore their passions. Consider starting a mixed-gender book club where the children read and discuss diverse books with all sorts of protagonists, or recruit dads to volunteer for classroom activities or lead homeschool co-op events while moms pitch at T-ball practice.

Some communities offer more opportunities for expanding our children's worlds in this way than others, but even if your geography makes these regular interactions more challenging, remain tenacious and get creative. Consider teaming up with diverse like-minded families to start inclusive groups within your area if none exist today. Start by picking a shared interest, and plan meetups around that topic (e.g., books, hiking, art, board games). Remain committed to having diverse leadership that can help ensure that the group truly has a multiethnic flavor from the very beginning and is seen as a safe and inspiring space for all.

Online communities are not substitutes for in-person relationships, but if your child's local opportunities are minimal, you can enhance their extracurricular learning experiences with diverse instructors and students in online classes from websites like Outschool. And some families who find themselves without frequent access to varied people and experiences have even chosen to relocate to make these opportunities more readily available for their children. Moving may seem like a radical response to social segregation to some and is certainly not possible for all, but I've never met a family who regretted the decision.

As you think about extracurricular offerings in your community, consider each one an opportunity for your child to make diverse connections. If you live in a homogenous area and sign them up for all the things your neighbors do at the same places where your neighbors do them, you may be setting your children up for a very vanilla existence. I'm the first to admit that researching diverse environments, teachers, instructors, and classes can be time-consuming. Sometimes I get annoyed at the need to exert so much effort for such a seemingly simple thing, but it's worth it every time.

Give your family's social and community interactions an honest look. If you find that you've somehow ended up in a place where everyone your kids have an opportunity to do life with looks just like them or never looks like them (equally unhealthy scenarios), consider making some changes. The possibilities are endless and are entirely dependent on each family's circumstances, but we owe it to our children to try our very best to make it happen.

AVOIDING TOKEN FRIENDSHIPS

Not too long ago, someone invited my kids on a hike with a group of local nature-loving families. Excited about the possibility of building more friendships with people who like to hang in the woods as much as we do, I jumped at the opportunity. All was going well until we stopped to rest for lunch and one of the moms said, "I'm glad that your family came out today because we've really been wanting more Black people to come."

Ouch.

I wasn't mad at the woman for saying what she said. We've even been hiking with them a couple of times since then because being offended is a choice, and forging cross-racial relationships requires a certain amount of grit coupled with a lot of forgiveness. Everyone doesn't show up the way we want them to, and I try to work with people until they've proven themselves malicious or resistant to demonstrating empathy and kindness. It doesn't always work out because some people aren't reachable, but I do try.

Her admission stung, though, mainly because it's an issue that I encounter time and again from well-meaning white people who don't understand that nobody wants to be a token friend. Black people don't enjoy serving as props so people can say, "Hey, look, everybody. I've got Black friends!" And the same applies to anyone else who can garner you brownie points if the right people witness your association. If you're reaching out to Black people expressly to "enrich" your child's worldview, rather than showing interest in a genuine friendship, just pop some popcorn, order a pizza, and watch a diverse movie instead.

So what should the hiking mama have said? How about, "Amber, I'm so glad that you and your kiddos were able to make it today. I really enjoy having you here." The end. That makes me feel like she sees me, Amber, as a multifaceted person. Not me, a random Black woman with brown-skinned kids to check one of her boxes. This doesn't mean that I wanted her to be colorblind. I'm glad that she saw me as a Black woman because that's what I am. It's more about my "other" status becoming why she wanted me in her space.

I've discussed this with some of my close white friends over the years (we literally talk about everything!), and they've shared that white people sometimes feel stuck. In some cases, they're learning that they need to expand their worlds, but they don't know how to do so. They don't regularly encounter people of color, so the attempts often feel forced or artificial as they try to manufacture opportunities or awkwardly jump at the infrequent prospects when paths do cross. That's real, and I get it. It's part of why I've said from the beginning that this work is not easy. Each person you encounter is different and will respond to your friendship efforts in their own way.

Others become angry and defensive at any mention of multiculturalism or inclusivity because they feel excluded. They think they're being blamed for sins of the past or even other white people's current behavior. Some white people feel ashamed or embarrassed about the past (and sometimes the present), or they're hypersensitive to saying or doing the wrong thing.

I've also encountered plenty of BIPOC who have no interest whatsoever in forming friendships with white people. Their reasons vary, but some of the things I've heard repeatedly are:

"I spend all day at work with them, so when I'm off work, I don't want to deal with all that comes with being around white folks."

"I've tried being in white environments, and it never goes well. I'll pass."

"White people are fake. They want to be my friend as long as I act white, but as soon as I say something indicative of my experience as a person of color, they clam up or pull back."

"I'm sick of white people parading around their racism while passing it off as patriotism. I don't trust them."

"I just want to be myself. I'm not in the mood to navigate 'white' world today."

I understand the sentiments underlying these comments, some of which are rooted in distrust or facades covering up years of pain. People of color who feel this way about white people have left the table, and they're not going to believe that they can come back until they see evidence of being understood and valued. So those people are not your best bets for friendship peeps right now. They're wedged into vulnerable, indifferent, or sometimes even angry places. No judgment here. It's just that they're not the people you should be inviting to integrate your all-white social scene. In fact, you really shouldn't be expecting *any* people of color to just join you in what you're doing the way you're doing it.

Instead, we all should be seeking opportunities to forge mutual relationships rooted in trust. Exactly how those friendships happen is as much of an art as a science. I thought through how my best cross-racial kinships have been birthed, and here are some of the qualities that came up again and again:

1. **BOTH PARTIES ARE OPEN TO THE IDEA OF DEEP CROSS-RACIAL CON-NECTION.** Neither of us was actively hunting for it, but we both live with hearts open to the possibility. So when we crossed paths and found that we had similar interests, it felt natural to pursue those interests together (in person) or discuss and share about them (online). Over time, those more surface-level encounters led to us intentionally making space for one another. There is much value in extending kindness to people who don't return the favor, and sometimes trust has to be earned, but when you think of digging deeply into friendship, consider investing in people who seem open to having you as a friend.

2. **OUR CONVERSATIONS ARE WIDE OPEN.** One of the first things that shuts me down in a potential cross-racial friendship is someone who constantly changes subjects or acts super uncomfortable whenever I talk about being Black. I am Black. How can we be friends if you don't want to see me? It's like you're asking me to leave my right arm at home when I meet you for tea. My close white friends are interested in all of who I am. And I feel the same about them.

3. **WE'RE STICKY.** This means that we stick around and keep digging in. Life, work, family, and a slew of obligations offer every reason for slacking off on friendships. But it feels like there's an unspoken understanding with my closest white friends that what we're engaging in is more significant than ourselves, and we're committed to seeing it through. It's not that the time we spend together is unpleasant, mind you, but busyness tries to disrupt our good intentions. Does this mean that you should prioritize cross-cultural friendships over others? Not at all. I'm only saying that these friendships are often harder to launch, and we should take care to fan the flames lest they blow into the wind.

4. **WE WORK ON DEVELOPING MUTUAL CULTURAL CONSCIOUSNESS.** Sometimes my white friends just get me. They've either been around many people of color, read and listened extensively, or can intuitively discern the intricacies of cross-racial kinship. But at other times, I've had to teach some of them that our friendship can't have a "white is

the default" vibe to it. I may do this by letting them know that I would appreciate them not always buying white books, dolls, and action figures for my kids. Reminding them that they can't chicken out on coming to an all-Black gathering at my house because I often go to all-white gatherings at theirs, and they've never considered how that might make me feel. Or reminding them that a fabulous girls' night out in my book might be snagging tickets to the stage performance of *The Bluest Eye* at a small community theater, followed by dessert at a restaurant where they'll be the only white person, and I need them to be okay with that. I also need full acceptance of the idea that we may spend time together without me exhibiting any signs of what they may consider Blackness.

But this cultural consciousness is not one-sided. People of color tend to understand a ton about white culture, so the learning curve is not as steep; however, there is nuance among white people that often goes unacknowledged. Even though white people are often seen as plain or "regular" while everyone else is ethnic (something I think is at the root of many of our racial issues), white people *do* have cultural markers. When I spend time with my white friends, I make room for them to be more than "just white." I listen to their family stories and history, show interest in their recipes and viewpoints, and remain alert for regional differences that may call forth certain behaviors or preferences. We learn to absorb ourselves in each other's worlds. Not as bystanders, but as active participants willing to put ourselves out there and show up for someone we care about and their community.

5.   **WE FORGIVE ONE ANOTHER.** If you spend enough time around someone with whom you're willing to be vulnerable, you'll inevitably put your foot in your mouth. Usually out of ignorance or carelessness, but sometimes out of malice you didn't even know you were harboring. Too often, I see people (white people and people of color) walk away from potential friendships because they're offended. And yes, if someone repeatedly or regularly shows a lack of regard for your emotional health, you should love them from afar. But if a person makes a mistake that isn't in line with their character, it's quite possible that calling them in with truth is a more radically loving act than walking away.

My friends and I don't pretend to be okay when we hurt each other. We talk about it, apologize, change, and grow. Sometimes we even share a good cry over it. But when the tissue box is empty and the wounds are licked, the friendship remains. And although I'd never sign up to hurt or be hurt, I can say that my cross-racial relationships are typically stronger after being forged in fire.

6.   WE LISTEN TO EACH OTHER CAREFULLY AND PUT WHAT WE LEARN INTO ACTION. This book is the result of me listening to what my friends need. All my beautiful, colorful friends, including the white ones. I've heard them when they've shared their insecurities and apprehensions. I've listened to them cry and get angry. I've helped pick up the pieces of their shattered dreams. And I've seen their hearts break when my heart breaks. I don't always agree with my white friends, but I don't always agree with my Black and Brown friends either. My Instagram friend Charaia Callabrass created one of my favorite T-shirts. It says, "Love your neighbor more than your opinion." That's what it takes if you're going to integrate your friend circle.

I hope one idea you take away from this book is that forging friendships across racial lines isn't too wildly different than building connections within your ethnic community. But it often requires more intention and a higher level of commitment. Broken aspects of our communities and the visible scars of hate can stress the cords of cross-racial friendships. And voluntary social segregation is a massive roadblock for families to overcome. It's something that researchers are still trying to grasp, and their findings are compelling.

Social segregation happens when people of varying socioeconomic groups in a city have little opportunity to be exposed to people different than them. The MIT Media Lab uses geospatial data collected from cell phones to measure social segregation in cities across the United States, and they look at how much individual citizens would need to change their behavior to make their patterns of exposure more integrated. Their research shows that small changes in the amount of time people spend in different categories of places—changes as low as 2 to 5 percent—can reduce their social segregation by half.[9] The idea that slight intentional choices can revolutionize relationships and communities is surprising and gives me so much hope. But in the meantime, we have to name, claim, and prioritize what we know is right.

For that to be done effectively, without launching a "token friend" campaign, the desire to connect with specific, individual people must be genuine. We need to model this authenticity for our children and give them early and frequent opportunities to practice it for themselves. The hope is that it will become second nature for our kids. Not just when they're little and willing to play in the sandbox with anyone, but for the long haul. For the times when standing up may mean standing out.

EARNESTLY SEEKING CROSS-CULTURAL KINSHIP

Children, white children especially, need to be consistently involved in diverse environments that promote cross-racial connections and friendships. These relationships help them learn how others see the world and normalize peer interactions with people who look or live differently. In fact, all kids benefit from opportunities to actively participate in inclusive communities where they can practice socializing with adults and kids from other backgrounds.

Building authentic relationships across racial, ethnic, and cultural lines requires self-awareness, humility, and a willingness to sit with the tension that often accompanies the melding of different viewpoints or even competing aims. Once children feel secure in their heritage and culture, they develop an understanding that everyone they encounter has a story as unique as their own. It should be heard, respected, and celebrated.

Separation and alienation are not paths to belonging, even if the separatists feel dandy about themselves. The goal is that our children feel intimately known and seen *so that* they can build genuine relationships with others when possible and stand in solidarity with those who are different even when friendships aren't forged. We're here to create a culturally conscious, inclusive, and colorful family culture where the celebration of heritage, diversity, togetherness, and multicultural ideals (those that include both people of color and white people together) emanate from our homes.

Our families can demonstrate committed engagement within our communities and around the globe with people who are easy to love, as well as those we may never fully understand. Our children's lives will be forever changed when we lead by example and invest in our families, homes, and communities. This change won't occur because of a rigid political stance or a controversial hashtag. It will be ushered in by people who love their children well and show them a better way.

Outside of our homes, organizations have formed to tackle the cross-racial relationship divide in various spaces from both sacred and secular perspectives. In her book *Be the Bridge: Pursuing God's Heart for Racial Reconciliation,* author Latasha Morrison says, "In the love of the family of God, we must become color brave, color caring, color honoring, and not color blind. We have to recognize the image of God in one another. We have to love despite, and even because of, our differences."[10]

And in her secular Theory of Enchantment framework, diversity and resilience training entrepreneur Chloé Valdary shares these three guiding principles:

1. Treat people like human beings, not political abstractions.

2. Criticize to uplift and empower, never to tear down, never to destroy.

3. Root everything you do in love and compassion.[11]

No matter how you approach the sensitive topic of relationships across ethnic and racial lines, many reasonable and truly committed people agree that we must include love in the mix. Lest you write me off as a hippie mama intent on giving a trite solution to a complicated problem, let me explain.

Ancient Greeks studied love and gave each type its own name. Philia is the type of love shared between close friends and family members who have a foundation of trust, respect, and shared values. Eros is a romantic love that doesn't come into play here. But agape love, which flows without any expectations of receiving anything in return, is the type of love that I believe both Morrison and Valdary are holding up. Agape gives us purpose beyond ourselves, and it directs our actions for the good of humankind instead of our own kind.

Can agape love be taught within our homes and spread throughout the world? I don't know. Perhaps it's unreasonable, but we must try. In this, as in many things, I can relate to the thoughts of Toni Morrison. In her book *The Source of Self-Regard,* she states, "Our past is bleak. Our future dim. But I am not reasonable. A reasonable man adjusts to his environment. An unreasonable man does not. All progress, therefore, depends on the unreasonable man. I prefer not to adjust to my environment. I refuse the prison of 'I' and choose the open spaces of 'we.'"[12]

If we want our children not just to accept but to actively embrace and pursue authentic and healthy cross-racial relationships, our families must choose "we." It's indeed an uphill battle, and at times it hardly seems worth fighting, but what war would we not wage on behalf of our children? Lives have been given for far less than the pursuit of universal brotherhood. To align our aims with agape love seems saner than giving up.

I want my children to take the time to dream. I want them to imagine how things could be and move through the world making choices that give life to the cause of togetherness and kinship rather than rob it. And truth be told, I want the same for all children, including yours. It's not too late for us big kids, mind you, but childhood is ripe for dreaming, and our homes are sanctuaries in which to seed dreams of agape love.

13

SOW, REAP, AND HARVEST

Launching Socially Conscious Changemakers

> If you have come here to help me, you're wasting your time. If you
> have come because your liberation is bound up with mine, then let
> us work together.
>
> —Lilla Watson, Aboriginal elder, activist, and educator

BE COLORBLIND. ACCEPT OTHERS. TOLERATE DIFFERENCES.
These strategies were once touted as politically correct ways to deal with
people of color, but the mindset of socially and culturally conscious parents
is rapidly progressing. Today's intentional parents want to raise children
who see color, embrace others, and celebrate differences among a sea of
similarities. Not as strategies to "deal" with people but as natural outflows
of empathy and genuine interest.

Parents have the unique privilege of using our homes as springboards to
launch our children into the world as changemakers and social leaders who
seek opportunities for solidarity, expansion, and progress. We lay a foundation for generational work by making the home a place for our children to
be seen, heard, and valued. As the saying goes, "We are planting seeds for
trees under whose shade we will not sit." This mission is our legacy.

A heart-centered parenting approach that's neither permissive nor oppressive offers children space to safely explore the world with curiosity and
confidence. Under our wings, our kids can gain years of practice reaching

out toward others and being enveloped in return, making solidarity and connectedness second nature. In our care, our most beloved little people can cultivate a thirst for inclusive community.

If we're honest, we must admit to ourselves and our children that demonstrating a deep, abiding love for our sisters and brothers around the world and right next door is no easy feat. The body of work spread before us is vast, and some parts are murky and impenetrable. But if we remain steadfast and diligent, our kids will be emancipated into the world feeling tethered to people who experience life differently, in more ways than we know.

There are many examples of people making big splashes and lots of noise about diversity, equity, inclusion, social justice, anti-racism, and the like in today's world. This kind of disruptive clanging is worthy and necessary because it often leads to positive change. But the people making the most noise aren't always the ones making the most significant difference. Screaming from the rooftops, telling everyone else what to do while making no attempts to live out what we preach breeds resentment as others look at our hypocrisy. Our family's hypocrisy. Our nation's hypocrisy.

As Malcolm X once said, "We can't teach what we don't know, and we can't lead where we can't go." We must roll up our sleeves and lead our children as socially conscious adults. We need to model what we expect from them by unlearning normalized bias and intentionally disrupting the ways society trains us to overlook injustice. It's our job to call out and challenge the status quo. Our kids need to hear us talk about important issues and take a stance on what's right as we direct their attention toward other people's experiences.

Leading well will require some heavy lifting on your children's behalf. Make socially conscious living part of your family's lifestyle. It should be part of who you are and what you stand for. Give your kids opportunities to be in diverse spaces, and explain that people are more complex and dynamic than it may appear at first glance. We can't label or sideline anyone based on the few facts we think we know about them.

Let your children know that it's not acceptable to think less of people who have different experiences. There are countless underlying reasons for disparities of all sorts. Teach your kids that everyone doesn't start from the same place and, importantly, your children have the power to help change those glaring inequalities. Explain disadvantages that people have simply because of how they look or where they live, and how sometimes systems operate for the advantage of some and the detriment of others, whether it's intentional or not.

Recognize the multifaceted nature of people's identities as you interact with them. Acknowledge that numerous viewpoints need to be honored and understood on every matter, major or minor, because each person experiences various freedoms and limitations differently based on their identities. A wealthy white woman with a physical disability and a poor white woman with that same disability will have different experiences navigating similar institutional and social challenges. Likewise, a young white male blaring loud music in his vehicle and a young Black male doing the same will have varied experiences, demonstrating how race impacts the level of ease or difficulty with which they'll each move through the world.

Help your children challenge long-held assumptions and beliefs. Normalize inclusivity by pointing out that fictional characters don't always have to be white, and the color peach is not synonymous with skin color because there is no default skin color. Make sure they understand that there are no bounds to the creativity, inspiration, and value of *any* group of people in this entire world. Expand your children's concept of beauty beyond the bounds of Eurocentric ideals. Dark skin and big curly hair that grows out more than down are gorgeous. Racially ambiguous people are not exotic and don't want to be asked, "What are you?"

Put your kids in front of influencers from all walks of life, letting them see that there's an amazingly diverse gamut of great thinkers and doers. And while you're at it, make sure your children understand that the world is much bigger than home, wherever that may be, and that most of the world looks and lives differently than they do.

Teach your kids that the words they use to describe people should come from the people themselves, and those descriptors are fluid. Acceptable and desirable adjectives for different people groups change over time. Sometimes they stick around for generations, and at other times words become passé before we even get the chance to use them. By the time this book is published, some of the terms I've used to describe various people may be outdated, despite how careful I was to aim for respectful language. What makes all the word changes even more complex is that multiple people within the same group sometimes prefer to be described differently. There's no simple solution for complex issues.

Words hold tremendous power, so keeping up with people's preferred vocabulary for describing themselves is part of socially conscious living. White people have been called white for as long as any of us can remember. But words used to describe people of color and oppressed or marginalized groups will likely continue to change for as long as stigma is attached to being Black, Brown, disabled, gay, or anything else. Learning to use words carefully and understanding that preferred language can change is part of training our children to navigate diverse spaces confidently and with compassion.

Gently but firmly correct your kids when they make prejudiced assumptions and ignorant conclusions. This requires you to recognize these things yourself, so you must become a lifelong learner. Read books, blogs, social media posts, news stories, and articles. Listen to podcasts, watch videos, and lean into the stories of people in your community and beyond. Build friendships with people who look, live, and experience life differently. Educate yourself on the issues experienced by predominantly unheard, underserved, and marginalized people and commit to an ongoing pursuit of growth and action. And bring your children along for the ride. Learning ahead of your children is ideal because you can guide them more easily when you're informed, but sometimes that's not possible. If today is your first day of linking arms in a quest for liberation for all, then you and your kids will get to experience this transformative work together.

Be sure that you're here to appreciate and center people of color and other overlooked groups, not to gawk at them or check a box. People can make assumptions based on your words and deeds, but only you know your heart. If you're patting yourself on the back because you volunteered at a soup kitchen, you'll need to examine what it would mean for you to help without getting recognition. The idea is not to pity people or walk around othering them. Instead, roll up your sleeves and help while appreciating the full breadth and depth of our diverse world.

Some people say that this work can wait. That change will eventually come naturally. They're content to sit on the sidelines because there's no point getting messy when time will heal all wounds. But this is not the way of the brave. Change is ushered in on the backs of people who give selflessly to the cause. Sitting in silent indifference while others do the work that you expect your kids and grandkids to benefit from is an expression of contempt for everyone who can't comfortably just wait things out.

And getting lost in the busywork of inviting folks to the table without pulling up a chair, breaking bread, and joining in the exchange isn't hospitable. It's a cop-out. This isn't about grand displays of performative action or seeking accolades over some good deed. And it's certainly not a public exercise to prove how "woke" or "progressive" you are. This work isn't even about you. Or me. It's for the collective, the greater good.

ALLIES, ACCOMPLICES, AND HARD WORK

Being an ally or accomplice is about standing in solidarity with people affected by disturbing, deeply seated societal norms. Allies commit to working through their discomfort, listening, and learning from their mistakes. They consistently stand alongside people of color and other underserved or marginalized groups, using their powerful voices and positions to positively impact the cause.

Accomplices deepen the commitment of allyship by intentionally disrupting the status quo by effecting real change through advocacy. They directly challenge inequity by blocking or impeding prejudiced, racist, and discriminatory people, policies, and structures. Accomplices name and disrupt injustice, even when doing so impacts their personal comfort, and they don't operate out of guilt or shame. They act and do the work because they believe in a world built on cooperation, compassion, and community. Working alongside BIPOC, accomplices actively listen with respect while understanding that oppression appears in many forms and that beliefs and priorities vary across and within communities.

Performative allyship is for the loud and proud. These people profess solidarity and claim allegiance to historically underserved groups to gain brownie points or avoid scrutiny. They don't do anything that explicitly challenges the pillars of injustice held up in our country or elsewhere in the world, but they say just enough to get a public pass. When performative allies lack an audience, the facade fades because their hearts aren't in it.

This is not to say that true allyship is undesirable—quite the opposite.

Allies and accomplices are not a part of the groups they wish to support, but their social advantages afford them unique opportunities to help. They understand that these advantages don't indicate a life free of hardship. It doesn't mean that they haven't worked hard to get where they are or that anyone handed them a free ride. It only means that there are things they'll never have to experience simply because of who they are. They will have other challenges, and some of them may be pervasive and devastating. Still, they won't be the *same* challenges experienced by people who lack one particular advantage. And that advantage is often, but not always, "white" skin.

If the idea of white people having privileges because of their skin color rubs you the wrong way, let me assure you that we *all* have privilege of some sort or another. I learned this quickly through my world travels. The first time someone said I could get away with something the locals could never do because I was a gringa, I was shocked. The idea that being American gave me opportunities and advantages that I didn't even realize other people don't automatically receive in their own country clued me into the world of privilege. And since then, I've noticed the privilege I have in other areas.

I have the privilege of homeschooling, something that is made easier by the fact that I have a spouse with a steady job that allows us to live on a single income in a place where homeschooling is legal. I have the privilege of displaying my affection for my husband in public without anyone staring or making hateful comments. That's not something I could safely assume if we were part of the LGBTQIA+ community. And this is just the tip of the iceberg. To deny my many privileges would be disingenuous and insensitive to those who are not afforded the same advantages. To deny your privilege would be the same.

Anyone has the potential to be an ally (or accomplice). The role is not just for white folks. It's a requirement for every single one of us in some way because racialized groups are not the only ones who need and deserve allyship. There certainly are many ways white people can uniquely advance the cause of equality for all, and they have a responsibility to do so, but they're not responsible for fixing everything alone. Our most formidable weapon is the power of the people, and we need to wield it together. Our strength lies in our ability to unite as an influential force that effects real change rooted in compassionate community and carried out in seamless solidarity. Mutuality is our superpower.

WORKING FOR THE GREATER GOOD

This idea of mutuality, something I suggest we teach our children early on, is a truth that some South Africans have long held on to, and it's connected to the word "ubuntu." The late Desmond Tutu said that it's the very essence of being human. He described a person who has ubuntu as generous, hospitable, friendly, caring, and compassionate—someone who shares what they have.

"It is to say, my humanity is caught up, is inextricably bound up, in yours. We belong in a bundle of life. We say a person is a person through other persons. It is not I think therefore I am. It says rather: I am human because I belong, I participate, and I share. A person with ubuntu is open and available to others, affirming of others, does not feel threatened that others are able and good, for he or she has a proper self-assurance that comes from knowing that he or she belongs in a greater whole and is diminished when others are humiliated or diminished, when others are tortured or oppressed, or treated as if they were less than who they are."[1]

Here, we see a link between our purpose and the well-being of our fellow persons, and this refrain echoes across culture, language, race, ethnicity, geography, and religion. It's a core universal value of humanity that many resist because accepting that we're bound to one another makes some people feel vulnerable or out of control. The idea that we aren't free to do whatever we please, even if it's legal, can feel confining if you haven't accepted that no one is free until we're all free.

In *Save Your City: How Toxic Culture Kills Community & What to Do About It,* author Diane Kalen-Sukra writes, "Human connection is based on trust, and it is trust that is continually violated when people do not practice setting aside their narrow self-interests in consideration of the needs and interests of others, such as their coworkers, family, neighbours, and community."[2] There are tangible ways that families can move through their communities, demonstrating their steadfast commitment to the greater good. Examples include:

- Raising funds for, donating money to, and volunteering for organizations with clear justice-minded missions directed by the people impacted.

- Attending meetings, hearings, and other public events to advocate in person on behalf of policies impacting the organizations and groups you support. Don't center your voice but add to the work of others as a show of solidarity.

- Using your job and other positions of influence to ensure that BIPOC have a seat at decision-making tables.

- Supporting BIPOC-owned businesses by hiring them or buying their goods and spreading the word through online reviews, social media, and word of mouth.

- Disrupting conversations, both public and private, when you observe or hear racialized microaggressions.

- Whipping out your phone and recording confrontations when someone is intimidated, harassed, or targeted with violence. Your evidence could very well be the determining factor between justice served or the incident being swept under the rug.

- Donating and campaigning on behalf of politicians who support equitable and inclusive practices that extend beyond their personal comfort at the federal, state, and local levels.

- Working with local families, schools, and civic organizations to create intentionally inclusive environments for all children.

- Organizing book clubs and fireside chats with people in your community as you share, learn, and grow together in your understanding of how best to embrace socially conscious living.

At first glance, many of these actions seem adult-led, but remember that our children are watching us. We're training them to be bystanders or upstanders, performative allies or accomplices, depending on what they see from us. But that doesn't mean that kids don't have the agency to enact change. We can usher them through the process of critiquing things they feel are unjust and developing and implementing plans for how they can become part of the solution. In addition to joining in the family efforts just described, kids can lead the charge with activities like these:

- **BECOMING A PEER EDUCATOR.** Kids can use their writing, music, art, and voice to share knowledge and insight on important issues with their peers. My oldest enjoys entering art and creative writing contests. I've noticed that she typically incorporates socially or culturally conscious messaging in the pieces she submits. I don't coach her in that direction, but she uses her voice to speak about the work we've centered in our home.

- **ADVOCATING FOR LEGISLATIVE CHANGE.** Our children are more than capable of pushing for important legislation by writing letters to their legislators, speaking up at public events, and working alongside groups with similar goals. This is something that I never thought of doing with my kids until I started doing it myself. I used to believe that one little letter couldn't possibly help, but when I began reading more widely and seeing the collective impact that seemingly small actions have had, I changed my attitude. Now we operate from the belief that our voices could be the drops that make the buckets of change overflow, and we have a responsibility to use the tools at our disposal to effect change.

- **PARTICIPATING IN A PROTEST.** Provide resources for your children to create posters, learn songs or chants, and practice demonstrating in ways that publicly convey their thoughts and feelings on issues they value. I attended my first protest in college. It was a small march at the courthouse, and the ability to connect with other people who felt passionate about the same cause was an empowering experience that I wish I'd had earlier.

- **RAISING MONEY.** Sometimes children are encouraged to collect toiletries or canned goods for people in need. While I think the end goal is good, adults often leave out part of the process. Money doesn't just appear, and I don't see much use in taking my kids to the store and paying for their donated goods. In that case, I'm doing some good, but my kids are just tagalongs. I already donate to organizations that support issues I value, and I want my kids to do the same. They can raise money with my support as needed and determine which people or organizations they'll serve. Whether they have a bake sale, sell handcrafted items, or request contributions from family and friends, the choice is theirs to make, and they need to drive the effort.

- **ELEVATING YOUR CONCERN.** When my son got frustrated that there were no brown-skinned military action figures in the toy store, I let him know that he could try to share his concern with the store manager. Unsure whether he would be given an audience, I was pleasantly surprised when the customer service desk paged the manager to the front. My son hesitatingly explained that he thinks people who protect our country are brave and strong, and he wants to play with some "army guys" that look like him. This incredible store manager listened attentively and told Beckett that he would find some brown soldiers, order them for the store, and have one shipped to our home free of charge. Wow. What a lesson my son learned that day about using his voice to make a difference, no matter how small. Along these lines, letter writing is another way kids can make their thoughts and ideas known to companies and organizations that they feel have done something unfair or biased. I don't write these letters for my kids, but I coach them to include a combination of facts and feelings in a persuasive tone while writing.

- **COMMUNITY SERVICE.** This is a big one for kids because giving their time is a concrete way to sacrifice on behalf of another. When I was a teen, I volunteered weekly at a women's shelter, watching the children who lived there while their moms attended a group meeting. This wasn't something anyone saw or praised me for, and I think that went a long way toward my understanding that serving others isn't about me. Service opportunities like these are endless, and I try to help my kids find ways to volunteer within their passion areas. We've dabbled with various organizations, but most of my kids' service hours involve alleviating food insecurity in families living in transitional housing. It's not necessarily what I would've thought of for my kids, but that's what they picked, and I love it. I'm happy to work alongside them in this worthy work.

So, what are we expecting of our children? We're hoping that they'll carry the torch of righteous living and help it burn brighter. That they'll speak up and live out their values, the ones they learn within their homes and those they may inherit elsewhere as they spend time under the tutelage of other voices. We're investing in them so they, in turn, will contribute to the betterment of humanity.

Our expectations transcend college majors, entrepreneurial endeavors, family choices, and chosen professions. This work involves our children's daily lives, what they're eager to stand for, and how far they're willing to go to elicit change. It impacts where they spend time and how they show up when they arrive, and it even affects those they invite along for the ride.

Essentially, we're looking for our children to stake a claim on culturally conscious living for all their days. We want this to be a part of who they are, something they feel in their core, something that doesn't feel awkward or burdensome. Successfully launching a socially and culturally conscious changemaker is not the cherry on top. It's the whole point.

Each child's path will be different, and that's more than okay. The world doesn't need shallow social justice automatons or factory model freedom fighters. We're looking to break the mold. Renowned cellist Pablo Casals is credited with saying, "The child must know that he is a miracle, that since the beginning of the world there hasn't been, and until the end of the world will not be, another child like him." This explains why our children's identity so profoundly impacts their ability to spread branches toward others. Our kids must know that there are unique contributions they can make in this world.

Raising kids this way can feel scary because when we teach them to think critically and to be guided by their hearts to propel change, we relinquish our power to command. And that's a good thing because although we hold great influence, they aren't ours to control. Our children are born whole. They just need loving guides to care for them and shepherd them as they learn to fly, lean in, and do hard things.

Our kids will chart unknown territory and trudge through the mundane on behalf of others because we choose to travel alongside them. Our homes matter. I matter. And so do you. As we train our kids in the way they should go, there are lessons for us to impart. These are things that we want to make sure our children inherit from us. Our kids should know this way of living so intimately that by the time they leave our homes, and even as they experience the world today, it becomes woven into the fabric of who they feel themselves to be. Some of the most important lessons we can teach our children include:

1. **BACK UP YOUR BELIEFS AND YOUR WORDS WITH TANGIBLE ACTS.** Not flashy ostentatious action but meaningful moves undertaken because everyone's freedom, including your own, depends on it. This world is a web of interdependent relationships. Inextricably insert yourself into the matrix.

2. **DON'T WAIT AROUND FOR THINGS TO GET BETTER.** The "do nothing" strategy is a losing one. If you feel comfortable enough in your circumstances to wait this thing out, you've disconnected yourself from humanity. How can you sit by while others are struggling just to breathe freely?

3. **WALK THROUGH LIFE AS AN ACCOMPLICE.** Carry out your work because it's what you need to do. Not because you're a do-good savior or because it feels nice to "make someone's life better." Decenter yourself. Understand that you're incomplete when you ignore the suffering and oppression of others.

4. **LIVE HOSPITABLY.** Walk with open hands as one who has ubuntu. Be yourself, but always remember that interdependence requires humility. Give freely, work with others to gain what neither of you has, and notice what you receive even when it comes in unfamiliar packaging. In her book *Mother to Son,* author Jasmine L. Holmes asks her child to be "the one who speaks calm into chaos. The one who pursues peace. The one who asks clarifying questions and seeks understanding. The one who will not rest until you can state your opponent's arguments in terms so compassionate that you finally understand where they're coming from."[3] This is the perfect expression of a hospitable life.

5. **SEE PEOPLE FOR WHO THEY SAY THEY ARE.** In Bill Konigsberg's *The Music of What Happens*, one of his characters says, "With my white friends, I'm always half-Mexican. They never say I'm half-Irish. Never say I'm half white. Like I'm tainted halfway from the standard. It's like when I was a kid and I thought vanilla ice cream meant no flavor, like it

was the base of all the flavors. But vanilla is a bean. Like chocolate is a bean. Like cinnamon is a root. All roots and beans. All flavors. There is no base. No ice cream without a flavor."[4] This is a fictional account, but its realness is what makes it so good. Don't box people in based on what you think you know about them. Give everyone you meet the freedom to be who they say they are, whether you see and understand it or not. Don't make people scramble for value and worth.

6. **IT'S NOT YOUR INTENT BUT YOUR IMPACT THAT MATTERS.** I know that your intent when dealing with others is good. But even with good intentions, you're going to make mistakes. I've been on a socially conscious path for years and I still mess up. Saying the wrong thing, even when you hurt someone, doesn't make you a bad person. But getting defensive or shutting down when people call you on your mistake is a major issue and a sign of immaturity. As soon as you see that your words, actions, silence, or inaction have negatively impacted a person or group, you need to own up to your mistake, learn from it, apologize well, and make every attempt to do better going forward. And when you're on the receiving end of someone's honest apology and sincere efforts to engage and grow, you should gracefully and genuinely accept their humble attempts to right their wrongs.

7. **EXPECT YOUR WORK TO MATTER.** Your contributions to the cause are unique and valuable. They make a difference when people notice, and they matter just as much when no one's there to offer you a fist bump or a pat on the back. Keep going.

It's our responsibility to help our kids stretch in purposeful and sometimes uncomfortable ways, but it's not our job to unearth miracles. We can't entirely manufacture thinking, feeling people whose liberation is bound up in others, but we can contribute meaningfully to their growth. The potential already resides within each of our children. We're here to sow seeds, water deep roots, and watch them grow. As we teach our children that the quality of their individual lives is inseparable from the vibrancy of the collective, the seeds we plant will yield ample, cool shade for generations to come.

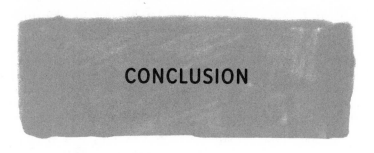

CONCLUSION

May we be gentle with our little heartlings. May we make our homes a haven for the precious ones growing in our care. May we offer our arms as a shelter from their fears. May we let our words be a guide for their feelings. And may we see our hearts as a compass for their own.

—Ainsley Arment, author of *The Call of the Wild and Free*

IT'S EASY TO GET SWEPT UP IN THE ENORMITY OF OUR CALLING to create an inclusive and colorful family culture, but I find comfort in remembering that we're not expected to slay dragons. Our real job is to create a home where our children feel tethered and seen as they grow and serve with confidence, grace, and humility. And that's something that intentional, loving parents are uniquely equipped to do. We were made for this.

It's unlikely that everything I've suggested in this book will appeal to you or work for your family. Some things will speak to you more than others based on your past, your personality, the needs and desires of your children, and your family dynamics. It's not even advisable that anyone tries to incorporate all these ideas simultaneously within a single home.

Self-reflection. Dinner table talk. Home library curation. Culturally rich learning. Community. Relationships. All of that takes time. The atmosphere of my home has been years in the making, and my family is molting, making way for new growth, even as I write this today.

The vision I cast for my family developed over time, and the progress was not linear. It was full of ups, downs, and periods of stagnancy while we adjusted to a new normal. Your journey will be different. In some cases, it will be radically different. And that's what makes all of this so liberating. There are no boxes to check. I haven't written a recipe for you to follow.

There are many ways to consciously weave color and inclusivity into the fabric of your home, multiple paths to culturally rich living. You are the master curator of your child's home environment, so think of this book as a grand buffet where you can fill your plate with as much or as little as you'd like, and you're free to season everything just right to suit your family's palate before handing it off to your children. Every parent possesses a "special sauce" that can be imitated but never perfectly duplicated because the main ingredient is you!

We're here because we share a vision for what childhood can be. Our kids, when left to maneuver on their own, will certainly grow, but wouldn't it be great if we as parents could be the ones to help usher them to true freedom? We can help them find a place of belonging where they can be deeply rooted and watered as they grow toward others.

Despite what the world would have us believe, we can choose to agree on the truth: We have much in common, our differences do not negate our shared humanity, and we can raise our children to be comrades. To enjoy one another. In the words of Dr. Martin Luther King Jr., "I refuse to accept the view that mankind is so tragically bound to the starless midnight of racism and war that the bright daybreak of peace and brotherhood can never become a reality. . . . I believe that unarmed truth and unconditional love will have the final word in reality."[1]

Many of us have already decided to go against the grain of what society tells us we must be and what others expect us to do with our children. This is nothing new for us. All I'm suggesting is that we take it a step further and solidify our rebellion.

As I raise my kids, I will infuse in them all the beauty of who they are and where they come from while ensuring that they see you and your children as friends and not foes. I'll give them windows into other families and their ways of life alongside the mirrors reflecting our own culture to them. I will lead them to love themselves. And I will teach them to love you.

I'm able to do this because I'm trusting you in your home (or on your homestead). While you walk down the aisles of Target with a latte in hand or count your guinea fowl after milking the goats. While you stop by the drive-through to pick up another late dinner or mix essential oils to soothe the days' insect bites. Whether you're parenting alone, living every moment with the love of your life, or firmly holding on to a marriage you barely recognize. No matter how you're showing up, I choose to trust you.

I trust that you have your children's best interest at heart because that's easy for me to do. But I also trust that you have *my* children's best interest in mind. And you can trust me to feel the same about your little loves.

My children do have a place to belong. Living, learning, growing, and changing hearts right alongside yours. Our children belong. Together.

ACKNOWLEDGMENTS

My beautiful children are the reason for this book. Nina, I will forever be grateful to you for granting me another chance to love you well and for helping me find myself in the process. You showed me what belonging is all about, and without your bold insistence, there would be no story to tell. You are incredible, and there's nowhere I'd rather be than on this journey with you.

Sweet Sasha, thank you for the long, lingering hugs that remind me every day that I'm your person. I've told you many times that you were the answer to fervent prayer. He created your inmost being and knit you together intentionally and perfectly. Don't ever forget that. The cover of your favorite journal says that you're a "book nerd" (and I love that!), so I'm confident that you'll be the first to read my words. Thank you for filling our home with laughter and scrumptious treats. They have kept me going.

Beckett, you made me a boy mom, and it's been the coolest thing ever. You've remained consistently excited that "Mama's writing a book!" but you've also made sure that I remained Mama above all else. Your early years have existed amid much turmoil as our nation grapples with boys like you becoming men. There have been times when I've wanted to hide you, to shelter you in every way, but your #BlackBoyJoy is too infectious to be hidden. You are a "go big or go home" adventurer, and I'm so honored that you're mine.

Little Brooks, you have been the best writing pal that a girl could ever hope for. You somehow learned to dial my phone ("Alexa, call Amber") just as I was beginning to draft this book, and you've called me at least a hundred times to find out what time I'm coming home and if I can make you pancakes. I want to say that the calls were distracting, but they were not. Each one made me feel more loved and appreciated than the one before. You are my sunshine.

There really is no way for me to fully express how thankful I am to my love, Scott Johnston, for making my dreams come true. You gave me a beautiful home filled with babies and good times, and you are our safe place. I appreciate how you never once doubted my abilities and especially how you held down the fort when I was away writing. Thank you for keeping me supplied with expensive tea. I needed it more than you know.

I'll never be able to thank my agent, Anna Knutson Geller, enough for so intimately understanding my message and helping me find my voice. None of this would have been possible without your diligence, wisdom, and care. Your timing was impeccable, and I'm incredibly thankful for your coaching and suggestions. You brilliantly challenged my early direction and helped me craft something more intriguing than I'd ever imagined. We make a wonderful team!

Joanna Ng, my editor at TarcherPerigee, is nearly too good to be true. Your steady encouragement and detailed feedback gave me confidence and helped me remain true to the vision. You understand me, and I've always felt how strongly you believed in my message. Working with you has made this feel so much bigger than just the book, and that has been an unexpected gift.

April Wells, I don't even know what to call you. My sister-friend, perhaps. Or my "framily." Thank you for thirty-seven years of ride-or-die friendship. You not only encouraged me to write, but you made me believe that I could do it.

Kristi Holm, thank you for being my biggest cheerleader. You have always been on Team Amber, and I hope you know that I feel the same about you. Our epic conversations fueled by blueberry pancakes are and have always been treasures, and your card arrived just on time.

Kristen Leigh, from the moment my children were born (literally), you've shown them that love has no bounds. It easily crosses racial lines and flows wherever it's allowed to flow. You were their first example of what it feels like to genuinely love and be loved by someone who chose them.

Kia Stephens, you made me face my fears and put on my big girl pants. A light bulb came on while sitting on the ground with you in the middle of that parking lot. You called me out, in love, and it spurred me to action. Thank you.

Alisha Miller, your desire to walk the walk rather than just talk the talk changed everything. You believed in me and gave me a path forward that eventually led to this book. I'll never forget that.

Ainsley Arment, you amplified my voice in a way that no one has ever done before. Thank you for trusting me and for loving on me so well. You are the queen of creating a place to belong, and I'm grateful to call you a friend.

Laura Marshall, thank you for putting everything on hold to read chapters when I really needed you. I've always admired your steadiness and honesty. Both are a breath of fresh air.

Jennifer Mahnke, your surprise writer's package brought tears to my eyes. It's an incredible feeling to be known and cared for so intimately. I will cherish the teapot and handmade cozy forever. The chocolate, on the other hand, never stood a chance.

Allison Humphrey, Jailyn Nicholson, Keisha Johnson, Tiffany Grimes, and Tisha Harper: When I say that I found women that I didn't even know I needed, I'm talking about you. Thank you for seeing this book on the shelves before I even knew I would write it.

Leslie Martino, just being around you makes me smile for no reason. I can't even explain it. Thank you for giving me the confidence to listen to my intuition, embrace connection, and savor the slow school joy undergirding this book.

Torrie Oglesby, Delina Pryce McPhaull, Susan Seay, and Brenaea Fairchild: Every time we connect, I feel like my game is tight. You are the ultimate encouragers.

Amanda Holt, thank you for being a sounding board and refuge while reminding me that genuine cross-racial friendships can form quickly and easily when both people choose to lead with love. As I wrote this book, I often had your children in mind because our conversations always remind me that our kids are worth fighting for.

Julie Bogart, thank you for believing in me enough to cast a life-changing vote of confidence and for writing such a compelling foreword. Your actions support your values, and I endeavor to live that way.

Erika Alicea and Nicole Cottrell, thank you for getting into "good trouble" with me. Going against the grain is not easy, but you both have made it your business to have influence in our community. Thank you for supporting my work and inspiring me with yours.

Leah Boden, the Modern Miss Mason, you may not have realized it, but I found comfort in knowing that I had a sister across the pond feverishly writing as I was. On the days when I felt like I could go no further, I thought of you and was reminded of why we do what we do.

Greta Eskridge, how can I ever thank you for tolerating my endless meanderings throughout the entire writing process? You are a gifted encourager, and I'm so glad to have you in my corner.

To all the families in Heritage Homeschoolers, thank you for giving my children space to just be. You've shown me what a sacred village feels like, and I love you for it.

To my sister, Traci O'Neal Ellis, you've been a place of refuge and sanctuary since the moment I was big enough to crawl into your bed. You have always been and will always be my "Nissy."

I'm so grateful for my brother, Ronald O'Neal Jr., who knew I had a book in me. You're always thinking two steps ahead, and you're always right. Thank you for your unwavering support and unshakable love.

Mom, you are the very best of everything, and I have always loved being your daughter. In Dad's last days, he asked me to keep him alive in the minds of my children, and with your help, I have. They never met him, but they know him well. His love endures.

And thank YOU, my readers, for joining me in celebrating diversity and kinship in the home and beyond. I can't wait to see who our children become!

INTRODUCTION

- What brought you to this book? Why are you reading it, and what do you hope to gain in the process?

PART 1: LAYING THE GROUNDWORK

CHAPTER 1 | EVALUATING YOUR FAMILY CULTURE:
What Are You Bringing to the Table?

- What does "identity is prismatic" mean to you? How does it relate to your family?

- As you evaluate what you're bringing to the family table, you'll likely be challenging deeply held beliefs and long-held assumptions. Which questions made you the most uncomfortable, and how did you deal with the tension?

- What do or would you find helpful as you humbly learn to see the world through someone else's eyes?

- On a scale of 1 to 10, how would you rate your willingness to set your self-interests aside in pursuit of understanding others? Why did you choose that rating?

- Define "anti-racist" in your own words. Is this something you wish to be, or do you find it problematic? Why?

- How is diversity multidimensional and intersectional?

- Do you ever worry that teaching your children about how others live will lead to them embracing undesirable values? Why or why not? How do your thoughts impact how you share about different people with your kids?

- Were you raised to be colorblind? How does the idea of walking away from that mentality make you feel?

- What does having a colorful family culture mean to you?

CHAPTER 2 | EMBRACING TOUGH TABLE TOPICS:
Normalizing Weighty Conversations

- Do you discuss discrimination, race, gender, and class with your kids? If not, what's holding you back, and when do you think you'll start?

- What can you do to become a more askable parent? What do you think your biggest challenges will be in this area?

- How comfortable are you discussing tough table topics with your kids?

- What are your thoughts on the *PBS KIDS Talk About: Race & Racism* questions? Would you use them as conversation starters with your kids?

- What about the examples from *Raising Race Conscious Children*? Do you already speak freely with your children in this way? If not, how does it make you feel to read the examples?

- How comfortable are you talking about race with other adults? What about with your kids?

- Do you see value in Du Bois's seven goals for *The Brownies' Book*? Do any of the goals surprise you, concern you, or especially resonate with you?

CHAPTER 3 | ESTABLISHING A BLUEPRINT:
Inclusive Family Ways and Home Culture

- Do you see yourself adopting any of the twenty family ways described in this chapter? Which ones feel most comfortable for your family? Are there any that don't seem relevant or worthwhile?

- What are some inclusive family ways that you'd like to pursue in your family?

- Are there any people in your life who don't uphold your family ways? How will you handle their comments or actions?

- Do you think your children have a strong sense of "intergenerational self"?

- Are you comfortable sharing family stories with your children on an ongoing basis? What would make it easier for you?

- Answer the researchers' questions for yourself:

  o Do you know where your mother grew up?

  o Do you know where some of your grandparents met?

  o Do you know the source of your name?

  o Do you know which person in the family you act most like?

  o Do you know the national background of your family (such as English, German, Russian, etc.)?

  o Do you know some awards that your parents received when they were young?

  o Do you know the names of the schools that your dad went to?

- How do you handle difficult narratives in your family?

- Does your family have a long or short timeline from which to pull? How does that make you feel? What can you do to maximize what you have to work with?

PART 2: CURATING THE HOME LIBRARY

CHAPTER 4 | MIRROR, MIRROR ON THE WALL:
When Children See Themselves in Their Books

- What are literary mirrors? Describe the role they play in your home today.

- Did the CCBC statistics on the primary characters in children's books surprise you? If so, what did you think of the publishing landscape before reading the stats?

- Describe the "apartheid of literature." How does the concept impact your thoughts on the availability of children's books?

- Had you ever thought about curating a home library before? If so, what types of selection parameters do you use (or are you planning to use)?

- What do you think of colorblind vs. colorful bookshelves?

- What other aspects of your child's personhood, beyond race and ethnicity, would you like to see reflected in some of their books?

CHAPTER 5 | PULL BACK THE CURTAINS:
Uncovering Books as Windows to the World

- What are literary windows? Describe the role they play in your home today.

- Which types of windows do you think your children need more of and why?

- Are there any barriers to you providing more windows in your home library?

- What is the issue with the single story? What can you do to prevent the proliferation of the single story within your home?

- If you have a son, does he hear or read stories that center the experiences of women? Do you believe that boys should read stories about girls? Why or why not?

CHAPTER 6 | LIFE-GIVING BOOKS:
What Makes a Book "Good"?

- What role do classics play in your home library?

- What are your thoughts on Newbery Award–winning books?

- What are your thoughts on the #DisruptTexts movement?

- How do you feel about the concept of "our own ideal libraries"?

- What do you think about eliminating generally accepted booklists?

- Describe your thoughts on classics, living books, life-giving books, and twaddle. What are the similarities and differences? Which types of books dominate your home library?

- What percentage of the diverse books in your home center on "the struggle"? Do you have books depicting the joyful, everyday life or fun adventures of children of color?

- Are #OwnVoices books important to you? Why or why not?

- How often do your children select their own books? How do you feel about the books they pick?

PART 3: SHAPING THE HOME ATMOSPHERE

CHAPTER 7 | DEEPLY ROOTED:
Leaning into Family Culture and History

- How do you connect your children to their cultural roots? Do you find this easy or difficult to do?

- Which of the projects described most resonates with you? Are there any that you can't relate to?

- Do you think you could comfortably integrate these types of activities into the rhythms of your home over time? If not, what do you see as the biggest barriers?

- What is a legacy mindset, and how can you best infuse it into your home?

CHAPTER 8 | REPRESENTATION MATTERS:
Navigating the Ups and Downs of Media and Pop Culture

- What are your thoughts on the #NotMyAriel outcry? Does it bother you when imaginary characters are reimagined as people of color?

- Define invisibility, distortion, and tokenism. Give examples of where you've seen these in children's TV shows and movies. What about the media you consume as an adult?

- Do you know exactly what your children watch or play on the TV or other devices?

- Do you approve your kids' shows ahead of time, or do they pick their own?

- What do you think about the distinction between consuming media and creating media?

- What are the media rules of engagement in your home? Do you think any of them need to shift or change?

CHAPTER 9 | FROM TRAGEDY TO TRIUMPH:
Bringing Hard History into the Home

- What is your relationship with learning history? Is it something you enjoy? Is it something confined to the school day or something that permeates other areas of your family time?

- Are your children learning hard history? If so, who's teaching it, or how do you decide what to share? If not, what's preventing you from sharing difficult truths with your kids?

- Is your child receiving an inclusive and balanced view of history? If not, what can you do to ensure that they're experiencing the fullness of voices throughout history?

- Do you visit local historical sites? Do you incorporate history into your family travels?

- How can you help make history come alive for your children?

CHAPTER 10 | CHOOSING JOY:
Finding Beauty Through Culturally Rich Learning

- What do you think are the best ways to balance the heaviness of hard history?

- Do you regularly incorporate art, music, and poetry into your home? If so, do your selections reflect the diversity of our country? Our world? If not, what would help you in that area?

- What do you think about incorporating the beauty of cultural foodways into your home? Is this a new concept or something that comes naturally to you?

- Were you aware of the history of exclusionary and racist practices in nature and environmentalism? What are your thoughts on how those past practices may be impacting families today?

- How important is it for you to seek out examples of beauty within underrepresented cultures? What have you already done? What do you plan to do differently going forward?

PART 4: MOVING BEYOND THE FOUR WALLS

CHAPTER 11 | THEORY TO PRACTICE:
Training Through Travel and Language-Learning

- What are your thoughts on global citizenship? Is this something your family values? Why or why not?

- Have you ever considered worldschooling? What do you find most and least appealing about the idea?

- Are your children learning other languages? If so, how are you leading them in the effort? If not, what would help you pursue that for your kids?

- How can you connect your children to the world from the comfort of home?

CHAPTER 12 | SACRED SPACES AND PLACES:
Cultivating Safe Villages, Inclusive Community, and Cross-Cultural Kinship

- What are your thoughts on racial affinity spaces or safe villages?

- If you disagree with the idea, what alternative solutions do you have for supporting children of color who live in mostly white communities?

- If you agree with the concept, how can you join or create that space for your family, or how can you advocate or support the creation and existence of these groups for others?

- What does it mean to be bicultural? Can you relate to that term?

- What is code-switching? Is this something that you do? Have you seen others do it? If so, how did/does it make you feel?

- Do any of the ten points on the rationale for cultural micro-communities make you uncomfortable? If so, which ones and why?

- How can you avoid seeking token friendships? Or, how can you avoid becoming a token friend?

- Do you have authentic cross-racial friendships? If so, how are they cultivated and maintained? If not, what can you do to better position yourself for organic connection?

CHAPTER 13 | SOW, REAP, AND HARVEST:
Launching Socially Conscious Changemakers

- What is a socially conscious changemaker?

- Do you believe that white people are afforded certain privileges due to their skin color? Why or why not?

- Do you benefit from any privileges simply because of who you are? If so, name a few and tell how you feel about them.

- Do you consider yourself an ally and/or accomplice? Why or why not?

- What is performative allyship? How can you avoid exhibiting it, and what can you do if you find yourself on the receiving end of it?

- Describe "ubuntu." How can you incorporate this concept into your family's value system?

- What can you do to demonstrate your commitment to the common good of your local community? Our nation? The world? How can you help your children to do the same?

- What are your three biggest takeaways from this book?

NOTES

PART 1

1. Maya Angelou, *The Complete Poetry* (New York: Random House, 2015), 189.

2. *My Sister's Keeper,* directed by Nick Cassavetes (Warner Bros., 2009), https://www.amazon.com/My-Sisters-Keeper-Cameron-Diaz/dp/B0093QJATE.

CHAPTER 1

1. Tembi Locke, *From Scratch: A Memoir of Love, Sicily, and Finding Home* (New York: Simon & Schuster, 2019), 245.

2. "prismatic," *The Oxford Pocket Dictionary of Current English*, Encyclopedia.com, accessed August 16, 2021, https://www.encyclopedia.com/humanities/dictionaries-thesauruses-pictures-and-press-releases/prismatic-0.

3. Corinne Gray, "Disability Fashion: Stephanie Thomas Is Shaking Up the Fashion Industry," June 20, 2019, URevolution, https://www.urevolution.com/disability-fashion-stephanie-thomas/.

4. Parker J. Palmer, *The Courage to Teach: Exploring the Inner Landscape of a Teacher's Life* (San Francisco: Jossey-Bass, 1998), chap 1, Subjects That Chose Us section, para 6, ebook.

CHAPTER 2

1. "Representation: Diversity & Inclusion," Center for Scholars & Storytellers, accessed August 21, 2021, https://www.scholarsandstorytellers.com/representation-diversity-inclusion.

2. Audre Lorde, "The Transformation of Silence into Language and Action," paper presented at the Modern Language Association's "Lesbian and Literature

Panel," Chicago, Illinois, December 28, 1977, Electric Literature, https://elec
tricliterature.com/wp-content/uploads/2017/12/silenceintoaction.pdf.

3. Ali Michael, "Raising Race Questions: Whiteness & Inquiry in Education,"
   accessed December 4, 2021. https://www.alimichael.org/featured-work/raising
   -race-questions.

4. "Talking to Young Children About Race and Racism: A Discussion Guide,"
   pbskids.org, accessed August 21, 2021, https://www.pbs.org/parents/thrive
   /talking-to-young-children-about-race-and-racism-a-discussion-guide.

5. "100 Race-Conscious Things You Can Say to Your Child to Advance Racial
   Justice," Raising Race Conscious Children, June 2, 2016, http://www.racecon
   scious.org/2016/06/100-race-conscious-things-to-say-to-your-child
   -to-advance-racial-justice/.

CHAPTER 3

1. Michael Allen Fox, "Home: A Very Short Introduction," December 30, 2016,
   https://blog.oup.com/2016/12/home-place-environment.

2. Albert Murray, *The Omni-Americans: Some Alternatives to the Folklore of White
   Supremacy*, accessed December 4, 2021, https://www.penguinrandomhouse
   .com/books/645336/the-omni-americans-by-albert-murray--with-a
   -foreword-by-henry-louis-gates-jr.

3. Bruce Feiler, *The Secrets of Happy Families: Improve Your Mornings, Tell Your
   Family History, Fight Smarter, Go Out and Play, and Much More* (New York:
   HarperCollins, 2013), 41–42.

4. Robyn Fivush, "The 'Do You Know?' 20 Questions About Family Stories,"
   Psychology Today, November 19, 2016, https://www.psychologytoday.com/us
   /blog/the-stories-our-lives/201611/the-do-you-know-20-questions-about
   -family-stories.

PART 2

CHAPTER 4

1. Nancy Larrick, "The All-White World of Children's Books," *Saturday Review*,
   September 11, 1965, https://brichislitspot.files.wordpress.com/2017/08
   /384larrick.pdf.

2. Madeline Tyner, "The CCBC's Diversity Statistics: New Categories, New
   Data," Horn Book Inc., February 2, 2021, https://www.hbook.com/?detail
   Story=the-ccbcs-diversity-statistics-new-categories-new-data.

3. Christopher Myers, "The Apartheid of Children's Literature," *New York Times*, March 15, 2014, https://www.nytimes.com/2014/03/16/opinion/sunday /the-apartheid-of-childrens-literature.html.

4. Clay Clarkson with Sally Clarkson, *Educating the WholeHearted Child* (Monument, CO: Whole Heart Ministries, 2019), 212.

5. Grace Lin, "The Windows and Mirrors of Your Child's Bookshelf," TEDx-Natick, March 18, 2016, https://www.youtube.com/watch?v=_wQ8wi V3FVo.

CHAPTER 5

1. Emily Style, "Curriculum As Window and Mirror," National SEED Project, accessed August 22, 2021, https://nationalseedproject.org/Key-SEED-Texts /curriculum-as-window-and-mirror.

2. Jamie C. Martin, *Give Your Child the World: Raising Globally Minded Kids One Book at a Time* (Grand Rapids, MI: Zondervan, 2016), 36.

3. Luther B. Clegg, Etta Miller, Bill Vanderhoof, Gonzalo Ramirez, and Peggy K. Ford, "How to Choose the Best Multicultural Books," *Scholastic*, accessed May 20, 2021, http://www.scholastic.com/teachers/article/how-choose-best -multicultural-books.

4. Chimamanda Ngozi Adichie, "The Danger of a Single Story," TEDGlobal, July 2009, https://www.ted.com/talks/chimamanda_ngozi_adichie_the _danger_of_a_single_story.

5. Caroline Paul, "Why Boys Should Read Girl Books," Ted.com, March 29, 2016, https://ideas.ted.com/why-boys-should-read-girl-books/.

6. Shannon Hale, "What Are We Teaching Boys When We Discourage Them from Reading Books About Girls?" *Washington Post*, October 10, 2018, https://www.washingtonpost.com/entertainment/books/parents-and -teachers-please-stop-discouraging-boys-from-reading-books-about-girls /2018/10/09/f3eaaca6-c820-11e8-b1ed-1d2d65b86d0c_story.html.

CHAPTER 6

1. Julia Torres, Dr. Kim Parker, Lorena German, and Tricia Ebarvia, "4 Core Principles to #DisruptTexts," #DisruptTexts, January 2, 2021, https://dis rupttexts.org/core-principles/.

2. Charles Augustin Sainte-Beuve, "Introductory Note," *Literary and Philosophical Essays*, vol. 32, Harvard Classics (New York: P. F. Collier & Son, 1909–14), www.bartleby.com/32/.

3. Valerie Strauss, "Are Newbery Winners the New Not-to-Read List?" *Los Angeles Times*, December 24, 2008, https://www.latimes.com/archives/la -xpm-2008-dec-24-et-newbery24-story.html.

4. Italo Calvino, "Why Read the Classics?" *The New York Review of Books*, October 9, 1986, https://www.nybooks.com/articles/1986/10/09/why-read-the-classics.

5. Antonio García Martínez, "Drowning in the Melting Pot: Secular Liberalism and What It Requires," Pull Request, December 9, 2020, https://www.the pullrequest.com/p/drowning-in-the-melting-pot.

6. Sonya Shafer, "What Is Twaddle?" Simply Charlotte Mason, September 3, 2009, https://simplycharlottemason.com/blog/what-is-twaddle.

7. Charlotte M. Mason, *Home Education* (Cambridge, UK: Tyndale House, 1989), 205.

8. Charlotte M. Mason, *A Philosophy of Education* (Cambridge, UK: Tyndale House, 1989), 117.

9. Charlotte M. Mason, *School Education* (Cambridge, UK: Tyndale House, 1989), 168.

10. Mason, *School Education*, 228–29.

11. H. D. M. Spence, Joseph S. Exell, and Charles Neil, eds., *Thirty Thousand Thoughts: Being Extracts Covering a Comprehensive Circle of Religious and Allied Topics* (New York: Funk & Wagnalls, 1885), 94, https://archive.org/details/ thirtythousandth03spen/page/94/mode/2up.

12. Kayla Whaley, "#OwnVoices: Why We Need Diverse Authors in Children's Literature," Brightly, February 23, 2016, https://www.readbrightly.com /why-we-need-diverse-authors-in-kids-ya-lit/.

13. Alpha DeLap and Laura Simeon, "White Kids Need Diverse Books," Voya, April 2017, http://teacherlibrarian.com/wp-content/uploads/2017/07/11F -delap.pdf.

14. Pamela Paul and Maria Russo, *How to Raise a Reader* (New York: Workman, 2019), vii.

PART 3

1. Gabor Maté and Gordon Neufeld, *Hold On to Your Kids: Why Parents Need to Matter More Than Peers* (Toronto: Vintage Canada, 2013), 217–32.

CHAPTER 7

1. Donald Miller, "How to Grow Strong Root Systems," SFGATE, April 8, 2012, https://homeguides.sfgate.com/grow-strong-root-systems-23697.html.

2. Simone Weil, *The Need for Roots: Prelude to a Declaration of Duties Towards Mankind*, trans. A. F. Wills (New York: Routledge, 1978), 40.

3. Amy C. Evans and Martha Hall Foose, *A Good Meal Is Hard to Find: Storied Recipes from the Deep South* (San Francisco: Chronicle, 2020), 11.

4. Edna Lewis, *The Taste of Country Cooking, 30th anniversary ed.* (New York: Knopf, 2012), 52.

5. Bryant Terry, *Afro-Vegan: Farm-Fresh African, Caribbean & Southern Flavors Remixed* (Berkeley: Ten Speed Press, 2014), 4.

6. Michael W. Twitty, The Cooking Gene: A Journey Through African American Culinary History in the Old South, accessed November 30, 2021, https://thecookinggene.com/.

7. "Field Trip Friday: Atlanta in Five Objects," Atlanta History Center, April 9, 2020, https://www.atlantahistorycenter.com/blog/field-trip-friday-atlanta-in-50-objects-your-atlanta-in-5-objects/.

8. Rachel Jepson Wolf, *Herbal Adventures: Backyard Excursions and Kitchen Creations for Kids and Their Families* (Stillwater, OK: Voyageur Press, 2018), 8.

9. Susan Moeller, "Quilters Are Weaving Personal Histories of the Black Experience: 'We're a People with a Lot of Stories to Tell,'" *Boston Globe*, March 11, 2021, https://www.bostonglobe.com/2021/03/11/magazine/quilters-are-weaving-personal-histories-black-experience-were-people-with-lot-stories-tell/.

10. Sally Clarkson and Sarah Clarkson, *The Lifegiving Home: Creating a Place of Belonging & Becoming* (Carol Stream, IL: Tyndale Momentum, 2016), 6.

CHAPTER 8

1. Justin Kroll, "Disney's Live-Action 'Little Mermaid' Casts Halle Bailey as Ariel," *Variety*, July 3, 2019, https://variety.com/2019/film/news/little-mermaid-halle-bailey-chloe-x-halle-1203234294/.

2. "The White Nostalgia Fueling the 'Little Mermaid' Backlash," *Washington Post*, July 9, 2019, https://www.washingtonpost.com/outlook/2019/07/09/white-nostalgia-fueling-little-mermaid-backlash/.

3. Elizabeth Hawkey, "Media Use in Childhood: Evidence-Based Recommendations for Caregivers," CYF News, American Psychological Association, May 2019, https://www.apa.org/pi/families/resources/newsletter/2019/05/media -use-childhood.

4. bell hooks, *Reel to Real: Race, Class and Sex at the Movies* (London: Routledge, 2012), 4.

5. Ralph Ellison, *Invisible Man* (New York: Knopf Doubleday Publishing Group, 2010), 25, ebook.

6. Yurii Horton, Raagen Price, and Eric Brown, "Portrayal of Minorities in the Film, Media and Entertainment Industries," Poverty and Prejudice: Media and Race, Stanford University, June 1999.

7. Natachi Onwuamaegbu, "The Importance of Representation," *Stanford Daily*, May 25, 2018, https://www.stanforddaily.com/2018/05/25/the-importance -of-representation/.

8. "What Is Media Literacy, and Why Is It Important?" Common Sense Media, accessed August 22, 2021, https://www.commonsensemedia.org/news-and -media-literacy/what-is-media-literacy-and-why-is-it-important.

CHAPTER 10

1. John Lingan, "Rhiannon Giddens Is Reclaiming the Black Heritage of American Folk Music," *Time*, February 21, 2019, https://time.com/5534379 /songs-of-our-native-daughters-music-review/.

2. Michael Rosen, *What Is Poetry?: The Essential Guide to Reading and Writing Poems* (Somerville, MA: Candlewick Press, 2019), 111.

3. "Ten Facts You May Not Know About Afghanistan," BBC News, July 5, 2011, https://www.bbc.com/news/world-south-asia-13931608.

4. "Feature: In Western Afghanistan, an Ancient Love of Poetry Thrives Again," UN News, October 5, 2017, https://news.un.org/en/story/2017/10/567862 -feature-western-afghanistan-ancient-love-poetry-thrives-again.

5. Maya Angelou, *Rainbow in the Cloud: The Wisdom and Spirit of Maya Angelou* (New York: Random House, 2014), 6.

6. Jedediah Purdy, "Environmentalism's Racist History," *New Yorker*, August 13, 2015, https://www.newyorker.com/news/news-desk/environmentalisms -racist-history.

7. David Scott Lee and KangJae Jerry Lee, "People of Color and Their Constraints to National Parks Visitation," *George Wright Forum* 35, no. 1 (2018): 73–82, http://www.georgewright.org/351scott.pdf.

8. *The Journal of Henry David Thoreau, vol II, 1850–September 15, 1851*, ed. Bradford Torrey and Francis H. Allen (Boston: Houghton Mifflin, 1906), 373.

PART 4

1. Esau McCaulley, Twitter post, May 26, 2021, https://twitter.com/esaumc caulley.

2. Chad Everett, "Truth or Dare?—NerdTalk 2017," ImagineLit, July 15, 2017, http://www.imaginelit.com/news/2017/7/12/nerdtalk2017.

CHAPTER 11

1. Charlotte M. Mason, *Parents and Children* (Cambridge, UK: Tyndale House, 1989), 4–6.

2. Natasha Miller, "How to Raise Your Kids as Global Citizens," Little Pim, May 3, 2019, https://www.littlepim.com/blog/how-to-raise-your-kids-as -global-citizens.

3. Emily Dickinson, *The Complete Poems of Emily Dickinson* (Boston: Little, Brown, 1924), https://www.bartleby.com/113/1106.html.

4. Mason, *Parents and Children*, 7.

5. Tappy Vera, "Raising Bilingual Kids," Instagram, June 10, 2021, https:// www.instagram.com/p/CP8ustzBNZq.

6. Elliot W. Eisner, "The Uses and Limits of Performance Assessment," *Phi Delta Kappan* 80, no. 9 (1999): 658–60. http://www.jstor.org/stable/204 39532.

7. Eli Gerzon, "Eli Gerzon: Writer, Traveler, Worldschooler," Eligerzon.com, accessed August 28, 2021, http://eligerzon.com/worldschooling.php.

CHAPTER 12

1. Elaine Welteroth, *More Than Enough: Claiming Space for Who You Are (No Matter What They Say)*. (New York: Viking, 2020), chap. 7, 83, ebook.

2. Welteroth, *More Than Enough*, chap. 6, 72, ebook.

3. Eugene Cho, Twitter post, February 2, 2017, https://twitter.com/eugenecho /status/827210981491093504.

4. Locke, *From Scratch*, 244.

5. Gena Minnix, "What Does Racial Reconciliation Mean?" Seminary of the Southwest, March 1, 2016, https://ssw.edu/blog/what-does-racial -reconciliation-mean/.

6. Ali Michael and Eleonora Bartoli, "What White Children Need to Know About Race," National Association of Independent Schools, Summer 2014, https://www.nais.org/magazine/independent-school/summer-2014/what -white-children-need-to-know-about-race/.

7. Sergio Troncoso, ed., *Nepantla Familias: An Anthology of Mexican-American Literature on Families in between Worlds* (College Station: Texas A&M University Press, 2021), introduction, ebook.

8. bell hooks, *Ain't I a Woman: Black Women and Feminism* (New York: Routledge, 2015), 99.

9. "Measuring and Reducing Social Segregation in Cities," MIT Media Lab, accessed August 28, 2021, https://www.media.mit.edu/projects/measuring -and-reducing-social-segregation-in-cities/overview/.

10. Latasha Morrison, *Be the Bridge: Pursuing God's Heart for Racial Reconciliation* (New York: Waterbrook, 2019), 23.

11. Conor Friedersdorf, "Can Chloé Valdary Sell Skeptics on DEI?" *The Atlantic*, January 31, 2021, https://www.theatlantic.com/ideas/archive/2021/01/can -chloe-valdary-sell-skeptics-dei/617875/.

12. Toni Morrison, *The Source of Self-Regard: Selected Essays, Speeches, and Meditations* (New York: Alfred A. Knopf, 2019), 47.

CHAPTER 13

1. "Mission and Philosophy," Desmond Tutu Peace Foundation, August 25, 2011, http://www.tutufoundationusa.org/desmond-tutu-peace-foundation/.

2. Diane Kalen-Sukra, *Save Your City: How Toxic Culture Kills Community & What to Do About It* (Victoria, BC: Tellwell Talent, 2019), chap. 5, location 1116, Kindle.

3. Jasmine L. Holmes, *Mother to Son: Letters to a Black Boy on Identity and Hope* (Downers Grove, IL: InterVarsity Press, 2020), 107.

4. Bill Konigsberg, *The Music of What Happens* (New York: Scholastic, 2020), 290, location 3974, Kindle.

CONCLUSION

1. Martin Luther King Jr., Acceptance Speech, December 10, 1964, NobelPrize .org, accessed December 5, 2021, https://www.nobelprize.org/prizes/peace /1964/king/acceptance-speech/.

INDEX

Amber O'Neal Johnston lives in Georgia, nestled among pine trees, hammocks, and zip lines with her husband and their four children. Her happy place is the back porch on a rainy day, preferably with a giant mug of hot tea and a good book. And although she was raised in the air-conditioning, somehow the woods is where she feels most at home these days. Amber is a regular contributor to the Wild + Free homeschooling community, and she writes and speaks about the beauty of an inclusive, culturally and socially conscious home environment. You can find her sharing diverse literary mirrors and windows at HeritageMom.com and on Instagram @heritagemomblog.